Adolescent Health

The role of individual differences

Patrick C. L. Heaven

London and New York

For William A. Scott
who loved doing research

First published 1996
by Routledge
11 New Fetter Lane, London EC4P 4EE

Simultaneously published in the USA and Canada
by Routledge
29 West 35th Street, New York, NY 10001

Routledge is an International Thomson Publishing company

© 1996 Patrick C. L. Heaven

Typeset in Times by LaserScript, Mitcham, Surrey
Printed and bound in Great Britain by
Biddles Ltd, Guildford and King's Lynn

British Library Cataloguing in Publication Data
A catalogue record for this book is available from the British Library

Library of Congress Cataloguing in Publication Data
A catalogue record for this book has been requested

ISBN 0–415–11578–7 (hbk)
ISBN 0–415–11579–5 (pbk)

Contents

Figures and tables

Foreword

Adolescence is probably the most turbulent, challenging, stressful, and uncertain of all phases in life, both for teenagers themselves and for their parents, teachers, and health professionals. Yet adolescence is also a period of great joy, excitement, and optimism during which the delights of autonomy, intimacy, and the future are fresh and possibilities are created for happiness, success, and psychological growth throughout the remainder of life. The theme of this book, adolescent health, reflects a similar interplay between difficult challenges and exciting new achievements and opportunities. On the one hand, the health issues of adolescence can be viewed as developmental danger zones. In contrast to younger children, contemporary teenagers must cope with a set of new health risks that may range from drugs and sexually transmitted disease to eating disorders or suicidal depression. While risks like these lend an element of urgency to the understanding of adolescent health, there are also exciting new insights to be gained from studying those positive aspects of health behaviour that set adolescents apart from children and, in some instances, from the adult generation.

As Patrick Heaven points out in this well-organised and gracefully written book, many teenagers today possess a sophisticated understanding of health as a multifaceted blend of physical and psychological factors stretching far beyond the mere absence of disease. Many likewise accept greater personal responsibility for immediate and long-term personal health than did teenagers of previous generations and are strongly motivated to maintain fitness and achieve optimal emotional wellbeing.

This book approaches the understanding of adolescent health from the perspective of individual differences. Through a set of well-chosen research findings and vivid examples, Patrick Heaven alerts the reader to the fascinating contrasts in health behaviour that exist not only between girls and boys but also as a function of personality, family life, poverty, homelessness, and cultural background. The underlying message is that the psychology of adolescent health cannot be fully appreciated unless the uniqueness that characterises each of us as a human being is taken into account. One of this book's great strengths is its ability to capture the complexity of this message in such an eminently readable, engaging, and practical manner.

The organisation of the book will appeal to health educators, practising health professionals, university instructors, and interested lay readers alike. The book begins with a carefully reasoned analysis of the meaning of health to adolescents and the special health risks arising during this stage in life, and successive chapters take up each of the major avenues of contemporary research into adolescent health, including health education, stress and coping strategies, eating and body image, sexuality, HIV/AIDS, substance abuse, mental health, and optimisation. Each chapter contains a rich blend of new research findings and the book concludes with a very pertinent discussion of how adolescents can be empowered to take control of their own health care. Suggestions on how to improve health care services for adolescents are also provided.

In short, this book is an indispensable resource for anyone who is concerned with the health and development of contemporary adolescents. It blends thoughtful accounts of the varied theoretical perspectives that researchers bring to the study of adolescent health with insightful summaries of their findings and a rich store of factual information on the health issues facing today's teenagers. Yet it is also a very practical book, full of useful ideas for educators, health professionals, parents, and adolescents themselves who strive to optimise physical health, mental health, and human individuality in our complex and changing society.

Candida C. Peterson
University of Queensland
Brisbane, Australia

Preface

This book is about how psychological factors are linked to illness among adolescents. Adolescence is enjoying increasing research focus and interest as evidenced by the number of publications on the teenage years. This book looks at those behaviours that have implications for the physical and mental health of young people. The theme in this volume is that one cannot divorce illness from the individual and the approach that is therefore taken is unashamedly psychosocial.

Chapter 1 sets the context for the discussions that follow. It introduces the reader to definitions of health as well as how conceptions of health and illness develop in young people. It also discusses the idea that the teenage years are a time of health risk. In the second chapter the need for and importance of health education are raised, as are various health education strategies that are available. The bulk of the chapter is taken up with models of health behaviour, that is, it discusses psychological models that have been proposed to explain why individuals engage in the health-related behaviours they do.

The rest of the chapters deal with specific behaviours and the risks they pose to health including the psychological factors that give rise to these behaviours. Included are stress and coping, body image and eating behaviours, sex and the threat of AIDS, substance use, schizophrenia, depression, suicide, and lifestyle factors, namely exercise and diet. Chapter 9, very briefly, makes some suggestions for enhancing adolescent health.

I am indebted to others who have assisted in one way or another with this book. Firstly, I thank Dr John Coleman who agreed to include this volume in his Adolescence and Society Series. I would also like to thank colleagues (and former colleagues) for their useful discussions. In particular, I would like, as always, to thank my family for their love and support.

Patrick Heaven
Wollongong, New South Wales
March, 1995

1 General introduction

1.1 INTRODUCTION

For some years now the adolescent or teenage years have been recognised as crucial for the later emotional development of the individual. This is evidenced by the proliferation of publications devoted to this stage of the life span (e.g. Conger and Petersen 1984; Dusek 1991; Furnham and Gunter 1989; Furnham and Stacey 1991; Heaven 1994; Rice 1992; Sprinthall and Collins 1988). It is only more recently that research attention in both the medical and social sciences has begun to focus exclusively on adolescent health. Indeed, this development has been characterised by the establishment of journals such as the *Journal of Adolescent Health* and the *Journal of Adolescent Health Care* as outlets for research into all matters related to adolescent health.

There are, no doubt, several possible explanations for the growing interest in adolescent health. Two will be mentioned very briefly. The first is the HIV/AIDS epidemic. It is well established that adolescents are increasingly at risk of HIV infection. Research data show that, although teenagers are aware of the dangers inherent in practising unsafe sex, this awareness is not matched by appropriate preventive behaviour (Crawford, Turtle and Kippax 1990; Moore and Rosenthal 1993). It is therefore crucial to understand all aspects of adolescent sexuality, adolescents' perceptions of risky behaviours, and the effectiveness of behaviour-change programmes. Another reason for the interest in adolescent health may be that the onset of some behaviours such as cigarette smoking occurs in adolescence (Hill, White, Pain and Gardner 1990). Given the links between cigarette smoking and cardiovascular and pulmonary diseases in later life, it is important to understand just why some teenagers are at risk from cigarette smoking.

Implicit in this interest in adolescent health is the notion of adolescence as a period of change. It is during the adolescent years that teenagers experiment with new activities, and Jessor (1984) reminds us that many behaviours relevant to health (such as smoking and sexual activity) occur for the first time during this period. For this reason, therefore, it is important to understand all aspects of adolescent health.

1.2 DEFINITIONS OF HEALTH

Just what does it mean to be healthy? Health can be defined in a variety of ways and definitions have undergone substantial change over the years. In the nineteenth century the focus was on the physical aspects and this was followed in later years by an emphasis on germ theory (Millstein and Litt 1990). Later definitions viewed being healthy simply as an absence of any physical ailment, while the current tendency is to view health as involving body, mind, and social factors (Gochman 1988; Taylor 1991). Thus, many writers today view health as a function not only of one's physical condition, but also of one's attitudes toward health, one's perceptions of risk, one's diet, and the environment. For example, a teenager who believes that he or she is unlikely ever to become HIV positive is more likely to engage in risky behaviours such as practising unsafe sex or sharing needles. This teenager's health status is therefore partly determined by cognitive as well as behavioural factors.

According to Gochman (1988), a definition of health should incorporate three perspectives. The first emphasises the biological aspect of health and is primarily concerned with such factors as physiological malfunctioning and germ theory. Also of relevance are certain overt symptoms of illness.

The second perspective concerns the social roles that individuals are expected to perform. Thus, those teenagers who do not perform the roles expected of them are likely to be labelled 'deviant'. The third perspective is the psychological approach. Not surprisingly, this view emphasises the individual's attitudes and perceptions. Thus, those who 'feel' well are likely to think of themselves as being healthy. According to this view, personal experience as well as cognitive factors therefore predict one's wellness or illness.

These perspectives of health raise two important issues which require closer attention. The first is the idea that one is responsible for or in control of one's health, and the second is a view of health referred to as the biopsychosocial model. Each of these will be briefly discussed.

Being responsible for one's health

It was pointed out above that one's health status may be determined, in part, by cognitive and behavioural factors. The teenager who *believes* that HIV infection is unlikely will be less inclined to adopt safe-sex practices. This suggests that many behaviours which have an effect on health are under the individual's personal control. That is, one can *choose* to live a healthy life, or not. According to this argument, many diseases (e.g. lung cancer or heart disease) reflect lifestyle and personal choice (see also Chapter 8).

The concept of 'locus of control' has had an important influence on psychologists' understanding of human motivation. So-called 'internals' take charge of their life events. They believe that they are in control and largely responsible for what happens to them. By contrast, those who are externally controlled believe that what happens to them is largely due to luck or chance. There is a large research literature which has implicated locus of control in a wide range of health behaviours and attitudes. In brief, those who have a sense of personal control are more likely to practise healthy behaviours (Lau 1988).

A related concept is attributional style which is based upon a reformulated learned helplessness model of depression. A pessimistic or negative attributional style has been shown to be related to personality traits such as low self-esteem and loneliness as well as poor health outcomes (Peterson, Seligman and Valliant 1988). Locus of control and attributional style have important implications for health status and will be discussed in more detail in the next chapter.

The biopsychosocial model

The view that physical, psychological, and sociological factors play an important role in determining an individual's health status is referred to as the biopsychosocial model (Engel 1977). According to Engel, the medical model that concentrates on the biological causes of illness is unable fully to explain all matters of health and illness. This is because the medical model excludes from consideration psychological and social factors and suggests that what deviates from the norm of biological variables must be 'disease' or 'illness'. Medical practitioners find it tempting to apply this reductionist taxonomy to all cases of illness and to look no further than a biological cause for the aberrant health status.

According to the medical model, mind is separate from body. In other words, this approach is a single-factor model of illness (Taylor 1991) focusing on a very limited range of causes (usually biological) that tends to overlook other possible causal elements such as cognitive or psychosocial factors. Some would suggest that, quite often, it would be appropriate when reviewing an individual's health status to consider psychological and social causes in addition to biological ones (Engel 1977).

The biopsychosocial model argues that the boundaries between 'wellness' and 'illness' are diffuse and that the medical model is therefore not always an appropriate yardstick for delineating the two. Unlike the medical model, the biopsychosocial model includes the patient as well as the illness. As Engel (1977: 133) suggests:

> By evaluating all the factors contributing to both illness and patienthood, rather than giving primacy to biological factors alone, a biopsychosocial model would make it possible to explain why some individuals experience as 'illness' conditions which others regard merely as 'problems of living', be they emotional reactions to life circumstances or somatic symptoms.

According to one recent review (Irwin and Orr 1991) there has, of late, been increasing communication across scientific disciplines. The authors found that many researchers are beginning to recognise that adolescent wellbeing, health, and illness are multidimensional in nature, comprising not only mind and body, but also environmental and legal elements. The biopsychosocial model of health and illness challenges medical practitioners to take all aspects of individual functioning into account when diagnosing and treating an illness (Engel 1977). Thus, they are being encouraged to acknowledge that health and illness are determined by multiple causes that interact with each other and that an adequate diagnosis can be made only once the biological, social, and psychological factors have been assessed (Schwartz 1982).

Practitioners are being challenged to show an interest in all aspects of the patient, to communicate with the patient, to take note of the patient's life circumstances, and to be more sensitive to the personal problems of the patient. Thus, the challenge to the medical practitioner is to adopt a *systems approach*, that is, to recognise that the biological, social, and psychological aspects of the individual form an integrated system and that they work in unison in determining health (see Figure 1.1). In other words, it is suggested that changes to just one element of the system have the potential to affect other elements in the system.

Consider, for example, the teenager who is rejected by her peers at school. Her class mates avoid contact with her as much as possible. She is hardly ever asked to join in class activities, nor is she invited to social gatherings. As a consequence, she feels isolated and lonely, she is not eating well and has lost some weight. Unaware of the school situation, the family doctor treats the physical symptoms, disregarding their social origins. Not surprisingly, her physical condition remains largely unaltered.

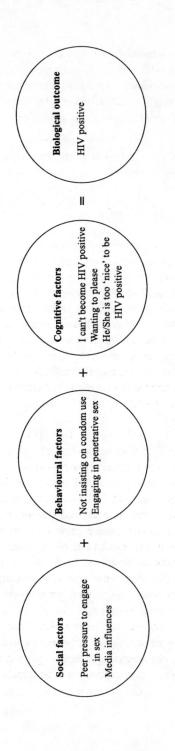

Social factors

Peer pressure to engage in sex
Media influences

+

Behavioural factors

Not insisting on condom use
Engaging in penetrative sex

+

Cognitive factors

I can't become HIV positive
Wanting to please
He/She is too 'nice' to be HIV positive

=

Biological outcome

HIV positive

Figure 1.1 A biopsychosocial approach to HIV infection among teenagers

The biopsychosocial model forms the basis for our definition of health. That is, it is recognised that biological and psychosocial processes play an important role in most manifestations of health and illness. In our examination of adolescent health, attention will be paid primarily to the psychosocial and individual difference variables that are involved.

1.3 CONCEPTIONS OF HEALTH AND ILLNESS AMONG ADOLESCENTS

This section will review adolescents' perspectives on health and illness. We begin by examining the development of health beliefs among young people.

The development of health beliefs

A relatively large number of studies have investigated the health and illness beliefs of young children (e.g. Campbell 1975; Dielman, Leech, Becker *et al.* 1980; Gochman 1971), although fewer studies have concerned themselves exclusively with the adolescent years. Nonetheless, what evidence there is suggests that, as with other beliefs and values, there is a developmental sequence in the establishment of health beliefs. It would appear that the development of these beliefs is closely allied to individual cognitive development.

Cognitive-developmental studies

Burbach and Peterson (1986) recently reviewed several research projects that attempted to shed some light on the developmental stages of illness conception. The studies found that cognitively mature children are more likely to feel that they have some control over illness and the healing process. Very often, younger children are likely to view illness as the outcome of their own bad behaviour and they think of illness as a form of punishment. Older children are able to be more specific about symptoms and diseases. They can describe more clearly the nature of the ailment or just where the pain is. Younger children, by contrast, describe illness in ways that are less clear and specific (e.g. 'I feel sore').

Research findings also indicate that older children, rather than younger ones, are more aware of the relationships between the psychological, social, and affective aspects of disease (Burbach and Peterson 1986). Older children have the capacity, it appears, to use internal cues when determining their health status. On the other hand, younger children are more reliant on external cues (such as a bleeding finger) or external verdicts (such as the opinion of the family doctor) to determine their health status.

It is therefore clear that as children mature cognitively and are able to think more rationally, their conceptualisations of health and illness change. There are subtle, yet quite important, differences in the perceptions of children at various stages of development. Older children, especially those functioning at the formal operations stage rather than at the concrete operational stage (Santrock 1990), employ abstract reasoning in their conceptualisations of illness. Whereas older children are able to view illness as having multiple causes, younger ones have more simplistic and unsophisticated notions of health and illness (Millstein 1991).

Themes in conceptualisations of health and illness

When asked to describe what it means to be healthy or ill, children differ in the themes they employ to describe what they mean. For instance, one study of children aged between 6 and 13 years found differences in illness conceptualisation between the younger and older children (Campbell 1975). The children were surveyed while recovering in hospital and asked the following question: 'Now I'm wondering about how you know when you're sick. When you say you are sick, what do you mean? On one day you know you are well; on another you know you are sick. OK, what's the difference?' (Campbell 1975: 93).

Several illness themes were uncovered and are shown in Table 1.1. Campbell (1975) found that there was some consensus between younger and older children as to the most salient or important themes. For instance, among both groups it was found that the vague and non-specific feeling states were more common definers of illness than questions of mood or altered role. It was also noted that older children were more likely than younger children to incorporate specific diseases or diagnoses in their definitions or to pay attention to altered roles. Despite some intergenerational similarities between mothers and older children, mothers' definitions were more sophisticated, that is, they were more psychosocially oriented, they were more exact, and also found to be more subtle.

The results of Campbell's (1975) research indicate that children even as young as 6 years of age have acquired consensus views as to the nature of illness. It also appears that, as children mature cognitively and acquire more advanced language skills, there is greater refinement or sophistication of their definitions of illness. Older children, for instance, are capable of recognising role performance. Thus, these results support those reported by

Table 1.1 Children's conceptions of illness

Themes	Examples
1. Non-localised, non-specific feeling states	'Feeling bad', 'not right'
2. Non-localised but specified feeling states	Non-localised 'soreness' or 'pain'
3. Specified and localised somatic feelings	'Stomach aches'
4. Visible external signs	'Swollen joints', 'spitting up stuff'
5. Objective signs not immediately visible	'Hot forehead', 'sugar in urine'
6. Disease concept or specific diagnosis	'Appendicitis', 'chicken pox'
7. Mood, motivational, attitudinal states	'Grouchy', 'irritable', 'unhappy'
8. Increase in sick role behaviour	'Want to lie down', 'go to bed', 'tell mother I am sick'
9. Altered conventional role	'Don't go to school'
10. Behaviour or intentions of others	'Mother gives me medicine', 'husband looks after me'
11. Explicit restriction of illness concept	'If I just have a cold, I am not sick'

Source: Campbell 1975

Burbach and Peterson (1986), which were discussed in the previous section.

When adolescents are asked to explain what 'being healthy' means to them, they typically suggest the following (Millstein and Litt 1990: 431):

- Living up to one's potential
- Being able to function physically, mentally, and socially
- Experiencing positive emotional states

One study examined the conceptions of health and illness of adolescents aged between 11 and 18 years. Students were interviewed individually about their understanding of what it means to be healthy or ill (see Campbell 1975 for the procedure used). The respondents employed various themes to define the concepts, as shown in Table 1.2. Of some importance was the finding that certain themes were associated with being healthy, but not with being ill. The table shows, for example, that health definitions focused more on general functional status (e.g. 'Easy to run a mile'), preventive-maintenance behaviours (e.g. 'A good diet'), and restriction-qualification (e.g. 'Not having too many illnesses') (Millstein and Irwin 1987: 518).

According to Table 1.2, illness profiles of the adolescent sample showed more emphasis on somatic feeling states (e.g. 'I feel sick'), indicators of illness (e.g. 'Swollen joints'), role functioning (e.g. 'Can't go to school'), and dependence on the evaluation of others (e.g. 'Mother says I am sick') (Millstein and Irwin 1987: 518). There were also other notable differences. For example, the authors found that younger adolescents focused on 'absence of illness', while there were some differences between the age groups in the range of themes used to define illness and health.

These findings suggest that the illness definitions of adolescents appear much more varied and diverse than their health definitions (Millstein and Irwin 1987). Thus, the researchers concluded that adolescents are more verbal about illness than they are about health, which might be suggestive of the fact that, for these respondents, illness is much more salient. It is also apparent that adolescents' conceptions of health and illness are not mutually exclusive, that is, aspects of one are incorporated into the other. Adolescents' definitions of health and illness therefore overlap to some extent. Health promotion and education schemes that focus only on the absence of illness may therefore be only partly successful (Millstein and Irwin 1987).

Source of health beliefs

Some writers (e.g. Lau, Quadrel and Hartman 1990) have argued that there are two models whereby health beliefs are learned. These are *enduring family socialisation* and *lifelong openness*. According to the first model, health beliefs are learned from the family, rather than from others such as the peer group. A primary method for acquiring a set of health beliefs is through social learning, that is, imitating the health beliefs and behaviours of other members of the family. As the authors explain (p. 242):

> [Parents] buy and prepare food for their children to eat, they engage in physical or sedentary leisure-time activities, they may drink excessively or may smoke, they bring drugs (both legal and illegal) into the home, they decide when a child should see a doctor.

In a longitudinal study that tested these two models, Lau and colleagues (1990) examined the extent to which parents and peers influenced the health beliefs and behaviours of adolescents as they moved into adulthood. A sample of adolescents who were still living at home completed a questionnaire concerned about the performance of a range of preventive

Table 1.2 Proportion of themes used in definition of health and illness by adolescents

Definitional themes	Health Mean	Illness Mean
Somatic feeling states	33.2	58.9
Indicators of health and illness	13.5	21.3
Objective indicators	12.0	16.5
Diagnoses	1.5	4.8
Functional capacity	16.4	7.1
General function	13.9	2.0
Role function	2.4	7.7
Affective states	6.5	8.0
Evaluation of others	0.0	0.9
Preventive-maintenance behaviours	17.9	0.3
Restriction-qualification	5.1	0.2

Source: Millstein and Irwin 1987

health behaviours and how effective they thought those behaviours were. Parents were asked similar sorts of questions as well as about their efforts at training their teenagers to perform those behaviours. Respondents were interviewed over a three-year period.

The evidence suggested that the two models in question must be rejected in their extreme forms. Lau and colleagues (1990) found that parents *do* play an important socialisation role in adolescents' health beliefs, although their influence is not as strong as first believed. It was also found that peers have some influence over adolescents, especially once they leave the home for university. This influence, however, is limited. Thus, the authors proposed a third model, namely, the *windows of vulnerability* model.

The authors suggest that parents play an influential role in the health beliefs and behaviours of their children, except during 'critical periods', or periods of vulnerability (Lau *et al.* 1990: 255). Such critical periods occur during adolescence (e.g. when teenagers experiment with different behaviours), when adolescents leave the home, and when the individual sets up his or her own home environment. During the adolescent's search for personal identity (Erikson 1968), it is not uncommon to experiment with different roles and behaviours. This is a critical period for the teenager when the influence of the peer group may be quite powerful. In summary, therefore, this model (Lau *et al.* 1990: 255):

predicts enduring parental influence *unless* the child is exposed during a vulnerable period to important social agents whose beliefs and behavior differ from those of the parents. In this case, beliefs and behavior should change to become more consistent with those of the new socialization agents.

It is quite clear from the above discussion that adolescence is a time of transition. In particular, it is clear that beliefs and conceptualisations about health and illness as well as preventive behaviours are in a state of flux. Research has consistently found age and sex differences in a range of behaviours that have a direct impact on health status. These include smoking, exercise, snacking, consumption of fast food, to name just a few (e.g. Cohen, Brownell and Felix 1990). These will be discussed in more detail in subsequent chapters.

Adolescent health concerns

Just as adolescents are able to conceptualise health and illness, so too they have specific health concerns. The Australian Longitudinal Survey (Department of Education, Employment and Training 1991) examined the health beliefs of over 5,000 teenagers aged 16–19 years. About one-fifth of respondents thought that their health had improved over the past year. Fewer than 10 per cent thought that their health had deteriorated while almost 70 per cent believed that their health had remained the same.

Sobal (1987) interviewed 278 young adolescents in the United States about their health concerns. Most of the respondents were white and from working-class backgrounds. Thirty-four per cent responded that they were in excellent health, 50 per cent in good health, and 16 per cent in fair or poor health. Ten per cent reported that they very rarely gave much thought to their health, whereas 35 per cent said that they often did; 55 per cent thought about their health only sometimes. The teenagers were also asked about the health issues that concerned them most. Although they noted a total of thirty such concerns, the ten issues that concerned them most were the following:

- Dental problems
- Getting along with friends
- Nutrition
- Sex
- Vitamins
- Getting along with adults
- Acne

- Sports injuries
- Sleep
- Headaches

Younger teenagers were found to be more concerned than older teen-agers about such issues as friends, vitamins, headaches, child abuse, car accidents, stomach pain, availability of health services, nervousness, drinking, dieting, venereal disease, frequent coughing, suicide, drugs, menstruation, and birth control. Girls, more than boys, were concerned about pregnancy, menstruation, birth control, acne, and being overweight. Boys were more concerned about sports injuries and sex. Those teenagers who believed that they were not as healthy as their peers were more concerned about depression, car accidents, drinking, and child abuse (Sobal 1987).

A similar study was conducted among a large group of over 700 Canadian adolescents (Hodgson, Feldman, Corber and Quinn 1986) aged between 12 and 20 years. Table 1.3 shows the percentage of respondents who indicated that they worry a lot or some of the time about various health issues. It also shows the proportion of respondents who had actually consulted a doctor or nurse about the problem and those who would have liked to have consulted someone about it. From the table it is clear that this sample of teenagers was most concerned about such issues as acne, followed by menstrual problems (girls only), nervous/emotional problems, and dental concerns. Some of these issues overlap with those uncovered by Sobal (1987).

It is perhaps noteworthy that both studies found adolescents to be concerned about sexual matters such as birth control and venereal disease. The Canadian study found that, although just over 22 per cent of the respondents reported engaging in sexual intercourse, only about 9 per cent were actually concerned about birth control. Girls were more concerned about this issue than were boys. Moreover, girls aged 16 years and older who had experienced sexual intercourse were more concerned about birth control than were boys of all ages or younger girls. Birth control and safe sex practices are important matters for adolescents and have important implications for health. They will be discussed in more detail in a sub-sequent chapter.

The health concerns of adolescents that have been discussed thus far indicate that they cover non-medical issues as well, such as inter-personal relationships. This seems to be supportive of other studies that have found that, whereas younger teenagers are more concerned about such issues as smoking and drug use, older teenagers are more concerned about school and career (Millstein and Litt 1990).

Perhaps not surprisingly, socio-economic factors play an important determining role in adolescents' perceptions of their health status and health concerns. Support for this view was found in a United States study of disadvantaged minority youth attending an inner-city school and students (mainly white) attending a private suburban school (Walker, Cross, Heyman *et al.* 1982). Although private and inner-city youth did not differ in the amount of time they spent thinking about their health, private students perceived themselves to be healthier than inner-city students (39.8 per cent vs. 26.8 per cent). Private school students tended to rate their own health as very good 51.8 per cent of the time compared to inner-city youth (31.8 per cent of the time).

There were also slight differences in these students with respect to their health concerns (Walker *et al.* 1982). Table 1.4 lists the five issues that concern these groups of students most.

What can one conclude on the basis of these results? Firstly, it would be wise to replicate the study in other cultures. One needs to check the cultural

Table 1.3 Health concerns of Canadian adolescents

Problem	% who worry a lot or some of the time	Consulted a doctor	Would like to consult a doctor
Acne	47.4	39.9	25.2
Menstrual	31.5	43.4	40.0
Nervous/emotional	26.3	54.2	38.6
Dental	25.9	54.1	66.7
Overweight	25.9	27.3	39.7
Eyes/vision	21.6	65.1	31.7
Sports injuries	19.7	18.0	37.8
Stomach aches	19.0	35.6	25.0
Birth control	9.2	26.2	44.0
Short for age	8.8	19.0	65.6
Underweight	6.8	31.1	40.0
Chronic health problem	5.1	71.0	31.9
Tall for age	2.6	16.7	24.8
Recreational drugs	1.6	20.0	19.4
Alcohol/drinking	1.2	14.3	42.9
Venereal disease	1.1	20.0	60.0

Source: Hodgson *et al.* 1986

specificity of these results and also determine what changes in health concerns have occurred since the original study was conducted over ten years ago. The results make clear that there are important socio-economic as well as ethnic influences on the way adolescents perceive their health status. Thus, health care services designed for teenagers should take note of just who their clientele are so that they can target their services more effectively (see next chapter).

1.4 ADOLESCENCE: A PERIOD OF HEALTH RISK

Adolescence is a time during which the young person is striving to achieve a personal identity. As such, it is a time during which the adolescent will experiment with different behaviours. Some writers view the adolescent years as a time of 'storm and stress' and of alienation. Others see it simply as a period of risk (Jessor 1984; Jessor, Donovan and Costa 1991; Kagan 1991; Mechanic 1991). Risky behaviours are those behaviours the outcome of which remain unclear. Such behaviours may have either harmful or non-injurious effects (Irwin and Millstein 1991).

Jessor and his associates propose a theory of *psychosocial risk* suggesting that a range of factors may predispose some teenagers to engage in problem behaviour, some of which may have direct effects on health status. These factors are (Jessor *et al.* 1991):

Social background factors
- Educational level
- Family composition and network
- Positive and negative life events, etc.

Table 1.4 Five health concerns of private school and inner-city school youth

Private students	Inner-city students
Depression-sadness	Acne
Tiredness	Health worries
Acne	Depression-sadness
How far to go with sex	Tiredness
Birth control	Headaches

Source: Walker *et al.* 1982

Social psychological factors
- Personality (values, beliefs, personal control)
- Perceived environment (e.g. parental control, role of social models, and peer approval)

Behavioural system
- Problem behaviour (drugs, smoking, general deviance)
- Conventional behaviour

According to this model, various factors of a personal as well as an environmental nature are closely interrelated in predisposing teenagers to engage in certain problem behaviours. As the authors indicate, however, there are also protective factors within each domain. For instance, a family in which there is communication between parents and adolescent, and in which parents adopt an authoritative parenting style, is likely to substantially reduce the risks of adolescent problem behaviours (Heaven 1994). Likewise, whereas some personality traits such as low self-esteem may be related to adolescent risk behaviours, others such as high self-esteem or religiosity may act as protective factors (Jessor 1993). As Mechanic (1991: 638) explains:

> children who grow up in decent neighborhoods and well-integrated families, who have parents and other close role models who communicate interest, caring, and support, but also convey high but realistic expectations and standards, are substantially protected against significant risks.

The model of psychosocial risk also distinguishes between proximal and distal factors in risk-taking (Jessor *et al.* 1991). Proximal factors have direct links to problem behaviour (e.g. the modelling effects of friends), while distal factors (such as self-esteem) have indirect effects on risky behaviours. There is empirical support for this psychosocial model of risk. In his longitudinal study, Jessor (1984) was able to predict the time of first sexual intercourse (a health risk) of a group of high school students. He identified a psychosocial pattern prior to first sexual intercourse. Thus, those virgins who engaged in sexual activity early were found to be high on expectation and value for independence, lower on value and expectation for academic performance, tolerated deviant forms of behaviour, were less religious, tended not to attend church, and were more critical of society. They were also engaged in other problem behaviours and seemed more aligned with the values of the peer group than with those of their parents.

One is able to delineate five different types of adolescents who are at risk primarily from three behavioural syndromes, namely, adolescent pregnancy, crime, and drugs. The five types at risk are (Kagan 1991):

- Those who have experienced chronic school failure
- Those in a family environment of indifference, abuse, and neglect
- Adolescents who are vulnerable to peer values and peer persuasion
- Adolescents who need to prove that they are not fearful of risk
- Those in families that communicate that stealing, drug use, and pregnancy is acceptable behaviour

Problem behaviours appear to be interrelated and it has been argued that health risks are implicated in many of these (Jessor 1984). Jessor and his colleagues have argued that many risky behaviours, in fact, occur *within* the same individual. They cite examples from their own research programme in support of this view. For instance, alcohol use in adolescence is related to involvement with other drugs, while drug use is related to involvement in other risky behaviours such as sexual intercourse (Jessor 1984). Although the health risks from some of these activities are quite apparent, others are less obvious such as insufficient sleep, lack of exercise, and poor diet, to mention just a few (Jessor 1984).

Health risks during adolescence can be defined from a number of different perspectives. It is possible, for example, to consider behaviours that have almost immediate health consequences (e.g. driving after alcohol consumption), or to consider behaviours that may have more long-term effects, such as a high-fat diet. On the other hand, one could consider behaviours that have both short- and long-term health effects, such as pregnancy. Jessor (1984), to whose ideas we shall return in the next chapter, discusses several of these perspectives on health risk. A number of these have been summarised in Table 1.5.

Adolescents' perceptions of risk

An important area of study is the examination of teenagers' ability to perceive risk adequately. To what extent do teenagers perceive risks to their own safety and health, and do they differ in their perceptions from adults?

There appears to be a generally accepted stereotype that adolescents perceive less risk than adults. Explanations for this view range from adolescents who focus on the benefits, rather than the risks, of some behaviours, to adolescent egocentrism as manifested by the *imaginary audience* and the *personal fable* (Elkind 1967). Imaginary audience refers to the fact that teenagers seem convinced that they are the centre of attention. Thus, they may spend long hours grooming themselves for their 'audience'. Adolescents also construct a personal fable, that is, they think of themselves as quite special people who experience events in a very intense way. They

Table 1.5 Perspectives on health risks in adolescence

Type of risk	Example
Immediate – within adolescence	Drink-driving
Post-adolescent period	High-fat diet
Immediate and post-adolescent	Becoming pregnant
Risk derived from behaviour	Cigarette smoking
Risk derived from personality	Locus of control
Risks derived from environment	Peer/media pressure
Gender-related risks	Alcohol consumption in pregnancy

Source: Jessor 1984

believe that no one else can feel as passionately about something as they do. As a consequence of these beliefs, it is suggested that adolescents view themselves as unique and invulnerable to risk.

Two recent research reports (Beyth-Marom, Austin, Fischhoff *et al.* 1993; Quadrel, Fischhoff and Davis 1993) found only partial support for suggestions that adolescents view themselves as less vulnerable than adults. One of the studies was designed to test the adolescent invulnerability hypothesis among groups of low-risk teenagers, their parents, and high-risk teenagers from juvenile centres. Each respondent was asked to evaluate their risk from eight possible adverse events, four of which were high in perceived controllability (e.g. an unplanned pregnancy), and four which were low in controllability (e.g. exposure to radiation). Each event was also evaluated in terms of target groups such as an acquaintance and a friend. In addition, parents rated their teenagers who, in turn, rated their parents.

Summaries of the data revealed that adults, more than the teenage groups, rated themselves as equally vulnerable compared to the target group. This appears to support the concept of adolescent invulnerability (Quadrel *et al.* 1993). However, when respondents were asked to differentiate between being highly vulnerable and less vulnerable, adults were, on average, more likely than low-risk and high-risk teenagers to perceive themselves as being less vulnerable: 34.5 per cent, 35.9 per cent, and 41.5 per cent respectively. Moreover, when the perceptions of parents and teenagers were compared, parents showed a higher trend toward a perception of invulnerability.

When consideration is given to each of the eight events mentioned in the study, low-risk teenagers were more likely to see an acquaintance at risk from alcoholism, while high-risk teenagers perceived acquaintances to be more at risk from alcoholism and unwanted pregnancy. Adults tended to view acquaintances at risk from alcoholism. All the other comparisons showed weak relative invulnerability. In conclusion, Quadrel and her colleagues (1993) found only limited support for the adolescent invulnerability hypothesis. As they explained (p. 111):

> Invulnerability was not, however, any greater for adolescents than for adults. Teens were more likely to distinguish their risk from that of the target. This might reflect a heightened tendency to overdifferentiate their personal situation . . . . However, it might also reflect more intense observation of friends and acquaintances than is possible for adults . . . . In any case, having made these additional distinctions, teens often judged themselves to have the greater risk.

In one investigation (Benthin, Slovic and Severson 1993), a sample of 15 year olds living in the United States was asked to rate the riskiness of thirty different behaviours, some of which could be considered to be problem behaviours (such as using cocaine or having sex), and others which could be viewed as socially approved risk-taking behaviours (e.g. downhill skiing).

The results showed that some behaviours (e.g. crack or cocaine use) were viewed as quite risky, while others (e.g. bicycle riding) were seen to be low in risk with high benefit. The teenagers also viewed having sex as risky, but that such a risk was as controllable as the risk involved in playing sports. The respondents were also more aware of the risks from sex than disease, but were more fearful of the risks from disease than from pregnancy. Interestingly, the respondents thought that their friends were more at risk from sexual behaviour than they were.

Finally, the authors were able to differentiate the various behaviours in terms of their riskiness *and* the extent to which the behaviours were admired. Those admired the most included some viewed as problem behaviours and some not so viewed: skiing, alcohol, sex, and marijuana. Those behaviours not admired were taking artificial sweeteners, diet pills, pain relievers, prescription drugs (not risky), and compulsive dieting and binge eating (very risky).

It has been argued that one way of understanding just why some teenagers engage in health-compromising behaviours is to examine the perceived costs and benefits of those behaviours. One such study examined the costs and benefits that adolescents associate with alcohol use and sexual behaviour (Small, Silverberg and Kerns 1993). The authors found that it is the perceived *costs* of engaging in a behaviour that are likely to differentiate sexually active from sexually non-active teenagers, and drinkers from non-drinkers. Females were more likely than males to perceive more costs in engaging in sexual intercourse and in alcohol use. Although non-sexually active adolescents perceived more costs attached to being sexually active than did those who were sexually active, the perceived costs to the non-active group tended to decrease with increasing age. Likewise, there was a tendency for older students at school to perceive fewer costs attached to alcohol consumption than younger teenagers. On average, however, non-alcohol using adolescents were likely to perceive more costs in drinking than those who used alcohol (Small *et al.* 1993).

These findings have important implications for changing the health compromising behaviours of adolescents. The main results suggest that most teenagers are aware of the benefits of certain behaviours, and that health education campaigns should rather focus on the *costs* of those behaviours. As the authors (Small *et al.* 1993: 84) argue:

> The present findings suggest that if we wish to discourage or delay such behavior in young people we should put our efforts into increasing and clarifying the perceived costs of those behaviors rather than trying to devalue the benefits.

The health risks to homeless youth

Homeless youth have been identified as particularly vulnerable to a variety of problem behaviours and as being quite susceptible to disease and infections. One reason for this susceptibility is that many homeless teenagers have to deal in drugs or prostitution to survive. Moreover, young females also face physical and sexual violence on the streets.

Youth homelessness appears to be a growing problem in many Western nations as well as some countries of the former Soviet bloc. It is estimated that there are 100 million street youth across the globe (Luna 1991). Family violence, rising levels of unemployment and poverty, and reduced levels of social welfare assistance seem to be some of the causal factors that have forced teenagers on to the streets. For those who have left conflict-ridden homes, however, being on the street has some distinct advantages such as freedom from conflict, companionship, and support from other teenagers (Noller and Callan 1991).

For many teenagers there are serious health risks to being homeless. One study of homeless individuals aged between the late adolescent and late adult years identified problems from influenza and bronchitis to depression and alcohol dependence (Ropers and Boyer 1987). That street youth are at risk from a variety of diseases is supported by several other studies. At one

United States clinic designed especially for street youth, almost 5,000 diagnoses were made over a five-year period. Nearly half of these were gynaecological, obstetric, STD (sexually transmitted disease), and dermatologically related. Dermatological problems included acne, scabies, pubic and body lice, head lice, boils, frostbite, atopic dermatitis, cellulitis, folliculitis, paronychia, and mouth lesions (e.g. herpes). Although psychiatric diagnoses constituted a relatively small proportion of all diagnoses, most of these were related to depression, anxiety, and suicide (almost one-third). Drug- and alcohol-related problems constituted over 20 per cent of diagnoses in this group (Deisher and Rogers 1991). The various diagnostic categories are shown in Table 1.6.

Street youth are at risk from a variety of STDs, including vaginitis, urethritis, venereal warts, genital herpes, gonorrhea, syphilis, cervicitis, and HIV/AIDS (Deisher and Rogers 1991). Researchers have noted rising trends of HIV infection among youth. For instance, almost 11 per cent of street youth at one New York clinic tested HIV positive, while a study in Rio de Janeiro found that almost 69 per cent of males aged 11–23 years who engaged in sexual activity for money were HIV positive (Luna 1991). Being HIV positive is an added stress factor for youth who already feel alienated from mainstream society. For them, being HIV positive increases the risks of depression, suicide, increased risk-taking, and social ostracism (English 1991).

The health risks to inner-city youth

Teenagers who live in large run-down metropolitan areas face their own peculiar health risks. According to some reports from the United States, homocide is the leading cause of death for males aged between 14 and 44 years (Schubiner, Scott and Tzelepis 1993). In many industrialised nations, minority youth are over-represented in inner-city areas. This fact, coupled with the availability of firearms and drugs, is likely to result in increased violent behaviour.

One study (Schubiner *et al.* 1993) attempted to examine these matters in more detail among a sample of 246 inner-city youth, most of whom were black. The authors were interested in respondents' exposure to and participation in violent acts. Fifty-seven per cent of the respondents were female. Of the respondents, 128 were aged between 14 and 18 years, while 125 were aged between 19 and 23 years. Most teenagers were from families classified as poor. At some time in their life, 42 per cent of the respondents had seen someone shot or knifed. While 22 per cent had witnessed someone being killed, 9 per cent had seen more than one person being killed. Table

Table 1.6 Diagnostic health categories for a sample of street youth

Diagnosis	% of sample
Sexually transmitted disease (STD)	16
Gynaecological and obstetric (non-STD)	18
Dermatological	13
Routine health maintenance	13
Respiratory	12
Trauma	7
Psychiatric	7
Gastrointestinal	4
Cardiovascular	2
Ophthalmological	2
Miscellaneous	7

Source: Deisher and Rogers 1991

1.7 details the exposure of the respondents to various other forms of violence over a three-month period.

Another study along similar lines was conducted by researchers in Boston (Vanderschmidt, Lang, Knight-Williams and Vanderschmidt 1993). Nearly half of the high school students in this sample reported being at risk from sexual activity and drinking, while 23 per cent and 25 per cent respectively reported being at risk from illicit drugs and cigarette smoking. More than half of the students reported being involved in violence over the preceding year, while about one-third reported carrying a knife. A gun had been carried by 11 per cent of the sample.

Run-down inner-city areas tend to be characterised by a culture of alienation, despair, and violence. Many of these youth appear overwhelmed by poverty, inequality, discrimination, and the availability of guns and drugs (Gibbs 1988). Table 1.7 suggests that weapons are easy to procure (especially in certain societies such as the US), thus putting the lives of others at risk.

1.5 SUMMARY

There is a growing interest in and awareness of the importance of research into adolescent health. Many behaviours that are risky in terms of their effects upon health have their origins during the adolescent years.

Table 1.7 Percentage of respondents exposed to forms of violence over three months

Type of violence	%
Witnessed one loud argument	81
Seen one physical fight	58
Seen someone shooting a gun	34
Seen at least one knife fight	19
Involved in loud argument	73
Involved in physical fight	32
Carried a knife	30
Carried a gun	18

Source: derived from Schubiner *et al.* 1993

We noted that definitions of health can be approached either from the biomedical or biopsychosocial perspective. Although the biomedical model has dominated thinking about health and illness for many years, we acknowledge the important role that psychosocial processes play in influencing an individual's health status. Whereas the medical model is a single-factor model of illness, the biopsychosocial model also acknowledges the important role that individual and environmental factors play in explaining illness.

This chapter also paid attention to the question of the development of beliefs about health and illness, adolescent health concerns, and adolescents at risk. Adolescents have well developed ideas about the nature of health and illness which reflect their level of cognitive development. They are able to think more sophisticatedly and in abstract terms about illness and to see disease as having multiple rather than single causes. Not surprisingly, some adolescents are concerned about their health status. It has been found that demographic factors such as socio-economic status are significant in shaping adolescents' perceptions of their health and of their health concerns.

Finally, the chapter discussed the view that some adolescents are at risk of developing health problems. Pre-eminent in this regard is the work of Jessor and his associates who have argued that three groups of variables predispose some teenagers to engage in problem behaviours, some of which are health-threatening. Benthin and colleagues (1993) have noted in their research that many adolescents are aware of the risks involved in some behaviours yet are reluctant to change their behaviour. They suggest that this calls into question the value of many information and education pro-grammes. They argue that, although teenagers may be *knowledgeable* about some behaviours, they believe that they are not *personally* at risk. If this is indeed so, it would seem to support the view expressed earlier that some youth adhere to a 'personal fable' and regard themselves as unique and unlikely to be affected by illness.

There are several psychological paradigms that have directed research into the role of attitudes, beliefs, values, and motivations *vis-à-vis* health behaviour. It is to some of these that we now turn our attention.

2 Health education

2.1 INTRODUCTION

It is imperative that adolescents acquire healthy behaviours if they are to reduce their risks of illness. To date, western nations have made significant advances in their control of disease and infection. Some diseases such as smallpox, common a generation ago, have been almost entirely eradicated. Technically, great advances have been made with respect to organ transplantations, genetic engineering, and so forth. Yet it is at the psychosocial level that we remain particularly vulnerable to disease. This would appear to be even more apparent among adolescents, who are susceptible to peer and media influences which may encourage them to experiment with different and sometimes risky behaviours.

There is empirical support for such a view. In one recent American study (Brown, Clasen and Eicher 1986), for example, adolescents were asked to nominate peer pressures that they had experienced. The evidence suggested that peer pressure can be categorised in clusters, the first being the pressure to engage in a variety of social activities such as going to parties. The second cluster, and of relevance to our present discussion, was the pressure to engage in misconduct, including drug use and sexual intercourse. It was found that older adolescents report more peer pressure than younger ones. The authors concluded that peer pressure appears to be an important component of adolescent misconduct. It is also clear that such pressure can have health implications.

Health education needs to be understood in the context of our definition of health. If one follows the biopsychosocial definition as we do, it follows that health education needs to be viewed in that light. In other words, we acknowledge the importance of such factors as personal beliefs and motivations about health and healthy behaviours in predicting the success or otherwise of attempts to influence behaviour. This chapter will examine some of the essential elements in health education among adolescents. It will also discuss some of the most important psychological models pertaining to health beliefs that recognise the centrality of individual values and personal motivation.

2.2 ADOLESCENT INJURY AND DISEASE: THE NEED FOR EDUCATION

Spurred on by the HIV/AIDS crisis, it is only in more recent times that governments have begun to acknowledge the importance of health education and health promotion campaigns. Weighed down by increasing financial costs, governments have slowly turned to advertising slogans and other methods in an effort to alert citizens to the benefits of adopting a healthy lifestyle, preventive behaviour, and regular medical or self-examination for such diseases as breast and testicular cancer.

Health education is particularly crucial among teenagers. Although it was pointed out in the previous chapter that young people are concerned about their health, it was also noted that adolescence is a period of heightened health risk. Thus, it was suggested that a range of environmental and individual factors predispose some teenagers to engage in certain problem or risky behaviours. In this section, we shall briefly review some of the risks faced by teenagers and the need for health education. This is not meant to be an exhaustive review of all possible injury or disease. Readers should consult later chapters in this volume.

According to some reports (e.g. Slap 1991), there are several individual factors which predict risk-taking behaviour among teenagers: gender, socio-economic status, family function, recent stress, and alcohol and drug use (see also Jessor *et al.* 1991). These risk factors are summarised in Table 2.1. According to the authors, it is likely that a combination of these factors will increase an adolescent's risk from health-compromising behaviours. In particular, it would seem that boys are more prone to injury and risky behaviour than are girls. It is interesting to note that governments have targeted some behaviours for educational programmes (e.g. alcohol and drugs), although very few, if any, educational messages are directed at the other factors shown in the table.

In the United States, injury rates for teenagers are quite high: 369 accidents per 1,000 adolescents (Kovar 1991). These are injuries that either require medical attention or limit activity for at least one day. Most accidents occur at school (37 per cent) and are sports-related (Slap 1991). Other accidents occur in the home (21 per cent) and on the streets (11 per cent). In this regard, large run-down metropolitan areas pose a distinct

Table 2.1 Individual factors predicting risk-taking behaviour

1. *Gender*	Males are 2.5 times more likely to die of injury. They are also more likely to suffer other non-fatal injury. Boys take more risks in decision-making.
2. *Socio-economic status*	Death rates from various accidents are 2 times higher in low-income areas than high-income ones. There are higher rates of homicide and assault in poorer areas. Fatal injuries are more common among black children.
3. *Family function*	Families at increased risk are those with medical problems, psychiatric illness, marital discord, unemployment, recent moves, separation of children from parents.
4. *Recent stress*	Stress is related to suicide.
5. *Alcohol and drugs*	Increase all types of risk. They also affect relationships with family and friends.

Source: derived from Slap 1991

threat. This situation is exacerbated by a mixture of drugs and weapons in the United States and the availability of arms in other cultures such as the black townships of South Africa. In the United States, for example, gangs control some areas of the larger cities such as Los Angeles, and these have become virtual no-go areas for other gangs and those with no interest in gang rivalry. In many instances, these youth are unlikely to be affected by slick advertising. In order to protect citizens' health, it seems more probable that governments will need to legislate to control the availability of weapons (particularly to teenagers) and to resort to all means at their disposal to control the spread of harmful drugs.

In other developing societies such as Brazil, rapid urbanisation has had a distinct effect on the health of adolescents. It is reported, for example, that youngsters in the rural areas are more likely to migrate to larger centres in an attempt to escape poverty and find employment. Because they lack legal status in the social system, they are likely to be excluded from health care (Silber 1984). At the same time, data show that, for females aged 15–24 years, complications resulting from abortion and pregnancy are a leading cause of death. Rural adolescents in Brazil are more susceptible to malnutrition and parasitosis, while many Brazilian youth suffer from tuberculosis, rheumatic fever, and so forth. Thus, in such cultures, governments and medical authorities have much to do, not only in terms of health education *per se*, but also in terms of providing primary health care.

In most industrialised nations external causes pose a greater threat to an adolescent's life than disease itself (Kovar 1991). Figures from the United States show that external causes were responsible for 48 per cent of deaths of 12 to 14 year olds. Among older adolescents, the figure was 54 per cent. The motor vehicle features very prominently among external causes, accounting for 27 per cent of deaths among the 12–14 year age group and 40 per cent of deaths among the 15–17 year age group. According to one report, there are several major risk factors for motor vehicle injuries among adolescents. These are young age, male sex, alcohol use, failure to use seat belts, and driving at night (Slap 1991).

A survey of more than 2,000 students in Iowa, United States, revealed that only 2 per cent reported using a helmet when bicycling. More students (54 per cent) used a seat belt when in the front of the car than when travelling in the back (15 per cent) (Schootman, Fuortes, Zwerling *et al.* 1993). Health education campaigns therefore need to take these factors into account when directing 'safe-driving' messages at young drivers. In particular, they need to stress the hazards of driving under the influence of alcohol, non-use of seat belts, as well as the risks of night driving. In addition to advertising, some governments (particularly in the United States) have raised the licensing age and introduced other legislation with respect to teenage driving. Many of these changes have dramatically reduced the accident rate (Slap, 1991).

2.3 HEALTH EDUCATION STRATEGIES

There are a variety of risk factors to adolescent health and it is clear that the methods of alerting youth to these risks will vary from culture to culture and risk factor to risk factor. Health authorities have at their disposal a variety of methods for promoting health. For instance, they can resort to fear-arousing warnings, they can simply provide vital information, or use various behavioural methods (Sarafino 1990).

Fear-arousing messages

Some would argue that too much fear is counterproductive and that individuals in such circumstances are likely to ignore, deny, or minimise the threat to their health in an attempt to rationalise their risky behaviour. However, most writers appear agreed that fear-arousing messages are generally quite effective in motivating people to alter their behaviour or to change their lifestyle. Moreover, it would seem that high fear-arousing messages are more effective in changing attitudes about health than are low fear-arousing ones (Sarafino 1990).

Although a fear-inducing message may change one's *attitudes*, is it likely to result in health-promoting *behaviour*? According to some (Sarafino 1990: 205), there are two methods by which changed attitudes are likely to result in changed behaviour. It is argued that:

> people are more likely to carry out a new preventive action if they receive specific instructions for performing it . . . [whilst] . . . A program may be more successful in changing people's behavior if it helps bolster their self-confidence before urging them to begin the plan.

Thus, fear-arousing messages must be coupled with practical advice about what to do as well as strategies to maintain or increase self-efficacy.

Providing information

The media play an important role in providing health-related information. The success, or otherwise, of media campaigns to promote healthy behaviour depends on the extent to which the following principles are adhered to (Egger 1986: 261–262):

- The media message should be targeted at the appropriate audience. Is the message suitable for an adolescent audience? Is it presented in language they can understand?
- The media message must be changeable. Public attitudes are not fixed and it is sometimes necessary to modify the message, particularly when dealing with adolescents
- The media should be used selectively and sensitively
- Sometimes it is appropriate to present both sides of the argument
- The message source should be credible
- The media message should be stimulating
- Fear inducing messages should be used carefully
- The message must set realistic goals

Some of the message characteristics referred to above can be further subdivided into other variables (Macdonald 1992). For example, message *source* can also refer to the credibility of the messenger, his or her likeability, the power of the message, quantity, and demographic factors. Thus, an important factor is the extent to which a prospective audience is able to identify with or believe in the messenger. Experts are likely to be more persuasive than those perceived to be non-experts, while attractive sources are more likely to be successful than unattractive ones (Baron and Byrne 1994).

Media campaigns can utilise one of two strategies (Egger 1986). One strategy is the communication-behaviour change framework. By this method, the media deliver information to the public who are free to act upon this or not. It has been found that this method is quite effective in changing behaviours that do not require much effort, such as condom use, the use of seat belts, sun screens, etc. This method is less useful for more complex behaviours such as attempts at reducing drug dependence.

The second method is the social marketing approach. This is based upon commercial marketing strategies and encompasses the following (Egger 1986):

- *Market research* This includes, for example, improving the accuracy of the communication directed at the target (adolescent) audience
- *Product development* This includes literature or special kits to assist with attitude and behaviour change or advice about what steps need to be followed to effect a change
- *Special incentives* These help to increase motivation to change attitudes and behaviour
- *Back-up support* This may include counselling sessions, meetings, and so forth

Thus, the social marketing approach differs from the first in a number of ways in that it makes use of product development, back-up support, and other strategies. Social marketing is a relatively sophisticated strategy. It is a systematic approach designed to convince the audience or 'consumer' that an appropriate (healthy) behaviour is more appropriate than other (unhealthy) behaviours. Social marketing is more than changing behaviour. As Lefebvre (1992: 154) explains:

[It] is a method of empowering people to be totally involved and responsible for their well-being; a problem-solving process that may suggest new and innovative ways to attack health and social problems.

Behaviour modification programmes

A final method for assisting in the adoption of healthy behaviours is the behavioural method (Sarafino 1990). This method employs principles of behaviour change to alter behaviours deemed to be at risk. Therapists who have responsibility for helping teenagers change their behaviour use a range of different strategies which may include helping individuals change the way they *think* about an issue, or changing the extent to which behaviours are *rewarded*.

In many instances, risky behaviours are unlikely to be abandoned unless the individual changes the thought processes surrounding the behaviour.

Table 2.2 Possible explanations for smoking by smokers

---

1. I am under a lot of stress, and smoking relaxes me.
2. Smoking stimulates me and helps me to be more effective in my work.
3. I have already substantially reduced my smoking.
4. I only smoke safe, low tar/low nicotine cigarettes.
5. I don't have the will power to give up smoking.

Source: Sarafino 1990

For example, those who smoke may rationalise their behaviour in a variety of ways, as shown in Table 2.2.

Professionals as well as parents and friends sometimes find it difficult to reason with teenagers who rationalise their behaviour in the ways described in Table 2.2. Very often, however, the use of commonsense counterarguments can have positive results in changing risky behaviours, according to Sarafino (1990). Take, for example, the adolescent who 'does not have the will power to change'. Possible responses might be: 'Sure it's difficult. But you may have to try different methods for quitting', or 'It's difficult on your own. Let me try and help you'.

Some professionals resort to behaviour modification techniques when trying to implement behavioural change among teenagers. This is done by changing the way behaviours are rewarded. These radical behaviourists make use of the principles of classical and operant conditioning. It is beyond the scope of this chapter to discuss these in any detail and interested readers should consult other sources (e.g. Hergenhahn 1988; Liebert and Spiegler 1990; Muuss 1988).

In brief, behaviourists contend that one quickly acquires or learns behaviours that are rewarded, while punishment leads to an extinction of behaviour. It was Pavlov (1849–1936) who first noticed that dogs salivate in anticipation of being fed. This led him to conduct several experiments on what he referred to as the *conditioning response*. In later work he showed that food could be associated with another stimulus, such as a tone, and that dogs would then salivate when they heard the tone. These ideas were later extended somewhat by Skinner in his work on *operant conditioning* (Muuss 1988). He suggested that the consequences of one's actions actually determine one's behaviour. That is, the rewards one receives enhance the original behaviour.

Of importance to the present discussion is the view that teenagers can learn health-threatening behaviours through reinforcement of that behaviour. For instance, someone might smoke so as to be more acceptable to the peer group. Being accepted or more popular, it is argued, acts as a reward that increases the smoking behaviour. In behaviour modification programmes where the aim is to eliminate smoking, the behaviour is usually associated with punishment (such as ridicule). Punishment is presented after the unacceptable behaviour, which has the effect of reducing the desirability of the unwanted behaviour.

Some writers (e.g. Liebert and Spiegler 1990) have argued that behaviour modification views human behaviour in rather simplistic terms, disregarding the fact that behaviour is multidetermined. By focusing on the stimulus–response components of behaviour, such therapists ignore individual differences, cultural influences, and free will. For example, some health-related behaviours (e.g. scarring of the body as a result of certain initiation rites) are culture-specific and cannot be accounted for in terms of stimulus and response.

2.4 ADOLESCENT HEALTH SERVICES

Health education for adolescents can occur in a number of different settings. To be effective, the delivery of health services should occur in those places most likely to be frequented by adolescents. The service should use materials (e.g. videos, pamphlets, etc.) that are appropriate for the teenager and that respect the anonymity and confidentiality of the client. Finally, staff should be sympathetic to the needs of the adolescents, while no financial barriers should be placed on those who decide to make use of a service (Klerman 1991). In other words, it is important that adolescents feel at ease in these settings and believe that they are accepted and respected. If not, educational strategies are not likely to succeed. The following are some of the major sources of health care and education for adolescents.

Community-based centres

Most of these centres or clinics provide their services free of charge. The main impetus for the establishment of these clinics was the rising numbers of street youth first evident during the 1960s (Klerman 1991). Klerman suggests that today, such clinics are an accepted feature of the medical landscape, providing an invaluable service to alienated youth who are unwilling and unlikely to use more traditional facilities such as outpatient sections of large hospitals. According to some medical practitioners (e.g. Deisher and Rogers 1991), the number of street youth in large urban areas appears to be growing. It is quite likely, therefore, that community-based centres will play an increasingly important role in providing health services and education to adolescents.

Whereas some community-based clinics provide only specialised care such as ante-natal care, others offer a broad range of medical services. One clinic described by Deisher and Rogers (1991) in the United States offers gynaecological and obstetric services as well as others such as psychiatric, dermatological, and cardiovascular services (see Table 1.6 in the previous chapter for the range of services offered).

It is important that adolescents who attend community clinics for the first time or very infrequently are given thorough physical examinations where possible. As Deisher and Rogers (1991: 502) explain:

> Physicians treating street youth in both outpatient and inpatient settings need to be aware of their often-neglected medical needs. All adolescents who have had lapses in their contact with physicians should have a thorough physical examination that includes both physical and sexual histories. Personal information must be gathered in an objective and nonjudgmental manner. The preeminent issues for adolescents involved in street life must be actively and constructively acknowledged.

School-based clinics and education

School clinics are gaining in popularity in some countries such as the United States. They provide general broad-based services to students ranging from physical examinations (usually for athletic participation), treatment of minor illnesses, immunisation, family planning, and weight control. Few, however, offer contraceptives to students because of vocal opposition from parents (Klerman 1991).

School health education

Although many schools may not have health clinics on campus, many more are involved in a programme of *health education*. Thus, these high school students are instructed in how to achieve physical, social, and emotional health. A health education study group reporting to the Australian Federal Minister of Health and Education recommended in 1980 that comprehensive health education programmes should be available to all Australian students. It suggested, moreover, that health education should be treated as a separate discipline in the schools. In the United States, it was suggested by the National Professional School Health Education Organization in 1984 that health education include the following components:

- Community health
- Consumer health
- Environmental health
- Family life
- Growth and development
- Nutritional health
- Personal health
- Prevention and control of disease and disorders
- Safety and accident prevention
- Substance use and abuse

Although the importance of health education in primary and secondary schools is generally acknowledged, it would seem that it suffers a rather unfortunate fate in some schools. The Australian Curriculum Development Centre (CDC) warned in 1980 that health education was being disadvantaged in a number of ways. For instance, many teachers are not adequately trained to teach the subject, while in other cases it is given to those teachers with 'light' loads. Some teachers fear that involvement in this sort of subject does not count toward promotion or career advancement and that they are really wasting their time. In other instances, health education is taught on an irregular basis, that is, it is often reserved for wet days or taught when there is a 'gap' in the timetable.

It would appear that the best way to raise the status of a subject such as health education in the school system is to treat it as a separate subject with its own specialist teacher and its own identifiable slot in the timetable. Like other subjects, it also needs its own resources. This would allow health education to be identified as an important subject equal in status to others that are taught in school. We shall return to some of these issues in Chapter 8.

2.5 MODELS OF HEALTH BEHAVIOUR

Why is it that some adolescents appear to respond favourably to health education programmes, while others do not? Are there psychological processes at work likely to enhance one's understanding of health-related behaviours? Social psychologists have proposed several models of health behaviour that, they believe, go some way to understanding such behaviours. As they are social-psychological in nature, they concentrate on the relationship between behaviour on the one hand, and attitudes, values, and beliefs on the other (Wallston and Wallston 1984). Some of these models will now be discussed.

The Health Belief Model

The Health Belief Model (HBM) originated among a group of health researchers in the United States. Key features of this model are the following (Becker 1974):

- *Perceived susceptibility*   Belief in a susceptibility to illness is likely to result in compliant behaviour.
- *Perceived severity*   The higher the perceived severity of the illness, the more likely it is that compliant behaviour will result
- *Perceived benefits and costs*   Perception of benefits following behaviour change is likely to lead to compliance
- *Motivation*   Positive health motivation is likely to lead to compliance
- *Modifying factors*   For example, relationship with doctor, demographic factors, and personality are important in determining behaviour

The HBM is embedded in expectancy-valence theory (Wallston and Wallston 1984). It is suggested that one is likely to take preventive action to protect one's health in line with one's perception of *susceptibility* to the disease as well as one's perception of its *severity*. Expectancies for one's effectiveness in avoiding risk and adopting healthy behaviours are also important predictors of whether we actually engage in preventive behaviour or whether we seek treatment for our illness. If one has no faith in a particular course of treatment, one is less likely to follow that treatment regimen. Thus, the likelihood of action is high if one's beliefs about efficacy are high (see also Rosenstock, Strecher and Becker 1988).

Implicit in the theory are *cues for action* (Mullen, Hersey and Iverson 1987) and these can arise in many different ways such as through reading about a disease or through one's perceptions. In summary, the HBM proposes (Rosenthal, Hall and Moore 1992: 166):

> that intentions and behaviour in health matters can be predicted from health-related attitudes and values . . . [and that] . . . preventive health action is influenced by the belief that one is susceptible to the disease or illness in question.

Janz and Becker (1984) reviewed several research studies of the HBM. The authors found substantial support for the importance of the HBM dimensions as predictors of health-related behaviour. Not all HBM dimensions were equally predictive of healthy behaviours, however. The predictors, in descending order of importance, were:

- Perceived barriers to action (89 per cent)
- Perceived susceptibility to disease (81 per cent)
- Perceived benefits of action (78 per cent)
- Perceived severity of disease (65 per cent)

The results of this review (Janz and Becker 1984) have important implications for health education programmes. Too often, health education focuses on the severity of the disease with less attention being paid to other dimensions. From the above, it is suggested that barriers to action and perceived susceptibility to disease need to be addressed more effectively. In addressing drug use among teenagers, for example, it is important to stress that adolescents are at risk from drug use given its availability, and that professional help is available to help overcome drug addiction. With respect to HIV/AIDS, for example, educational messages should stress that those who practise unsafe sex risk infection, while barriers to action (such as an unwillingness to use condoms) should also be addressed.

Some studies do not support the validity of all aspects of the HBM. A study among Australian 18 year olds applied the model to their responses to the threat of AIDS (Rosenthal *et al.* 1992). According to the model, the authors predicted that those teenagers who viewed the AIDS threat as serious and themselves as vulnerable would practise safe sex. They also predicted that those who perceived more benefits than costs in safe-sex behaviour would be more likely to practise safe sex. Finally, they predicted that condom use would be significantly related to the individual's level of health motivation.

The results showed only partial support for the model. For example, female adolescents viewed the AIDS threat as more serious than did the male respondents. Females, more than males, perceived more benefits than barriers to condom use, while males encountered fewer cues to action (condom use) than females. Although there were no significant differences between the sexes on measures of health motivation and susceptibility to infection, these factors did not predict males' sexual risk with casual partners. Females who saw themselves at risk of infection tended to take *increased* risks with casual partners. Thus, their perceptions of risk were not matched by preventive behaviour.

It is not clear to what extent these findings are disease specific. That is, is the overall poor predictive ability of the HBM attributable to factors such as the nature of the disease in question? Rosenthal and her colleagues (1992) suggest that because of the time-lag involved between HIV infection and actual manifestation of the disease, some individuals may be tempted to under-estimate or downplay its seriousness. Because risky sexual behaviour does not have health outcomes that are immediately apparent, some teenagers do not make rational decisions about preventive behaviours.

Evaluation

Some writers view the Health Belief Model not as a model *per se*, but rather as a collection of variables (Wallston and Wallston 1984). Indeed, the authors suggest that far too many variables or elements constitute the Health Belief Model, not all of which are included in every piece of research. Another factor that often detracts from the validity of the Health Belief Model is the fact that researchers employ different measures for the constituent elements. Thus, one researcher's measure of health motivation may differ from that used in another study. This makes it difficult to compare studies that have used different measures of the same variable.

Control of reinforcement

According to social learning theory we can learn behaviours by observing the actions of others and by noting whether or not they are rewarded (reinforced) or punished for their actions. Four constructs form an integral part of social learning theory. They are (Wallston and Wallston 1984):

- Behaviour potential (BP)
- Expectancy (E)
- Reinforcement value (RV)
- Psychological situation (S)

The relationship between these factors can be described in the following terms (Wallston and Wallston 1984: 31):

the potential of a specific behavior (BP) occurring in a given situation (S) is a function of the expectancy (E) that the behavior will lead to a particular reinforcement in that situation and the value of the reinforce-ment (RV) to the individual in that situation.

According to Rotter (1966; 1975) *expectancies* about events are shaped by *reinforcements*. Thus, important to understanding behaviour are the nature of the reinforcement, whether the reinforcement is positive or nega-tive, as well as the *value* that one attaches to the reinforcement (Rotter 1975). In other words, one is more likely to engage in healthy behaviour

(BP) if one expects (E) to be reinforced for the behaviour and if one values the reinforcement.

According to the model, generalised expectancies about reinforcement are crucial to understanding health behaviours. If one believes that rewards are contingent upon one's *own* behaviour, such a belief is referred to as *internal control*. If one believes that rewards are linked to forces outside oneself, then such a belief is referred to as *external control* (Rotter 1966). A vast literature has developed that documents the individual differences between so-called externals and internals, suggesting that locus of control has implications for many behaviours and attitudes (e.g. Lefcourt 1976).

A review (Strickland 1989) of the health locus of control literature has highlighted the extent to which expectancy variables are related to health outcome. In short, studies have found that those who have derived a sense of control and meaning in their world are more likely to engage in health-promoting behaviour. That is, those classified as 'internal' (see p. 3) are more likely to take an interest in messages about health, and are more likely to take active steps to control their health status. For example, one study (e.g. Slenker, Price and O'Connell 1985) found joggers to be more internally controlled than non-joggers. In a study among two groups of late adolescents, researchers found that internals who *valued* health highly were more likely to engage in information-seeking than were externals and those internals who did not value health as highly.

It is generally assumed that one is likely to engage in health protective behaviours if one perceives some threat to one's health. One study among Dutch adolescents aged between 15 and 18 years (Hoorens and Buunk 1993) examined the interaction between locus of control and perceptions of vulnerability to disease. Respondents completed a general locus of control scale as well as a health behaviour scale. They were also asked to estimate their own and others' chances of getting such diseases as AIDS, developing a drinking problem, and suffering a heart attack before age 40 years. The other person in question was either the average high-school student, their best same-sex friend, or an arbitrary high-school student.

Results showed that those who rated themselves as being internally controlled tended to perceive their health risks as lower than those of others. Moreover, the healthier the behaviour of respondents as indicated on the health behaviour scale, the lower was their perceived risk. Thus, the authors suggested that internals are more likely than externals to believe that they have the capacity to reduce risks to their health. Alternatively, it is possible that internals are more likely to engage in health protective behaviours than externals who may believe that chance and fate play an important determining role in their life (Hoorens and Buunk 1993).

Table 2.3 Health locus of control measures

Arthritis helplessness index
Alcoholic responsibility scale
Belief in pain questionnaire
Cancer locus of control
Children's health locus of control
Children's recovery from illness
Control of recovery from physical disability
Dental health locus of control
Depression locus of control scale
Diabetes locus of control
Dieting beliefs scale
Drinking-related locus of control scale
Dyadic sex regulation scale
Fetal health locus of control
Health locus of control
Health-specific locus of control beliefs
Heart disease locus of control
Hypertension locus of control
Labour in childbirth
Locus of control inventory for the deaf
Mental health locus of control and origin
Mental health locus of control
Multidimensional health locus of control
Perceived control of diabetes mellitus
Perceived control of tablet-treated diabetics
Smoking specific locus
Staff perceived control of diabetes
Weight locus of control

Source: Furnham and Steele 1993

Measures of health locus of control

Several locus of control measures have been developed. A recent review (Furnham and Steele 1993) identified twenty-eight such instruments. Some are quite short (e.g. only four or five items), while others are a little longer, comprising several dimensions. The measures identified by Furnham and Steele cover the whole spectrum of health locus of control (see Table 2.3). One of the better known measures is the Multidimensional Health Locus of Control (MHLC) scale (Wallston, Wallston and DeVellis 1978). It is an eighteen-item scale divided into three sections: internal control (e.g. 'If I take care of myself, I can avoid illness'); powerful others (e.g. 'Having regular contact with my physician is the best way for me to avoid illness'); and chance locus of control (e.g. 'No matter what I do, if I am going to get sick, I will get sick'). Research evidence suggests that how one responds to each of the dimensions is determined by several factors such as the individual's current health status and cohort effects (Furnham and Steele 1993).

Attributional style

Closely related to control of reinforcement is the concept of attributional style. First introduced into the psychological literature in the 1970s (Abramson, Seligman and Teasdale 1978), attributional style is based on a reformulated learned helplessness model of depression. The authors are of the opinion that three dimensions, namely locus, stability, and controllability, are important when attributing causation. This negative attributional style is referred to as a 'negative cognitive set' and has been shown to be related to a range of health outcomes.

In one retrospective study spanning thirty-five years (Peterson, Seligman and Vaillant 1988), a link was demonstrated between physical health from ages 30 to 60 years and explanatory style at 25 years of age. The authors found that those young males who attributed negative events to stable, global, and internal causes experienced health problems in later life. This finding held even when controlling for respondents' earlier physical and emotional health.

These are important results that demonstrate an association between a particular cognitive mind-set and physical health. Two questions remain unanswered, however, and need to be addressed in future research. In the first instance, the relationship between attributional style and health status among adolescents needs research attention. For example, what is the relationship between attributional style and suicide ideation or negative body image, to give just two examples? Secondly, it is not clear just *why* a negative attributional style should lead to poor health outcomes in some individuals (Peterson *et al.* 1988).

Evaluation

The concept of locus of control has had an enormous influence in research in social cognition. In the area of health-related behaviours, however, it has been pointed out that this variable explains very little unique variance beyond that already explained by the Health Belief Model (Wallston and

Wallston 1984). As these authors note, some locus of control variables may not be specific enough or may show only very little correspondence with the health behaviour in question.

Another important issue concerns the dimensionality of external and internal control. Furnham and Steele (1993) have noted that externality has been classified into the factors of chance and powerful others. Can the same be applied to internality? Thus, the writers (Furnham and Steele 1993: 473) suggest that:

> It may well be that the behaviourally and attitudinally predictive power of locus of control beliefs is greater enhanced not by content specificity but rather dimensional clarity. That is, it may be wiser to have a moratorium on sphere-specific measures until further work clarifies the facets of locus of control.

It would seem that attributional style offers distinct possibilities as a predictor of health status (Peterson *et al.* 1988). Its utility as an explanatory tool among adolescent samples needs further examination and verification.

The theory of reasoned action

According to the theory of reasoned action as proposed by Ajzen and Fishbein (1980), humans are rational beings who make use of the information at their disposal when engaging in behaviour. The authors are of the view that individuals consider the implications of their actions and that this determines their behaviour. In other words, individuals make rational decisions about their behaviour and consider the consequences of a particular course of action. They act in a considered way, making 'reasoned behavioural decisions' (Terry, Gallois and McCamish 1993a). Thus, this model relies heavily on rational decision-making, leaving little room for arousal through fear and perceptions of susceptibility to disease (Mullen *et al.* 1987).

The theory maintains that it is possible to predict behaviour from the individual's *intention* to commit the behaviour or the extent to which one is motivated or willing to perform the behaviour. Terry and her colleagues (1993a) review several research projects that have found very strong evidence for this link, with some correlations in the order of 0.96. Indeed, they report that the role of intentions is much stronger in predicting behaviour than one's attitudes. Of course, external circumstances or the social context may change with resulting changes in intention, thus weakening the once strong relationship between behaviour and intention.

There are other factors that may weaken the behaviour–intention link. Terry and her colleagues (1993a) discuss two. Firstly, individual intention is relatively unstable. One's intention to engage in a behaviour may alter depending on the social context in which one finds oneself. For instance, one may accept the offer of a cigarette not because one wants to smoke, but rather through fear of feeling embarrassed in front of one's friends. Secondly, the importance of intention is largely dependent upon the behaviour in question. There is likely to be a stronger intention–behaviour link if the behaviour is under volitional control than if it is not.

Intention is the function of two factors. These are positive or negative evaluation of actually performing the behaviour, and subjective norms that reflect the individual's perceptions of social pressure. These components are not always equally important in explaining behaviour. Rather, it would seem that their importance varies depending on the behaviour in question and the population under study (Terry *et al.* 1993a). Attitudes are predicted by *beliefs* about the consequences of engaging in the behaviour and one's *evaluation* of those consequences. Thus, if you believe that using a condom will reduce sexual pleasure and you are opposed to that, you will be less inclined to use condoms. Subjective norms are determined by one's *perception* of the extent to which we believe others want us to perform the behaviour as well as our own *motivation* to engage in that behaviour. For example, the decision not to smoke is likely to be a function of one's perception of community norms not to smoke and one's personal motivation in that regard.

Several recent research studies have examined the validity of the theory of reasoned action in explaining a range of health-related behaviours including safe-sex behaviour (e.g. Terry, Gallois and McCamish 1993b; Terry, Galligan and Conway 1993). In one study among university students, the authors determined the extent to which intentions, attitudes, and norms predicted three different behaviours, namely, engaging in an exclusive sexual relationship, avoiding casual sex, and asking sexual partners about their sexual and intravenous drug use histories (Terry *et al.* 1993). Actual behaviours were then assessed three months later.

The authors found that the intention to avoid casual sex and the intention to ask partners about their sexual and drug histories were significantly predicted by subjective norms and attitudes ($R^2 = 0.39$ and 0.14 respectively; both $p < 0.01$). Moreover, intentions best predicted all three actual behaviours, while in the case of engaging in an exclusive sexual relationship, attitudes were also a significant predictor of behaviour. Terry and her colleagues (1993: 366) concluded thus:

> the fact that the theory of reasoned action had some utility in the prediction of the safe sexual strategies . . . suggests that this model may

be a useful framework not only for future research in the area, but also for the development of safe sexual education programmes.

Not all writers agree with the utility of this model. Some have argued that the theory of reasoned action is asocial in that most of the salient processes determining behaviour are said to occur *within* the individual. According to Kippax and Crawford (1993), this theory relies too heavily on cognitive structures while ignoring the important role of social relations and social structures. In the authors' view, it is the social context that gives meaning to individual behaviour. By contrast, the theory of reasoned action seeks to remove the social context and social transaction from individual behaviour.

Kippax and Crawford (1993) take issue with many of the concepts as defined by the theory of reasoned action. For instance, they argue that the theory reduces subjective norms to mere cognitions leaving little contact with 'social'. In reality, subjective norms are part of wider cultural norms. Norms governing the use of condoms, for example, vary according to the cultural context within which the individual resides and will differ for a homosexual youth in an inner-city area, and a homosexual youth residing in a small rural community. The authors (1993: 262) explain their position as follows:

> Meanings are shared and derive from cultural values and norms govern-ing sexual practices, such as condom use, which are situated within discourses of sexuality. Normative rules are not fixed; they differ across sub-cultural groups and are modified by collective action.

The theory of planned behaviour

Ajzen (1991) has extended the theory of reasoned action and formulated a theory of planned behaviour. This was necessitated by the fact that some behaviours are not always under complete volitional control. In addition to the important role played by attitudes to behaviour and subjective norms, the reformulated model incorporates perceived behavioural control as an added predictor of the behaviour in question. Ajzen (1991) argues that perceived behavioural control refers simply to the extent to which people believe that it is easy or difficult to perform a certain behaviour.

Attitudes to behaviour, subjective norms, and perceived behavioural control are best understood in the context of beliefs. Specifically, they are predicted by behavioural beliefs, normative beliefs, and control beliefs, respectively (Ajzen 1991).

Perceived behavioural control differs from the locus of control concept discussed above. Whereas locus of control is a generalised expectancy that remains fairly stable across situations, perceived behavioural control can vary from situation to situation and be quite specific for the behaviour under question. As such, perceived behavioural control closely resembles the concept of self-efficacy (Ajzen 1991).

Evaluation

The theory of reasoned action is an important social psychological model that seeks to explain individual health-related behaviour. It makes use of attitudes, subjective norms, and intentions to commit behaviour as predictors of behaviour. By including subjective norms, this model strives to include both cognitive and social processes governing behaviour. Not all writers agree with the success of this aim, however, arguing that the model disregards the social context within which behaviour occurs.

2.6 SUMMARY

This chapter has reviewed important aspects of health education among adolescents. Teenagers are vulnerable to injury and infection and it is therefore important that educational strategies and models be adequately understood.

There are several strategies that can be employed in educational programmes. In this regard, the media often play a crucial role. The chapter reviewed the value of fear-arousing messages, provision of information, as well as behaviour modification programmes. Not all of these strategies are always appropriate and they need to be varied according to the behaviour in question and the target group in mind. Of importance too is the particular adolescent health service in question. There are a variety of services in which health education can take place and each of these serves a quite distinct, but useful and necessary, function.

Finally, a large section of the chapter dealt with models of health behaviour. Three models were considered, namely, the health belief model, control of reinforcement, and the theory of reasoned action. Each of these seeks to relate social psychological processes to individual behaviour. An interesting feature of these continually developing models is their inclusion of concepts such as self-efficacy, that is, the individual's belief in his or her ability to perform the desired behaviour (see also Rogers 1983). To some extent, therefore, there appears to be a slight convergence of ideas by those actively shaping these theoretical perspectives. It is doubtful whether any one model can ever fully explain the complexities of human action. Nonetheless, these models do go some way in illuminating some of the underlying processes that need to be grasped when explaining individual health behaviours.

3 Stress and coping

3.1 INTRODUCTION

As we move toward the next millenium, young people appear to be increasingly affected by stress. Whereas it was earlier assumed that stress is something that mainly affects adults, it is now widely accepted that teenagers, and even children, face stressful events that have the potential to severely disrupt their lives and negatively affect their psychological adjustment and health. Acute and chronic stress plays an important part in understanding normal as well as disrupted adolescent development (Compas, Orosan and Grant 1993). Stress has been shown to be linked to wide-ranging maladaptive behaviours such as depression, suicide, and substance abuse (Compas *et al.* 1993; Siegel and Brown 1988; Wills 1986).

Stress is linked to unexpected, demanding, and novel situations and young people face stressors in a variety of ways. For example, being bullied at school or disliked by one's peers can be extremely stressful for a child or adolescent. It is stressful living in a conflict-ridden home where mother and father constantly disagree and argue. It is stressful living with a physical disability that may serve to remind an impressionable child of how he or she differs from others. It is also very stressful to lose a loved one (e.g. parent, sibling, or close friend) and to have to cope with grief and feelings of despair. Events such as these have the potential to affect the health and emotional wellbeing of the adolescent. It is not surprising, therefore, that clinical and developmental psychologists have become increasingly aware of the importance and value of studying stress and coping mechanisms among teenagers. Thus, there is now a rapidly developing literature in this regard, as evidenced by recent important reviews (e.g. Colten and Gore 1991; Compas 1987).

In this chapter we shall review the nature of stress during the adolescent years. We shall also examine the coping strategies that young people adopt in reacting to stressful situations. It will become clear through the course of our discussion that stress is multifaceted. Moreover, teenagers vary in their susceptibility to stress: not all teenagers are negatively affected by the same events, while some are more adaptive in their responses than others. In other words, there are important individual differences at work that may exacerbate stress or act as buffers against stress. We turn our attention first to the importance of studying stress during the adolescent years.

3.2 THE NATURE OF STRESS

Our understanding of the nature of stress has undergone considerable change over many years. For instance, in the mid-1900s stress was regarded simply as a set of bodily defences or physiological responses to undesirable stimuli, while by the 1970s it was seen as a 'state of the body' (Lazarus and Folkman 1984). Recently, writers have proposed more formal definitions of stress incorporating aspects of the stressor and the individual. For example, Brooks-Gunn (1991: 134) sees stress as an *individual* response to events which is:

> said to occur when an individual is confronted with an event that is perceived as threatening, requires a novel response, is seen as important (i.e. needs to be responded to), and for which an individual does not have an appropriate coping response available.

Lazarus and Folkman (1984: 19) defined stress thus:

> Psychological stress is a particular relationship between the person and the environment that is appraised by the person as taxing or exceeding his or her resources and endangering his or her well-being.

It is clear from both these definitions that stress involves more than the stimulus or stressor and the individual's response. These writers emphasise the *relationship* between person and environment (Lazarus and Folkman 1984), acknowledging that some individuals are more susceptible to stress than others.

We need also to distinguish between *chronic* and *acute* stress. By discussing both the nature of stressors and various coping mechanisms, it is the aim of this chapter to highlight the importance of individual differences in stress and coping.

3.3 STRESS DURING THE ADOLESCENT YEARS

The teenage years are a time of transition and change. It is now well accepted that adolescents face a multitude of *developmental* challenges incorporating social, cognitive, and physical change. Social change refers, for example, to events such as the transition to high school. For some, this is a critical period when the security and familiarity of primary school is exchanged for new and uncertain friendships in high school. Cognitive change refers to the fact that teenagers have acquired the ability to think abstractly. This is an important developmental change, for adolescents are now in a position to contemplate the unknown as well as the possible long-term effects of events. They are now able to consider 'what if' and for some this can be stressful. Physical changes include the many hormonal and biological changes taking place in the body. The teenager must now adapt to a changing body and for some this change is occurring faster (or slower) than it is for others. Thus, for late or early maturers a *normative* transition is taking on *non-normative* dimensions with added stress.

Some changes reflect a combination of events. The gradual awakening of interest in members of the opposite sex reflects, no doubt, biological and social change. It is important to note, as some writers have, that single developmental events such as those described above are not normally responsible for inducing stress in adolescents. Rather, it is quite often a combination of normative *or* non-normative events that, in some youth, lead to experiencing stress.

Adolescence has traditionally been viewed as a time of 'storm and stress'. In this regard, psychoanalytic writers have tended to hold sway, viewing adolescence as a period of emotional turmoil and as a period of 'disarray'. Thus, for instance, Anna Freud stressed the importance of Oedipal feelings within the teenager, linking these to anxiety and certain behaviours such as running away from home or spending long hours alone in one's bedroom (Muuss 1988). Notable characteristics of the teenage years, according to the psychoanalytic point of view, are a host of drives, instincts, and motives that can become problematic and stressful during the adolescent years when, for example, a developing sexuality needs to be incorporated into the overall structure of personality or one's personal identity (see Coleman 1992).

More recently, some theorists (e.g. Petersen 1988) have questioned the view that adolescence is a time of 'storm and stress'. It is acknowledged that individuals in this stage of the life span face unique and important developmental tasks. For those aged 12–18 years these may include adjusting to a changing body image, accepting volatile emotions and mood swings, joining peer groups, etc. Older adolescents, it has been suggested, should be developing autonomy from parents, developing a sex-role identity, making career choices, etc. (Newman and Newman 1987). However, it is acknowledged that most adolescents will meet these challenges successfully. This has led Petersen (1988) to argue that there is little support for the view that adolescence is 'stormy', while Susman (1991) has pointed out that only a minority of teenagers risk stress and maladjustment. As Conger and Petersen (1984: 26–27) explained:

> While many adolescents face occasional periods of uncertainty and self doubt, of loneliness and sadness, of anxiety and concern for the future, they are also likely to experience joy, excitement, curiosity, a sense of adventure, and a feeling of competence in mastering new challenges.

In similar vein, Papalia and Olds (1989: 352) described the much heralded generation gap between parents and teenagers in the following terms:

> the rejection of the parents' values is often partial, temporary, or super-ficial. Teenagers' values remain closer to their parents' than many people realize, and the 'adolescent rebellion' is often little more than a series of minor skirmishes.

A major challenge that all adolescents must confront is the development of a personal identity or a sense of psychological wellbeing. According to Erikson (1968), teenagers live in a 'no-man's-land', caught between child-hood and adulthood. Adolescents face the sometimes daunting task of discovering their awakening sexual, socio-emotional, and physical identities. In this process, they must deal with the conflicting demands of parents and peers, each of which set somewhat different boundaries for acceptable behaviour. Both these influences play a vital role in shaping the formation of individual identity. Developing a sense of worth as a unique individual in which the appropriate developmental tasks have been mastered, therefore, has the potential to be a stressful process for some teenagers (Susman 1991).

3.4 TYPES OF STRESSORS

One study of over 1,000 American teenagers (Newcomb, Huba and Bentler 1986) asked respondents to rank the most desirable and least desirable life events (see Table 3.1). This study is noteworthy as it highlights possible sources of stress among young people. The authors found that the most desired events included starting to drive a motor car and owning one's own television or stereo set. Most of the desired events listed in the table refer to being able to demonstrate one's independence or autonomy. This supports the views of Youniss and Smollar (1985) who asserted that most adolescents seek to be independent of their parents. Table 3.1 also shows that the least desired experiences relate mainly to issues regarding sexuality

Table 3.1 Most and least desired life events for adolescents

Most desired	Least desired
1. Started driving	Got or gave VD
2. Got own stereo or TV	Death in family
3. Making own money	Serious accident or illness
4. Fell in love	Family accident or illness
5. Started dating regularly	Had a gay experience
6. Met a teacher I liked a lot	Trouble with the law
7. Holidayed without parents	Parent abused alcohol
8. Joined a club or group	Parents argued or fought
9. Decided about university or college	Thought about suicide
10. Got religion	Family money problems

Source: Newcomb *et al.* 1986

and family matters. Very few sex differences were noted between the rankings of males and females.

In the discussion above we alluded to the fact that there are different types of stressors. Writers differentiate between normative stressors, non-normative stressors, and daily hassles (Hauser and Bowlds 1990; Rice, Herman and Petersen 1993). *Normative* stressors are those events that all adolescents must confront. These are also referred to as generic stressors (Compas *et al.* 1993) and include physical changes, the transition to high school, and awakening sexual interest in others, to name just a few. As noted earlier, these stressors are amplified in combination with other events. Thus, the shift to a new school is exacerbated in combination with biological and physical change or by parental divorce.

Other normative stressors that should receive special mention are the important and varied effects of the peer group (see Hauser and Bowlds 1990). It will become evident in subsequent chapters that peers and friends can be very influential in adolescents' decisions to experiment with a wide range of behaviours that are potentially risky to their health. Peers indicate behaviour that they regard as acceptable, and thus help establish norms within which behaviour can occur.

Non-normative stressors refer to those events that can occur at any time. Included in this category are parental divorce, the death of a loved one, a bad grade at school, and so forth. By their very nature non-normative stressors can occur unexpectedly, sometimes during an important transition (Rice *et al.* 1993). As such, they often amplify or exacerbate the impact of the transitional experience. Of course, not all teenagers who experience parental divorce are likely to suffer stress and maladjustment. However, research evidence indicates that those teenagers who are able to vividly recall parental conflict or family tensions are more at risk from health and behavioural problems such as depression, impulsive, aggressive and sexual behaviours, and relationship problems (Hauser and Bowlds 1990).

Other non-normative stressors that have important implications for adolescent behaviour and mental health are parenting styles and parental psychopathology (Heaven 1994). For example, it has been well documented that adolescents who are raised in authoritative homes are higher on competence and adjustment and lower on problem behaviours. By contrast, those teenagers residing in neglectful homes risk mental anguish and problem behaviours.

Another category of stressors is *daily hassles*. These are day-to-day events that, cumulatively, result in stress for the individual. It has been argued that normative and non-normative stressors multiply the number of daily hassles that teenagers have to contend with (Rice *et al.* 1993). In other words, a major stressor (such as parental divorce) has a number of associated consequences (feelings of guilt in the adolescent; adaptation to new family circumstances; possible financial strain, etc.) that complicate the adolescent's life and also have the ability to affect behaviour and health.

Some have suggested that the best predictors of psychological symptoms during adolescence are an accumulation of daily hassles and acute, severe (usually non-normative) stressors (Compas *et al.* 1993; Compas, Howell, Phares *et al.* 1989). Some acute (sudden, short-term) stressors can be quite traumatic and can have negative consequences for adolescent functioning. Non-normative events can be chronic, such as living in poverty or in a conflict-ridden home (Compas *et al.* 1993) and can have serious implications for individual stress levels. In some instances, major events do not predict levels of stress, but are mediated by daily hassles. That is, daily hassles are often much more accurate as predictors of stress than are major events (Compas *et al.* 1989).

One research team examined the impact on adolescents of experiencing several major life transitions concurrently (Simmons, Burgeson, Carlton-Ford and Blyth 1987). Included were school change, pubertal change, early dating, moving to a new neighbourhood, and major family disruption such as death of a parent or divorce. The researchers were interested in the effects of these events on adolescent self-esteem, school performance (grade point average), and extracurricular activities.

It was found that as the number of transitions increased, so adolescents' school performance and extracurricular activities declined. Moreover, girls' but not boys' self-esteem was negatively affected. The findings suggest that teenagers who experience several major transitions over a short period of time are at greater risk of negative consequences than those teengers who do not have such experiences. As the number of transitions increases, so it becomes inceasingly difficult for young people to cope with their situation.

3.5 CAUSES AND CORRELATES OF ADOLESCENT STRESS

Thus far, our review has made clear that adolescents are subjected to normative and non-normative stressors as well as daily hassles. In this section we shall examine more closely the specific causes and correlates of adolescent stress.

Age differences in negative emotions

Evidence to date indicates that there are substantial changes in the experience of negative emotions between pre-adolescents and adolescents. Negative emotions arise when there is a gap between what adolescents expect to happen and what actually occurs. It is believed that negative emotions are linked to stress, although the causal direction is not altogether clear.

Larson and Asmussen (1991) demonstrated that certain life domains elicit negative emotions in adolescents. They asked the young respondents in their study to describe their emotional states across several life domains. These included the self, family, friends, school, and media. Some significant changes were noted on some of the domains as shown in Table 3.2. For example, older adolescents experienced fewer negative emotions on the domain 'non-school activities', although negative emotions increased on the diffuse 'other' category for boys (this includes jobs, time, and environmental issues). Both boys and girls experienced an increase in negative emotions on the domain 'friends'. Further analysis revealed that these negative emotions related to friends of the opposite sex. As the authors (Larson and Asmussen 1991: 28–29) noted:

> As children move into the adolescent years, a larger portion of their anger, frustration, and worry emanates from the area of heterosexual concerns. . . . They have acquired a new area of concern, a new area of 'what matters', and along with this they have a new source of vulnerability to hurt.

To some extent, these findings lend some support to the information provided in Table 3.1. It suggests that life events can be categorised into

Table 3.2 Changes in emotional states for boys and girls

	Boys		Girls	
Domain	Pre-adolescent	Adolescent	Pre-adolescent	Adolescent
Non-school activities	30.7	19.4[2]	17.2	9.4[2]
Friends	4.3	11.1[2]	14.4	25.4[2]
Other	2.0	4.9[1]	2.4	2.5

Notes: 1 p < 0.05   2 p < 0.001

Source: derived from Larson and Asmussen 1991

different domains, some of which include normative and non-normative stressors. As Larson and Asmussen (1991) indicate, friends take on added significance as a source of non-normative stress for older adolescents.

Family stressors

Although there is little support for the view that parent–adolescent relationships are characterised by the so-called 'generation gap' or as being conflict ridden (e.g. Noller and Patton 1990; Petersen 1988), it is agreed that most families experience disagreements and daily hassles that, cumulatively, can be stressful for adolescents as well as their parents.

Parents and their children often have quite different views and expectations about family rules, authority, and inter-personal relationships (Smetana 1989; Smetana, Yau, Restrepo and Braeges 1991). Sometimes, the views that children and parents hold can be unrealistic or irrational and can lead to family conflict. As Roehling and Robin (1986) have suggested, family members adhere to these beliefs rigidly and they tend to defend their views emotionally. This, in turn, elicits angry emotion from other family members, which only serves to reduce the likelihood of problem solving.

Teenagers and their parents are usually agreed as to the sources of conflict within the home. Smetana and her colleagues (1991) found that conflict was most likely to occur over chores (18 per cent of the time), inter-personal relationships (16 per cent), the regulation of teenagers' activities (12 per cent), personality characteristics (11 per cent), homework (9 per cent), bedtime and curfew (9 per cent), regulating social relations (8 per cent), and appearance (8 per cent). These reasons for conflict cover activities inside and outside the home, but are important to adolescents, who are likely to interpret the conflict as falling into the following domains (Roehling and Robin 1986):

- *Ruination*   Adolescents believe that parental regulations will ruin the adolescent's teenage years
- *Unfairness*   Adolescents believe that parents treat their teenagers unfairly
- *Autonomy*   Adolescents believe that they should have complete freedom
- *Approval*   Adolescents believe that parents should approve of their teenage children

The nature of parent–child conflict varies depending on the age of the child (Smetana 1989). With pre-adolescents, conflict usually revolves around rule-governed issues such as when to turn off the television, while teenagers are stressed by their perceptions of parents' regulation of their inter-personal relationships. Parents and teenagers also differ with respect to the *meaning* they attach to issues and the way they *reason* about these conflictual issues. It is not exactly clear, however, to what extent these differences in perception are related to stress levels.

Parents tend to think about family conflict from a conventional or moralistic point of view. Adolescents, on the other hand, view family disagreements in terms of their own personal authority or jurisdiction. In other words, they believe that they are capable of making their own decisions without parental influence.

Some researchers have adopted a *social ecological* perspective in examining stress in adolescents. Accordingly, it is held that behavioural processes are affected by one's immediate surroundings, of which the household and family members are a part. It is believed that other members of the family play a salient part, and in fact are crucial, in determining adolescents' mental health. There is much support for this view (e.g. Downey and Coyne 1990; Keitner and Miller 1990). It is well documented, for example, that clinical depression in parents is linked to social dysfunction in their children, and that parenting styles are associated with adolescent adjustment and behavioural styles.

Parental reports of stress and psychological symptoms are positively related to emotional and behavioural adjustment in adolescents (e.g. Compas *et al.* 1989; Compas and Wagner 1991). Compas and his colleagues demonstrated that fathers, more than mothers, play a critical role in shaping adolescent adjustment. They found that fathers' and mothers' reports of daily hassles were significantly related to their psychological symptoms. However, only fathers' psychological symptoms were related to adolescents' emotional and behavioural problems. Moreover, the influence of fathers' daily hassles on adolescent behaviour was affected by the strength of fathers' psychological symptoms.

Why should the psychological symptoms of mothers in this study not be related to the adjustment of their adolescent children? According to Compas and Wagner (1991: 77):

fathers' symptoms may hold considerably greater emotional meaning for their . . . children than do symptoms of psychological distress experienced by their mothers . . . indicating that fathers' symptoms may be more salient and have greater impact because they occur less often.

Another explanation concerns the power differential that exists in some families. In those homes where the mother enjoys less status than the father, her distress may be ignored or discounted, thus enhancing the salience or the importance of the father's hassles for the adolescent (Compas and Wagner 1991).

Ethnic differences in the perception of events

Important school-based events are likely to occur among some ethnic groups more than others. Munsch and Wampler (1993) examined the occurrence and perceived stressfulness of school-based events among a large multi-ethnic sample in the southern United States. Included in the study were black and white teenagers, as well as a sample of Mexican-American adolescents. The authors found that the prevalence of stressful events differed for the groups. For example, white students were more likely than other ethnic groups to be selected for an important school activity, while black students were likely to experience school suspension or have trouble in getting along with their teacher. Mexican-Americans, on the other hand, tended to experience academic problems more frequently. However, there were few ethnic differences in perception of the stressfulness of these events. The authors found that whites and Mexican-Americans viewed being chosen for an important activity more positively than did the black students. White students also indicated *not* being chosen for an important activity to be significantly more stressful than black students (see Table 3.3).

Gender influences

Several writers have noted that adolescent boys and girls differ in their experience of stress. One reason may simply reflect differences in the timing of the 'growth spurt'. On average, girls tend to encounter the growth spurt earlier than do boys (Tanner and Davies 1985) and this may result in higher stress levels for girls. Moreover, girls who mature physically earlier

Table 3.3 Occurrence of selected school events and perceptions of stress by ethnic group

School event	Blacks %	Whites %	Mexican-Americans %	F value
In-school suspension	17.6	2.3	8.2	–
Chosen for activity	60.8	77.9	54.1	4.93[1]
Not chosen for activity	25.5	32.4	33.3	5.26[1]
Trouble with teacher	47.1	29.3	37.7	–
Failed test	64.7	64.4	81.1	–

Note: 1 $p < 0.01$

Source: derived from Munsch and Wampler 1993

than average are likely to suffer greater negative body image and to have more eating problems compared to girls who mature on time or later (Rice *et al.* 1993). By contrast, boys who mature earlier than average tend to suffer less from a negative body image than boys who mature later (see the next chapter for more on body image).

All girls experience menarche, but not all will experience this major event without stress. It has been reported that girls who are early maturers but who did not discuss pubertal change with their mothers are more likely to view menarche negatively. It is also probable that these girls had fathers who were not immediately informed of their daughters' menarche (Brooks-Gunn 1991).

Adolescent boys and girls differ in their experiences of family- and inter-personal-related stress. In a recent review of some of this literature, Compas and Wagner (1991) reported that females are more prone to report major negative events that are related to family, peers, and sexuality. Is it possible that this is evidence of greater honesty on the part of girls? In any event, females appear more sensitive to stress-inducing changes in friendship and inter-personal networks than males. It has been suggested that central to males' friendship patterns are issues of autonomy and separateness, while females' friendship patterns can be described in terms of inter-personal relationships. For example, females are more likely to use social support and more emotional expression strategies than males (Frydenberg and Lewis 1993). Thus, those aspects of friendship likely to be involved in stress and coping strategies are different for males and females.

Another gender difference in stress concerns the incidence of depression, with young adolescent females experiencing higher levels of depression than their male counterparts (e.g. Brooks-Gunn 1991; Petersen, Sarigiani and Kennedy 1991). One explanation that has been offered is related to differences in hormonal changes during puberty, it being suggested that these hormonal changes play a more prominent role in girls' affective states than boys'. Increases in the hormone estradiol are believed to be important in explaining girls' higher depressive symptomatology. It is important to note, however, that statistical analyses indicate that hormonal influences are important, but not as important as the impact of negative life events (Brooks-Gunn 1991).

3.6 COPING WITH STRESS

Adolescents face many challenging experiences and they need to acquire effective coping mechanisms. Just how young people cope with major life events and transitions will play an important determining part in their emotional adjustment.

One can define coping in a variety of ways. For example, some authors view coping simply as all the responses that an individual will make in the face of an event or transition. According to Compas (1987: 393), such a view is too vague and not entirely useful. Rather, he recommends that we differentiate the three aspects of coping described below.

Effortful versus non-effortful responses This includes attempts at minimising the influence of the stressor or other attempts at mastering the environment. In other words, the individual constantly adapts his or her behaviour or cognitive strategies in an attempt to meet the challenges of the environment. This aspect of coping seems to be related to what Band and Weisz (1988) refer to as primary–secondary coping. Whereas primary control is directed more at attempting to influence conditions or stressful events, secondary coping refers to such strategies as cognitive flexibility. In the authors' view this is a more mature form of coping.

These conceptions of coping appear quite valid. For instance, one research study (Frydenberg and Lewis 1993) assessed adolescents' ability to use one of the following coping strategies: solving the problem, reference to others, and unproductive coping. The first refers to direct efforts to deal with the problem, while the second seeks to draw on resources offered by other people. The third strategy does not necessarily solve the problem, but does assist with tension reduction.

Coping's function According to Compas (1987), coping can be classified as problem-focused and emotion-focused coping. Taken together, their function is to modify the relationship between the stressor and the individual. For instance, in problem-focused coping one attempts to modify the source of the stress, while in emotion-focused coping one can change the emotional state which accompanies the stressor.

Resources, styles, and specific coping responses   This refers to a variety of individual difference and environmental variables that assist in coping. Included are such factors as social support networks (a resource), as well as problem-solving skills, inter-personal skills, self-esteem, etc. (Compas 1987).

Roth and Cohen (1986) differentiate between approach and avoidance coping styles. In their view, some coping mechanisms are oriented toward the stressor, while others are oriented away from the stressor. By avoiding the stressor completely, one reduces stress, although this approach may result in behaviours that can be disruptive (such as staying away from school to avoid a teacher). The approach strategy allows one to confront the issue and one's emotions associated with the event. According to the authors, this strategy also creates circumstances whereby the event is integrated into a much fuller self-awareness.

Respondents with deficits in some coping strategies are at risk from maladaptive behaviours such as alcohol use. For example, teenagers low in both emotion-focused and avoidant coping are likely to drink more heavily than are other teenagers (Fromme and Rivet 1994). They are also likely to drink more than teenagers who are high on emotion-focused coping, but low on avoidant coping.

In the following sections we shall examine some of the factors that may have an influence on the sorts of coping strategies that one adopts.

Developmental trends in coping

Several writers have demonstrated that children of different ages vary in the coping strategies that they adopt. As expected, older children are much more likely to engage in *secondary* coping mechanisms while younger children tend to use *primary* strategies, concepts that will become clearer below. These general strategies are very much dependent on the nature of the stressful situation, however. For example, Band and Weisz (1988) showed that school-related factors are more likely to elicit primary coping responses (be on your best behaviour with a certain teacher) among young *and* older children, while medical situations such as receiving an injection will elicit secondary responses (think of a holiday while receiving an injection) in older children and primary responses in younger children.

Compas and his colleagues (Compas, Malcarne and Fondacaro 1988) examined the extent to which adolescents of different ages use problem-

and emotion-focused coping strategies. Their research evidence indicated that younger teenagers are much more likely to engage in the former, that is, they are more likely to attempt to change the stressor than are older children. For example, young children are more likely to try and avoid the stressor altogether. Older children, on the other hand, appear to have the cognitive flexibility to engage in emotion-focused coping whereby they attempt to modify their emotional state associated with the stressor.

These findings were upheld for different stressful events except academic stressors where both age groups were found to use problem-focused coping. An explanation for such a finding is that younger as well as older adolescents perceive that they have much more control over school-based problems. They are, therefore, more likely to attempt first to change the stressor (e.g. to try and please the teacher, study for the next assessment, etc.) before attempting other strategies.

One can speculate from these findings that children differ in their use of approach and avoidance coping styles, and that approach strategies (a form of problem-based coping) are more likely to be reserved for *controllable* situations. In support of this prediction, Altshuler and Ruble (1989) found that when children aged 5 to 12 years are presented with uncontrollable situations, such as having to wait for a desired or unpleasant event, they tend to use avoidance strategies. In fact, the children often resorted to forms of behavioural distraction, such as counting or the use of guided imagery. In line with our earlier discussion, it was also found that older children used cognitive distractions, such as trying to control one's emotions, more often than younger children.

In line with some of these findings, a study of Israeli adolescents found that older adolescents were more likely than pre-adolescents to use cognitive coping styles (Hoffman, Levy-Shiff, Sohlberg and Zarizki 1992). The following were regarded by the authors as examples of this style:

• Concentrated on good things that might come out of the situation
• Tried not to think too much about the problem

The authors explained their finding in terms of Piagetian theory which asserts that older teenagers progressively engage in formal operational thought. That is, as they get older they are more able to engage in abstract thought and it is possible for them to contemplate the possible result of a particular course of action. The authors (Hoffman *et al.* 1992) explain the implications for coping as follows:

A positive outcome of cognitive development would be an expected increase in coping efficacy due to an enhanced ability to flexibly and differentially formulate, moderate, and integrate multiple forms of coping in a goal-directed fashion.

The influence of close relationships

Having a social support network is crucial in assisting individuals to cope with stress. Thus, a close circle of friends or a warm and loving family moderate the anxiety and anguish that stress induces and assist the individual in adjusting to stressful situations. We begin by first discussing the role of the family, followed by friendships and the peer group.

Family relationships

It is widely held that a supportive family network is an important buffer against the effects of stress and that parenting style is related to social competency among adolescent offspring. In one Australian report (Noller and Patton 1990), for example, the authors noted that supportive parents tend to use lower levels of coercion resulting in socially competent children. By contrast, coercive child-rearing practices that are combined with a lack of support are much more likely to lead to behavioural problems among adolescents.

These issues have also been addressed by other writers such as Hauser and Bowlds (1990) who noted that authoritarian, traditional, and authoritative parenting styles have important implications for adolescent adjustment and behaviours. These and other research reports suggest that family dynamics are also related to adolescent coping. Indeed, it has been noted that family relationships play a vital role in the direction and unfolding of adolescent development paths. Furthermore these different paths are associated with different coping styles in teenagers which ultimately lead to different behavioural outcomes (Hauser and Bowlds 1990).

In an Israeli study (Shulman 1993), it was noted that different types of family relationships are directly related to the coping strategies that adolescents adopt. The research identified four different types of family climate, as shown in Table 3.4, and the authors noted that each family climate generated its own set of unique coping behaviours. The unstructured conflict-oriented type of family usually results in teenagers who lack adequate models of coping, while families perceived as supportive and emotionally warm, in which self-esteem is encouraged, tend to produce teenagers who are better equipped to deal with stress. Authoritarian-type families in which rules are clear but in which there is little emotional warmth tend to produce teenagers who are passive and rely on the family to make most of the decisions.

Table 3.4 Relationships between family climate and coping behaviours

Family climate	Coping behaviours
1. Unstructured conflict oriented E.g. High degree of conflictive interaction; lack of support within family; no support for personal growth	High level of dysfunctional coping characterised by withdrawal and passivity
2. Control oriented E.g. Structured family activities; explicit family rules; emphasise achievement; supportive family, but do not express emotions	Rely on family decisions; tend to be passive
3. Unstructured expressive-independence oriented E.g. Cohesive and unified; express feelings; support individual independence; no pressure to achieve	Turn to óthers for advice and information; adolescents plan course of action
4. Structured expressive-intellectual oriented E.g. Emphasis on family relationships; independence encouraged; clear rules	Turn to others for advice and information; adolescents plan course of action

Source: Shulman 1993

Significant numbers of adolescents experience parental separation or divorce. For many teenagers this can be a painful and stressful experience, and they may react with anger, aggression, or depression. Parents and professionals have a duty to assist adolescents who cannot cope with this major transition. In this regard support groups (such as friends or community groups) may have to be relied upon to help the teenager through what is often a difficult time.

For other teenagers, parental separation signifies the end of a long period of parental dispute and conflict which heralds new opportunities in a conflict-free environment. For these youngsters there are now increased chances for personal growth and development (Barber and Eccles 1992).

Peer relationships

Close friends and the peer group are also important sources of social support in times of stress. The peer group bolsters self-esteem, helps avoid loneliness, and provides valued support and friendship. Likewise, close friendships provide companionship and emotional intimacy. Friends share beliefs, values, and information and are therefore an important buffer against stress (Heaven 1994).

The relationship between attachment to parents and friends and coping differs for males and females (Shulman 1993). Whereas males tend to choose their parents as a source of support with respect to active coping (such as information-seeking), girls use parents and friends as sources of support. According to Shulman, these gender differences reflect the different functions that friendships fulfil for males and females. It has been documented, for example, that boys' friendships are less intimate and more guarded than girls', who are more likely to verbalise and engage in self-disclosure. They often characterise their friendships as mutually intimate, whereas boys tend to de-emphasise affection (Heaven 1994). These friendship patterns are reflected in different coping strategies for boys and girls suggesting that, while 'closeness' is not a prerequisite for coping (Shulman 1993), close relationships with parents and friends are important for girls' coping behaviours.

The Type A Behaviour Pattern (TABP)

The essential character of the TABP is a behavioural pattern that emphasises striving and control (Byrne, Reinhart and Heaven 1989), incorporating aspects of competitiveness, time urgency, impatience, and hostility (Thoresen 1991). According to Thoresen, the TABP forms an important coping mechanism in some individuals and is the result of the individual's experiences as a child and teenager (but see Kliewer 1991).

Why should the Type A behaviour syndrome be an effective coping mechanism for some individuals? Bryant and Yarnold (1990) propose that the TABP is characterised by what they refer to as *psychological vigour*, which tends to be associated with self-confidence, and global self-assessments of happiness. In other words, TABP individuals often experience their lives as more satisfying and fulfilling even though, unbeknown to them, they risk coronary heart disease. Although Type As report higher levels of positive experience than other Types, they do not differ in reported negative experience. It is therefore possible that the TABP acts as a source of positive experience rather than to reduce sources of negative experience (Bryant and Yarnold 1990).

As the TABP is an important coping mechanism, it is necessary to discuss it in some detail. It is now recognised that the TABP is an important predictive variable in coronary heart disease. Consequently, adolescents with elevated levels of TABP are at risk from coronary heart disease in adulthood (Thoresen 1991). More recently, it has been demonstrated that such teenagers are also at risk from behavioural problems (e.g. delinquency) and alcohol consumption (Reifman and Windle 1993).

Researchers have identified a range of physiological and psychosocial correlates of the TABP. For instance, compared to low-TABP individuals, high-TABP adolescents manifest enhanced systolic blood pressure in response to difficult, frustrating, and slow-paced tasks (Matthews and Jennings 1984). It has also been found that high-TABP adolescents report significantly higher self-ratings of stress and tension than do low-TABP subjects (Eagleston, Kirmil-Gray, Thoresen *et al.* 1986), while Siegel (1982) found anger to be predictive of the physical and psychological measures of cardiovascular risk.

Thoresen (1991) asserts that some of the physiological reactions demonstrated in laboratory studies are also observable in natural settings. He cites examples where adolescent perceptions of the environment as being hostile or demanding have been shown to be related to changes in individual blood pressure. Another study demonstrated that teenagers engaged in public speaking activities in front of their class mates (a stressful experience for some) experienced changes in blood pressure and heart rate.

It is quite likely that the TABP can be learned in the home and that parents who exhibit behaviours and attitudes typically associated with the TABP often transmit such values to their children (Matthews and Siegel 1982; Thoresen 1991). In fact, some studies have found significant associations between this behaviour pattern in fathers and sons, while there is evidence of a link between mothers' levels of verbal hostility and adolescent TABP. Other findings demonstrate that parents of TABP children are far more 'encouraging' or 'supportive' of their children's activities than are the parents of non-TABP offspring. As Thoresen (1991) suggests, these children are constantly encouraged to 'try just a little harder' and in many cases they have parents who are likely to be more critical of their achievements.

An important component of the TABP with respect to predicting cardiovascular disease is anger/hostility (Byrne *et al.* 1989; Thoresen 1991). In this regard, research findings suggest that TABP youngsters experience anger in a greater variety of situations than do non-TABP teenagers. They also tend to be angry more frequently and for longer periods of time. In addition, these teenagers report relatively low levels of self-esteem and life satisfaction, and tend to be overweight, smoke more cigarettes, and be more passive than non-TABP individuals.

Perceived controllability

Adolescents who believe that they are in control of their lives are better equipped to deal with stress than are those who believe that what happens to them is pre-ordained or just bad luck. Psychological research into the 'locus of control' concept has generated considerable insight into the link between control beliefs on the one hand and attitudes and behaviours on the other.

We noted in Chapter 2 that expectancies about events are shaped by reinforcements and that if one expects to be rewarded for a behaviour one is more likely to engage in that behaviour. Those who believe that rewards are contingent upon one's own behaviour are said to have a sense of *internal* control, while those who believe that rewards are linked to forces outside oneself are said to have a sense of *external* control.

Many studies that have examined the link between locus of control and coping conclude that internal locus of control is significantly related to emotional adjustment and acts as a buffer against stress. For instance, one study of life stress among American high school students (Cauce, Hannan and Sargeant 1992) found that those classified as 'internal' were better adjusted in terms of anxiety, as well as general, school, and physical competencies, than were 'externals'. Thus, a sense of control acted as a buffer against stressful experiences by reducing students' anxiety, thereby helping them to maintain adequate levels of competency.

Similar findings have been reported by Kliewer (1991). She found that internality was related to enhanced coping skills, although she did find some interesting differences between the sexes. For example, whereas internality was significantly related to cognitive avoidance as a coping strategy for both sexes, girls labelled as internal were also found to be more likely to engage in avoidant action. Kliewer (1991) explains her results in terms of differing socialisation experiences between the sexes, suggesting that while girls are often encouraged to 'walk away' from the source of stress, boys are encouraged to confront the source of stress.

3.7 SUMMARY

Should adolescents perceive different experiences as threatening or as requiring a novel response, then the event can be regarded as stressful (Brooks-Gunn 1991). Some stressful events are normative. Included in this category are physical change in the teenage years, the transition to high school, etc. Non-normative events include the death of a loved one, etc. Some researchers have argued that the best predictors of psychological symptoms in the teenage years are an accumulation of daily hassles.

According to this point of view, daily hassles are more accurate as predictors of stress than are major one-off events.

This chapter reviewed several major causes and correlates of adolescent stress. Included were changes in the experience of negative emotions across the teenage years, family stressors, ethnic differences in the perception of events, and the role of gender differences. Thus, for example, parents sometimes differ from their children in how family rules and expectations are perceived. Such differences in perceptions can, for some individuals, be a source of stress. Other writers have noted gender differences in the experience of stress. Although it is not entirely clear why such sex differences occur, it has been argued that physical/biological factors could be important. In this regard, the influence of certain hormones and the growth spurt may be important in shedding light on how males and females experience and react to stress.

Finally, this chapter reviewed the importance of adolescent coping strategies. Several important factors were mentioned including age-related changes in coping, the influence of close relationships (family and friendships), the Type A Behaviour Pattern, and a sense of control. All of these have been shown across several investigations to be related to adjustment and must therefore be considered as useful buffers against the effects of stress.

What is the outcome of faulty or inadequate coping? There are several possible outcomes ranging from substance use to depression, eating disorders, and suicide, to name just a few. These outcomes have important implications for adolescent health status and will be examined in more detail in subsequent chapters.

4 Body image and eating behaviours

4.1 INTRODUCTION

During the teenage years one's body undergoes rapid and marked change. One is maturing sexually, emotionally, cognitively, and physically. The former slender child has entered the 'growth spurt' (Tanner and Davies 1985) and may suddenly find that he or she is taller or 'bigger' than most others in class. Not surprisingly, this can be an anxious time for some youth and a few resort to a variety of strategies to cope with these physical and emotional changes. One strategy is weight control.

Our society seems to emphasise a particular body build (Spillman and Everington 1989) and, for many teenagers, being physically attractive is important. Contemporary western culture seems to favour thinner figures, and thin people are often regarded as having a favourable personality and other positive qualities. Teenagers are particularly susceptible to media and group pressure and some consciously vary their eating habits in order to control their weight. Others exhibit more deviant and serious eating behaviours such as bulimia or anorexia nervosa. For some of these teenagers, their condition can be life-threatening.

This chapter will discuss some eating behaviours that are characteristic of the teenage years. Given the emphasis in the media on 'being attractive', on 'having a beautiful body' and so forth, it is perhaps not surprising that some teenagers may feel pressured into modifying their eating habits so as to emulate well-known idols of popular culture. Some teenagers may equate success with having that elusive 'perfect' body shape and may therefore adjust their food intake in the hope that they too might acquire attractiveness and popularity. Whatever the reason, it is now generally accepted that, for many teenagers, deviant eating behaviours have social-psychological antecedents. It is therefore appropriate that we discuss some of these issues in detail and consider their implications for adolescent health.

We begin by discussing how the body reacts to drastic weight reduction.

4.2 CONTROLLING ONE'S WEIGHT

Most adolescents manage to maintain a relatively stable weight regime. One factor that has been identified to account for this phenomenon has been referred to as 'set point' (Mrosovsky 1984). According to this approach, each person has an ideal weight or 'set point' and it is suggested that the body attempts to maintain its weight and keep it as close as possible to its set point. Set point varies from individual to individual, with obese people having a set point that is somewhat higher than that of most other people. Thus, one can view set point as an 'internal thermostat' (Brannon and Feist 1992) that is able to 'monitor' the weight of the individual. A sudden gain or loss in weight of several kilogrammes may affect set point.

Experimental evidence has shown that, when the body loses (or gains) weight and set point is disturbed, the body may react in a variety of ways. These reactions depend on the extent of weight loss or weight gain. Indeed, extremes in weight loss or gain are associated with varied psychological, physiological, and behavioural changes to the individual (Mrosovsky 1984). These trends have been observed in a series of experimental studies in which respondents volunteered to lose weight (e.g. Keys, Brozet, Henschel, Mickelsen and Taylor 1950) or volunteered to participate in weight-gain research (e.g. Sims 1974; 1976). The study by Keys and colleagues (1950), which was conducted during the Second World War, is a classic piece of research and will be briefly described.

Conscientious objectors who resisted going into battle on religious grounds volunteered instead to participate in a study on starvation. During the first few weeks of the research programme volunteers were provided with regular meals and were monitored as to their daily calorie intake. At the end of this phase, the group was provided with reduced food intake. In fact, it was the aim of the experiment to reduce the body weight of each volunteer to 75 per cent of his previous level. This would be achieved by reducing the number of calories in the participants' diet while at the same time maintaining an adequate level of nutrients (Keys *et al.* 1950).

Initially, weight loss was quite rapid, but in order to achieve their targets, the men were later forced to consume even fewer calories. Although most of the men in the study lost 25 per cent of their body weight as designed, some of the participants found this much more difficult to achieve than others, while some took much longer than average to reach their target.

Of interest to the present discussion are the behavioural and physiological changes that were observed among the research volunteers. Although the men were initially rather enthusiastic about the research, this gave way to fights and feelings of disgruntlement during the later stages of the experiment. For instance, the men did not volunteer for extra exercise and became neglectful of their surroundings and personal appearance. Not surprisingly, they also became obsessed with thoughts of food and eventually it became necessary to place restrictions on the men so as to prevent them obtaining food by devious means. As Brannon and Feist (1992: 394) explained:

> These dedicated, polite, normal, stable young men had become very abnormal and very unpleasant under conditions of semistarvation.

Not only do behavioural changes accompany severe weight loss, but the body also undergoes important physiological and endocrinological changes. For example, Mrosovsky (1984: 104) has noted the following:

- Elevated blood cortisol
- Lower levels of lutenising hormone (LH)
- Blunted response to thyrotropin releasing hormone
- Abnormal dexamethasone suppression tests

It is worth noting that, in those instances where lost weight is either wholly or partly regained, physiological rehabilitation is not always complete. Indeed, weight recovery does not always lead to 'normalisation' of LH levels (Mrosovsky 1984). Moreover, there is some evidence to suggest that metabolism of brain norepinephrine may be dysfunctional or irregular for some period after weight gain. That such physiological dysfunction can lead to behavioural aberration gains some credence from the results of the last phase of the research by Keys and colleagues (1950). During this final stage of the experiment, the men were to regain their original weight. In order to achieve this, it was proposed that their food intake be systematically increased over a period of three months. However, it was found that the men remained obsessed with food and were quite irritable and unhappy. Consequently, all restrictions were lifted and the men were allowed to eat as much as they desired, with some even exceeding their original weight. Importantly, it was observed that, for some of the participants, pre-experimental levels of happiness took longer to return.

We now proceed to discuss the perceptions young people have of their own body before discussing specific eating disorders.

4.3 SELF-PERCEPTIONS OF BODY IMAGE

In reviewing eating behaviours, it is appropriate that we also consider self-perceptions of body image. After all, it is reasonable to argue that assumptions about one's level of physical attractiveness may be directly related to specific eating patterns and may also have important implications for the teenager's personality and level of social adjustment (Davies and Furnham 1986a). It is important to note at the outset that, although women tend to be more concerned than men about such matters as body weight and shape, there are societal influences on the body image perceptions of *both* sexes.

Perceptions of body weight

It appears to be a well-established fact, certainly among teenagers in the industrialised west, that females tend to be more sensitive than males about such matters as weight and body shape. They are also more sensitive to obesity in others than are males and more frequently express a desire to lose weight (Davies and Furnham 1986a, 1986b; Desmond, Price, Gray and Connell 1986; Paxton, Wertheim, Gibbons *et al.* 1991).

A variety of external agencies shape adolescents' attitudes about weight control. Females, for instance, appear to be strongly influenced by television, magazines, friends, and family members. Males, on the other hand, nominate television, family, their physician, and coach as important sources of information about weight (see Table 4.1). Thus, females look to more unreliable sources of information about weight and weight control (Desmond *et al.* 1986).

One study conducted in the United States (Desmond *et al.* 1986) found that males were more likely to classify themselves as normal weight or as thin, while females were more likely to classify themselves as heavy or of normal weight. Moreover, 6 per cent of females, but no males, who were classified as thin were in fact dieting to control their weight. Thus, females were more likely to regard themselves as 'overweight' and therefore to be dieting. Generally, many females view being thin as a distinct advantage and believe that thinness leads to greater happiness, more success, more friends, and more dates. They also believe that they are likely to be healthier and better looking. Boys, on the other hand, do not view thinness as an advantage (Paxton *et al.* 1991).

A similar study was conducted among a group of British girls aged 12–18 years (Davies and Furnham 1986b). In particular, the authors were interested in how the girls assessed their own weight, whether they desired to gain or lose weight, and whether they would alter the amount and type of food intake so as to gain or lose weight. It was found that older girls were less likely than younger girls to view their weight as 'just right'. More older (49.1 per cent) than younger girls (26.1 per cent) thought that they were

Table 4.1 Sources of information for weight control

Source	Males %	Females %
Television	34	34
Radio	10	6
Family members	41	61
Friends	16	48
Physician	25	16
Newspapers	4	7
Magazines	24	49
School	0	1
Teacher	4	6
Counsellor	0	1
School nurse	9	6
Coach	28	9
Books	6	20

Source: derived from Desmond *et al.* 1986

overweight. More older (17.0 per cent) than younger girls (8.7 per cent) considered themselves to be underweight.

The results of this study also showed that older girls, more than younger girls, were very keen to lose weight. More importantly, older rather than younger girls considered altering the amount and type of food eaten so as to lose weight, and high on their list of possible omissions were chocolate, cakes, and biscuits. There were also some interesting social class differences. It was found that 16-year-old middle-class girls were more likely to want to *lose* weight, while lower-class girls were more likely to want to *gain* weight. By age 16 years, middle-class girls were more likely than lower-class girls to use exercise as a method of weight reduction (Davies and Furnham 1986b).

It would appear, therefore, that the ages 14 to 16 years are most crucial for young females with respect to changes in their perception of body weight. It is during this time that they may begin altering food intake so as to control their weight (Davies and Furnham 1986b). Thus, the evidence points to clear developmental trends in this regard, suggesting that, at this young age, females may be especially susceptible not only to media images about what is attractive or not, but also to the actual physical changes that they themselves are experiencing.

What strategies do young girls use to control their weight? The results of an Australian study (Paxton *et al.* 1991) suggest that they are more likely than boys to attempt crash diets, calorie counting, meal skipping, drinking water, and not eating between meals.

Perceptions of body shape

Reviewers have shown that research into body image dissatisfaction has taken different directions for males and females. Furnham and Greaves (1994) note that three primary components underly women's body image. These are sexual attractiveness, weight concern, and physical condition. Among men the three components are physical attractiveness, upper body strength, and physical condition. Whereas physical condition among men refers to physical activity, among women it refers to how they are viewed as 'objects'. It therefore seems that there are different societal messages about male and female attractiveness, with male attractiveness being related to muscular strength and female attractiveness being related to thinness (Furnham and Greaves 1994).

Some researchers (Davies and Furnham 1986a) have examined body satisfaction in adolescent girls. In their study among British girls, Davies and Furnham (1986a) found that dissatisfaction with various body measurements increased among older girls. Table 4.2 shows the results of this study in which girls in four different age groups were asked to rate their satisfaction with bust, waist, and hip measurement. Although dissatisfaction was higher in all categories for older girls, the differences were significant only for hip measurement.

Younger girls differ in their attitudes from older girls in another important respect. Concern about body shape also undergoes developmental change. It would appear that younger girls are more concerned about the shape of teeth, hands, and feet and it is only later that concern develops about bust or hip measurements. Davies and Furnham (1986a: 285) explain this change in the following terms:

> Thus it seems that as pubescent growth occurs girls become not unnaturally most concerned with changes in their body measurements, while features that prior to puberty have caused distress become less important . . . with increased age, girls show more concern for those features of their bodies signifying sexual attractiveness. Previous work has demonstrated that females view their bodies primarily in terms of their sexual attractiveness.

These general sentiments find support in another research study among university undergraduates (Furnham and Greaves 1994). Females were

Table 4.2 Females' satisfaction with body measurements as a percentage

	Age in years				
	12.1	*14.0*	*16.1*	*18.1*	x^2
Bust measurement					
Yes	65.2	65.0	65.1	60.4	
No	28.3	32.5	34.9	37.7	0.73
Waist measurement					
Yes	63.0	65.0	62.8	52.8	
No	34.8	32.5	37.2	43.4	1.57
Hip measurement					
Yes	76.1	65.0	55.8	37.7	
No	21.7	32.5	44.2	62.3	17.48[1]

Note: 1 $p < 0.001$

Source: Davies and Furnham 1986a

found to be more concerned about such body parts as thighs and hips, and were keen to change their stomach, weight, and legs. Males were more keen to change biceps, chest, and shoulders, and to disguise their shoulder width.

Slightly different trends have been reported in a study of Finnish adolescents. Rauste-von Wright (1989) found that dissatisfaction with various body parts such as nose, profile, shoulders, legs, skin, and weight peaked around 15 years of age, but that satisfaction increased quite significantly by age 18 years. The author explains this result as the teenagers having accomplished one of the major developmental tasks of adolescence, namely accepting and coming to terms with one's body.

Although several studies of the perceptions of the ideal female body shape have been conducted (e.g. Brenner and Hinsdale 1978; Davies and Furnham 1986a, 1986b; Gitter, Lomranz, Saxe and Bar-Tal 1983), fewer studies have examined sex differences in the perception of male and female body shapes. An exception, however, is a study by Furnham and Radley (1989) among a sample of 16 year olds. These researchers used sketches of naked males and females that were quite detailed in showing all of the salient body features such as thighs, neck, shoulders, stomach, and so forth. Each adolescent in the study was presented with twelve male and twelve female stimulus figures and was then asked to rate them on sixteen bipolar constructs (e.g. attractive–unattractive) using a nine-point scale.

The authors found that around the middle of the range (that is, figures D–I) female figures were rated much more *negatively* than were male shapes. Only on figure F were no significant differences observed. The figure that showed the largest difference between male and female raters was figure G, a 'middling' figure: the female figure was rated much more *negatively* than the male figure. It was seen as unattractive, emotional, not confident, unfriendly, tense, unhappy, insecure, unsociable, unpopular, affectionate, warm, unassertive, feminine, unintelligent, passive, and unathletic (Furnham and Radley 1989: 660). These authors went on to conclude that (p. 661):

Male figures then, within the normal range, have a greater latitude of acceptability with regard to ratings of attractiveness and favourability.

It is interesting to note that the respondents themselves were mainly in the D to I range. The results of this study therefore suggest that males are generally more satisfied and accepting of their own individual body shape (Furnham and Radley 1989). This may be one reason why so much research of this nature is directed toward examining females' attitudes toward female shapes and why eating disorders are prominent among females.

In conclusion, much empirical evidence points to the fact that female adolescents are concerned and sensitive about body weight and shape. A significant proportion of those classified as of 'normal' weight are dieting or exercising in order to lose weight. By contrast, males seem to be much more accepting of their weight and shape and do not necessarily regard being thin as a personal advantage.

Cross-cultural differences in body image

One may ask whether the results discussed above pertain only to youth living in the industrialised west. Can these findings be generalised to teenagers who live in other cultures? It would appear not. As western notions of attractiveness have changed over time, so too there are cultural differences regarding what is viewed as physically attractive and less desirable.

In one examination of the attitudes of Nigerian university students, women were more satisfied than men with their body parts, but specifically with their ears, body weight, general muscle development, chest/breast, size of sex organs, and appearance of sex organs (Balogun, Okonofau and Balogun 1992). The data with respect to body weight do not support those obtained from western samples. The authors explain that Nigerian culture promotes masculinity and aggressiveness in men and it is therefore not surprising that the male respondents in this study tended to be dissatisfied with their bodies.

Another African study was conducted by Furnham and Baguma (1994) who contrasted the attitudes of British and Ugandan university students. The authors found that figures E, F, and G were most positively rated by both groups of respondents. However, the Ugandan rather than British subjects rated those figures at the heavier end of the scale as more attractive *and* healthy. This suggests that in poorer and less developed countries such as Uganda, the health risks of being obese have yet to be recognised (Furnham and Baguma 1994).

Finally, racial differences in body perception have been observed among a large sample of adolescents in the United States (Levinson, Powell and Steelman 1986). Although black and white males were found to be less critical of their weight than black and white females, whites as a group were more critical of their weight than blacks. It was noted that white teenagers were more likely than blacks to view themselves as heavier than a doctor would view them. Likewise, black were more likely than whites to think of themselves as thinner than a doctor's estimate. In conclusion, there appear to be distinct cultural and racial differences in our perceptions of what constitutes physical beauty.

The role of personality factors

Tiggemann (1994) has argued that how a woman perceives her body is integrally related to her feelings of satisfaction with herself. It is suggested that women who are dissatisfied with their weight or body shape are also likely to have lower self-esteem. Empirical evidence supports this view. Tiggemann found that females who perceived themselves as overweight not only dieted much more, but also had lower self-esteem. Interestingly, the reverse was found for men. She found that the bigger men were (or perceived themselves to be), the healthier was their self-esteem. Indeed, it was the underweight men who were observed to have low self-esteem.

The link between self-esteem and acceptance of the physical self varies between cultures. The results of one research study found that although low self-esteem was associated with poor physical image among university students in Japan, as predicted, this was not necessarily the case for younger Japanese still at school (Lerner, Iwawaki, Chihara and Sorell 1980). One explanation might be that younger Japanese are more susceptible to prevailing cultural and traditional norms, while those in university are more influenced by and prepared to embrace values emanating from other cultures.

Another personality trait identified as having important implications for body image perception is locus of control. Those identified as internals have been shown to have a perceived need to lose weight and have also demonstrated confidence in their ability to meet their target weight (Stotland and Zuroff 1990). Using a Body Shape Belief locus of control measure, Furnham and Greaves (1994) found that externals tended to be dissatisfied with their body shape, and have irregular eating patterns, lower self-esteem, and higher depression scores. Internals, on the other hand, tended to exercise for specific body shape reasons. The authors explain the results in the following terms (Furnham and Greaves 1994: 196):

> External-fate beliefs are most likely to suffer given the existence of society pressures. Since they feel that there is nothing they can person-ally do to alter their body shape towards the ideal, the resulting feelings of helplessness and hopelessness are likely to be associated with depres-sion and low self-esteem.

4.4 EATING DISORDERS

Two well-known eating behaviours that are cause for concern among lay and professional people alike are anorexia nervosa and bulimia nervosa. In the scientific literature both are referred to as *disorders* and are considered to be serious health problems. Recent epidemiological studies suggest that their incidence among teenagers is increasing (particularly in the indus-trialised west), giving rise to serious medical and behavioural conse-quences (Mitchell and Eckert 1987).

Bulimia nervosa

According to Muuss (1986) the word bulimia is derived from the Greek which means 'ox' and 'hungry'. Thus, the bulimic is so named because she (most bulimics are female) goes on an eating binge and eats like a 'hungry ox'. The bulimic is characterised by periodic and unrestrained eating during which the individual gorges herself, usually in secret and sometimes for up to two hours (American Psychiatric Association 1994). During this time up to 10,000 calories can be consumed (Muuss 1986) before she purges herself. Bulimia occurs in a small proportion of the population, namely about 1–3 per cent of adolescent females. Among males the incidence is even lower (American Psychiatric Association 1994).

Bulimics are usually within the normal weight range yet are dissatisfied with their weight. Thus, the period of gorging is followed by self-induced purging to control weight. Usually, the eating spree is associated with a sense of loss of control (Sheridan and Radmacher 1992). Weight control is achieved by a variety of methods including vomiting, laxatives, fasting,

Table 4.3 Diagnostic criteria for bulimia nervosa

---

1. Recurrent episodes of binge eating and characterised by
   a) large intake of food (more than what most people would consume) usually within a 2 hour period
   b) Sense of loss of control during the eating binge
2. Recurrent inappropriate compensatory behaviour. Main aim is to reduce weight gain. Methods may include self-induced vomiting, laxatives, enemas, fasting, excessive exercise.
3. Binge eating and compensatory behaviour occur about twice per week for 3 months.
4. Body shape and weight are crucial in self-evaluation.
5. This experience does not only occur during a period of anorexia nervosa.

Source: American Psychiatric Association 1994

excessive or vigorous exercise, enemas, and weight-reducing drugs (American Psychiatric Association 1994; Muuss 1986; Sheridan and Radmacher 1992). Although they are concerned about weight control, bulimics tend to maintain normal body weight.

The American Psychiatric Association (1994) has proposed a set of diagnostic criteria for bulimia nervosa. These are shown in Table 4.3. Crucial elements of these criteria are that the behaviour should occur about twice a week for three months for it to be classified as bulimia. The Association also specifies two types of bulimics. These are the *purging* and *non-purging* type. In the former, the compensatory behaviour may include self-induced vomiting or the use of laxatives, enemas, and so forth. Bulimics of the non-purging type may make use of fasting and vigorous and excessive exercise in order to control their weight.

Binge eating often follows an external event such as inter-personal stress, but may also be the result of intense hunger due to dieting. Although binge eating may act as a device to cope with a variety of events, it is not unusual for bulimics to experience depression and severe self-criticism after the eating spree (American Psychiatric Association 1994).

Muuss (1986: 261) interviewed bulimics and records the experiences of one of them:

> The first vomiting period perpetuated itself into a five-year-long habit in which I had daily planned and unplanned binges and self-induced vomiting sessions up to four times daily. I frequently vomited each of the day's three meals as well as my afternoon 'snack' of three or four hamburgers, four or five enormous bowls of ice cream, dozens of

cookies, bags of various potato chips, packs of Swiss cheese, two large helpings of french fries, at least two milkshakes, and to top it off, an apple or banana followed by two or more pints of cold milk to help me vomit more easily. . . . Then I tiptoed to the bathroom to empty myself. Sometimes the food did not come up as quickly as I wanted; so, in panic, I rammed my fingers wildly down my throat, occasionally making it bleed from cutting it with my fingernails.

Medical consequences of bulimia

It seems that periodic yet consistent purging of the body has serious medical consequences for the individual. Among the most common noted effects are the following (American Psychiatric Association 1994).

Among the purging type there is a significant or permanent loss of tooth enamel, particularly to the front teeth. Sometimes teeth may be chipped with evidence of an increase in the incidence of dental cavities. Among females, menstrual irregularity or amenorrhea are not unknown, and those who persistently use laxatives may become overly reliant on them. Evidence also indicates that purging results in fluid and electrolyte imbalances that can have serious consequences.

Other noted implications of constant purging include:

- Oesophageal tears
- Gastric rupture
- Cardiac arrhythmias

Psychological and social factors associated with bulimia

A wide variety of factors have been found to be associated with bulimia. These will be discussed below.

High standards

According to Heatherton and Baumeister (1991), bulimics and binge eaters set high standards for themselves. Earlier, we referred to media presentations of the 'ideal' or 'perfect' body. Many people take their cues from media portrayals of desirable behaviour and acceptable standards.

Physical attractiveness for women in contemporary western culture is equated with 'thinness'. We have seen that women tend to regard themselves as fatter than their weight would suggest and that more women than men are dissatisfied with their weight and body shape. Because being overweight is generally viewed as a disadvantage, some women are pressured into frequent bouts of dieting. Bulimics and binge eaters are especially dissatisfied with their body and have a stronger desire for 'thinness'. They are therefore more likely to suffer from eating-related difficulties. Thus, it is this fear of being 'fat' that may be central to the cycle of binge-eating and restraint. Attie and Brooks-Gunn (1989) assessed the role of body image in the later development of eating problems in a longitudinal study. They interviewed almost 200 white 13 year olds and their mothers in the United States and then followed them up two years later. The authors found that the best predictor of eating problems over time was negative body image during the puberty years. It was argued that it is during puberty that females' body fat increases significantly and that this may trigger concern with body image.

These women also have high standards that are not related to eating. They tend to be high achievers, have unrealistic expectations of performance, and a very strong need for approval (Heatherton and Baumeister 1991).

The role of personality and family climate

Family functioning is one of several factors that has been identified as being associated with bulimia. Indeed, mothers' ratings of family climate as less cohesive, less organised, and less expressive are significant predictors of later eating disorders (Attie and Brooks-Gunn 1989).

One review of some of the literature in this area endorses the view that family dynamics may be implicated in eating problems (Fisher and Brone 1991). These writers support the view that, during the childhood years, family enmeshment and rigidity are important precursors to abnormal eating patterns. In an effort to avoid family tension and to reduce hurt feelings, family conflict is often left unresolved, or remains deliberately hidden. Perhaps parents reason that this will ensure that their children stay 'close' to the family. However, in many cases these youngsters find it difficult to establish their own identity and may use the eating disorder as a means of negotiating conflict or as one way of asserting independence. Control over their weight is viewed as a sign of personal control and as being effective (Fisher and Brone 1991).

Research among slightly older bulimics (Johnson and Flach 1985) supports the role of family dynamics in the etiology of bulimia. Compared with the control subjects in their study, bulimics came from rigid and enmeshed families that were also conflict-ridden. These families were thought *not* to encourage self-sufficiency, self-reliance, or assertiveness in their individual members. In the authors' view, such dynamics, besides leading to eating problems, are also likely to result in feelings of helplessness, ineffectiveness, low self-esteem, perfectionism, and tension management problems.

A major review of research into binge eating also identified low self-esteem as a major factor in understanding this behaviour (Heatherton and Baumeister 1991). Because society at large and women in particular have been conditioned to view obesity in a negative light, the perception of oneself as overweight is often associated with a lowering of self-esteem. Thus, Katzman and Wolchik (1984) observed bulimics to have lower self-esteem as well as poor body image, higher self-expectations, higher need for approval, and greater dieting tendencies compared with control subjects. Another study suggested that a range of family and social factors have a negative effect on self-esteem and self-efficacy which then best predict eating problems (Strober and Humphrey 1987).

Other personality factors believed to be associated with bulimia are depressive affect, anxiety, and general emotional distress (Heatherton and Baumeister 1991). Those manifesting the disorder have been shown to score more negatively than normals on measures of depression, while anxiety has been related to feelings of rejection.

Anorexia nervosa

Although most anorexics are female, an increasing proportion are male (currently estimated to be around 10 per cent; Romeo 1994). Indeed, it is possible that prevalence among males may be substantially higher, as most practitioners who treat anorexics don't expect them to be male.

The American Psychiatric Association recently released a new set of criteria for the diagnosis of anorexia nervosa. These are summarised in Table 4.4.

Table 4.4 Diagnostic criteria for anorexia nervosa

1. Refusal to maintain minimal normal weight. Body weight is less than 85% of that expected for age and height.
2. Fearful of becoming fat or gaining weight.
3. Disturbance in body weight and shape perceptions. Body image linked to self-esteem.
4. Absence of at least three normal non-drug induced consecutive menstrual cycles.

Source: American Psychiatric Association 1994

Like bulimics, those suffering from anorexia nervosa have a distorted body image, perceiving the size of their body to be much larger than it actually is (Penner, Thompson and Coovert 1991). They are fearful of gaining weight and are unable to maintain what is referred to as a 'minimally normal weight' (American Psychiatric Association 1994: 539). In fact, fear of gaining weight continues even while weight is reducing. It has been suggested that self-esteem is closely linked to body image, with any failure to lose weight being interpreted as a sign of weakness or as a loss of self-control (American Psychiatric Association 1994).

Anorexics are so preoccupied with the shape and size of their body that they will diet to the point of near-starvation. Some engage in strenuous exercise to lose weight, but once very low weight levels have been reached, they become fatigued and weak. Not surprisingly, anorexia nervosa results in serious medical complications, some of which are outlined in Table 4.5. Allbutt (1910; cited in Kaplan and Woodside 1987: 645) described the appearance of the anorexic in the following graphic terms:

> A young woman thus afflicted, her clothes scarcely hanging together on her anatomy, her pulse slow and slack, her temperature two degrees below the normal mean, her bowels closed, her hair like that of a corpse dry and lustreless, her face and limbs ashy and cold, her hollow eyes the only vivid thing about her.

Anorexia nervosa seems to peak between the ages of 14 and 18 years and affects about 0.5–1 per cent of the population. More than 90 per cent of anorexics are female. Very rarely does the onset of this illness occur during middle age or among pre-pubertal girls. In most cases, this condition results from a stressful life event and may require hospitalisation due to electrolyte disturbance or severe weight loss. It is estimated that mortality rates are around 10 per cent and most deaths are caused by starvation, suicide or electrolyte disturbance (American Psychiatric Association 1994).

Anorexics, although slowly wasting away, become totally obsessed with thoughts about food and about being in control of their body. As Garfinkel and Garner (1982) have suggested, exceeding one's desired weight by even one or two kilogrammes is interpreted by the anorexic as having lost control of one's body. Indeed, some authors have noted that anorexics do not 'trust' their own body and may, in fact, be afraid of it (Garfinkel and Garner 1982).

Those who suffer from this illness often continue to complete daily tasks such as school work and many can be characterised as 'overachievers'. However, one early indication of the illness is a loss of contact with friends. Garfinkel and Garner (1982: 8) explain as follows:

Table 4.5 Some medical complications of anorexia nervosa

Affected body part	Symptoms
Endocrine system	1. Amenorrhoea can persist for 5 years after premorbid weight has been regained
	2. Thyroid function affected
Central nervous system	1. Cognitive function appears diminished
	2. Cortical atrophy
	3. Hypothermia; as low as 32.2°C
	4. Non-normal production of neurotransmitters
Cardiac	1. Pulse rate below 50/min
	2. Hypotension
	3. Changes in electrocardiogram
	4. Possibility of congestive heart failure
Gastrointestinal	1. Constipation
	2. Perforation of oesophagus or stomach possible during forced feeding
Haematological	1. Iron deficiency anaemia
Renal	1. Elevated blood urea nitrogen (BUN), haematuria and pyuria
	2. Protein in urine
General	1. Osteoporosis

Source: derived from Litt 1991

dieting which has begun to enable the person to feel better about herself and to be more involved with others does not lead to improved relationships but to withdrawal and isolation.

Possible causes of anorexia nervosa

Muuss (1985) has listed the following five possible explanations for anorexia nervosa.

Social theory

The view that societal influences are implicated in anorexia nervosa is a thread that runs through much of our discussion in this chapter. According to this theory, media portrayals of slim figures and the equating of slim and attractive people with success is a key factor in the etiology of disorders such as anorexia nervosa. At the same time, we live in a 'fast food' high fat culture. Many magazines show tempting ways to cook interesting and exotic meals. Much entertaining is conducted around the dinner table and one is encouraged to consume food and drink to demonstrate that one is being sociable. Thus, many women receive conflicting messages about food (Muuss 1985; see also Garfinkel and Garner 1982).

Psychosexual theory

This viewpoint holds that anorexics are unable to accept their sexuality or their role as a woman. It is contended that they fear sexual intimacy and want to resist sexual maturity (Muuss 1985). This theory is supported by some of the physical effects of the illness such as amenorrhoea.

The role of the family

Evidence suggests that a link may exist between anorexia in adolescent children and affective disorder among parents. Garfinkel and Garner (1982) reported that 14 per cent of fathers in one study suffered from manic-depressive episodes. Some research has also found evidence of higher than average alcohol misuse in families with anorexics.

Perhaps the most profound research into the family functioning of anorexics is that conducted by Minuchin and his colleagues, who adopted a systems approach (Garfinkel and Garner 1982). They are of the view that family members are interdependent, that is, the behaviour of one family member invariably affects the behaviour of other family members. It has been argued that families of anorexics tend to be 'enmeshed', with few attempts at conflict resolution. Moreover, coalitions are sometimes formed within families such that the anorexic teenager is expected to side with one parent against the other. It is argued, therefore, that anorexics are more likely to be found in dysfunctional families where few attempts are made to resolve conflict.

It is also possible that anorexia nervosa may be the result of a genetic factor. Strober and Humphrey (1987) report that the chances of a sister of an anorexic suffering from the same illness is 3–10 per cent, which is much higher than for the general population. However, it is not clear whether this is due to genetic factors or the skewed inter-personal relationships within the family as mentioned above.

Biological theory

According to this theory, disturbances in the functioning of the hypo-thalamus are a possible cause of anorexia nervosa. There is much experimental evidence, for instance, that has documented the link between damage to parts of the hypothalamus and anorexic behaviour (Muuss 1985). The hypothalamus is involved in important hormonal functioning which is disturbed during severe weight reduction (Kaplan and Woodside 1987). This explains the presence in these patients of amenorrhoea as well as the reduction of their oestrogen and testosterone levels. Whether disturbed hormonal functioning follows the anorexic behaviour or is a cause thereof is not clear, however.

Psychobiologic regression hypothesis

This view was first offered by Palmer (Muuss 1985). It is suggested that a critically low body weight leads to low nutritional levels and hence to neuroendocrine malfunction. It is asserted that the anorexic adolescent finds it difficult to cope with the demands of the teenage years and that, through endocrinological dysfunction, the body restores or regresses toward its pre-pubertal state (e.g. lack of menstruation).

Factors associated with general eating problems

We have thus far considered some of the factors associated with bulimia and anorexia nervosa. In this section we discuss factors associated with general eating problems.

The influence of social class

Several writers have suggested that eating disorders such as bulimia and anorexia nervosa tend to occur within specific social classes. Thus it is argued that anorexia is more prevalent among middle- to upper-class teenagers, while bulimia is found more among lower-class girls. A review of some of these studies, however, suggests that findings are ambiguous.

A recent study attempted to shed further light on this issue by examining the attitudes of over 11,000 Norwegian adolescents aged between 13 and 20 years (Wichstrom, Skogen and Oia 1994). Although these authors assessed eating problems rather than eating disorders, they found very little evidence of an association between social class and eating problems. Children from the higher social classes were found to have significantly higher scores on the EAT inventory compared to those from the lower classes.

Why does social class not have a strong effect on eating problems? One suggestion is that in homogenous societies (such as Nordic countries) the effect of factors such as social class is likely to be reduced somewhat.

Eating problems therefore permeate the whole of society so that there are small differences not only between the social groupings, but also the various regions of that society (Wichstrom *et al.* 1994).

The role of culture

There is also evidence that indicates that immigrant children may have higher scores on inventories such as EAT. Indeed, this was observed by Wichstrom and colleagues (1994) in Norway as well as by one research team who compared Asian immigrant children to native-born Britons (Mumford, Whitehouse and Platts 1991). There are two possible explanations for this trend. Firstly, immigrant children may adopt western ideals of a particular body image quite quickly and also pursue it steadfastly. Secondly, immigrant families, particularly from certain cultures, may be more concerned about minimising family conflict. Such families with hidden conflict may be at greater risk from eating problems than are families in which conflict is openly resolved (Wichstrom et al. 1994).

In a noteworthy report, Ahmad, Waller and Verduyn (1994) caution against assuming that cultural differences necessarily imply that some immigrant groups (such as Asians in Britain) are at risk from eating problems. In their view, cultural differences can quite simply be explained by noting the religious practices of groups such as Muslims and Hindi. They argue that teenagers in these religious groups may develop what westerners define as abnormal eating patterns purely as a result of their religious practices. These could include eating particular types of food that are cooked in a particular way, or periodic fasting (e.g. Ramadan).

4.5 THE TREATMENT OF EATING DISORDERS

Although different methods have been proposed for treating those with anorexia nervosa and bulimia, Mitchell and Eckert (1987) remind us that actual *controlled* trials of these treatments have been scarce, for the following reasons. Firstly, psychotherapy is difficult because anorexics very often are simply unmotivated. Those who are very ill might be too fatigued, thus rendering therapy ineffective. Secondly, other factors such as the influence of medication or the influence of family members may confound the effects of therapy.

As was discussed earlier, Minuchin suggested that disorders such as anorexia nervosa can be explained in terms of dysfunctional family relationships. It is therefore not surprising that he consequently proposed a treatment strategy that involves the whole family (Fisher and Brone 1991).

Family members need to realise that each is an individual with unique competencies and abilities. Thus, the enmeshment so typical of these families needs to be dismantled; families need to be 'disengaged' (Fisher and Brone 1991). Closely allied is the question of conflict or family disagreement. Members need to learn how to deal with conflict; rather than hide conflict, families must resolve disputes through warm, honest, and open communication. It has been suggested that those who adopt such a strategy can expect normalisation of weight in about 86 per cent of cases within one to seven years (Fisher and Brone 1991).

One treatment strategy that has been used for both bulimic and anorexic individuals is behaviour modification programmes (Fisher and Brone 1991; Leon 1990; Mitchell and Eckert 1987). Among anorexic patients the treatment involves controlled weight gain strategies and this is particularly useful during the early part of the treatment programme when it is vital to gain weight so as to ensure medical stability. Reinforcers are used and these may include ward privileges and social opportunities (Mitchell and Eckert 1987). The following example illustrates this quite well (Leon 1990: 184):

> she had to gain at least one-half pound per day in order to earn and accumulate points for special privileges. At first, the privileges consisted of time outside her room, which was barren except for a bed, table, and chair. Janet was weighed each morning, and if she did not meet the minimal weight gain requirement for that day, she remained alone in her room with the door closed until she was weighed again the following morning.

One treatment strategy for bulimia is a cognitive-behavioural process for helping individuals change their behaviour and thinking about their illness (Huon and Brown 1988; Leon 1990). Huon and Brown, for instance, propose a series of steps or exercises designed to function very much like a self-help programme. It includes the following (Huon and Brown 1988: 30):

- Contemplation or thinking about change
- The determination to make an informed and deliberate decision to change
- The action that will change things, and
- Maintenance to ensure that any changes are adhered to

An integral component of such a programme is monitoring binges and making notes about thoughts, feelings, and emotions during the binge. Another central tenet of this programme is 'mind control' (Huon and Brown 1988). Thus, the strategy involves assisting the individual to understand how she came to experience a sense of having little control as well as helping her to regain control, and also to understand what her thoughts and emotions were about certain events as they occurred in her life that may have caused stress and binge eating. This can often be achieved in group therapy sessions where discussions are held with other bulimics.

According to one review (Mitchell and Eckert 1987), many therapists attempt cognitive-behavioural therapy. These authors note that although therapists differ in the strategies that they adopt, it is possible to identify the following themes (p. 632):

- Nutritional counselling with emphasis on instituting normal eating patterns
- Assertiveness training and relaxation training
- Stimulus control, response delay, and problem-solving strategies
- Self-monitoring

It is also possible to treat anorexia nervosa patients with medication, although the results have been equivocal (Mitchell and Eckert 1987). The following have been attempted with mixed results: anti-psychotics (e.g. pimazide and sulpiride) as well as anti-depressants and lithium, although lithium should be used with caution with anorexics who have electrolyte imbalances or cardiac problems. Some success has also been reported for treating bulimics with anti-depressants (Mitchell and Eckert 1987).

4.6 SUMMARY

It seems to be generally accepted that there are strong sociocultural norms for defining physical attractiveness in males and females. Among females there are pressures to be slender and attractive. Among males there are pressures to be muscular with wide shoulders. Although norms are operative for both sexes, research has shown that females are much more sensitive than males to these ideals of physical beauty. Certainly, this appears to be the case among adolescents.

We know that the teenage years are a time of physical and emotional upheaval. At the same time adolescents experience pressure to conform to ideals of attractiveness emanating not only from the media, but also from the peer group. It is therefore not surprising that dissatisfaction with body weight and body shape has been identified in those who are quite young (in their early teens). One suggestion is that puberty, with its associated physical changes, acts as a signal triggering a concern with body image. Whatever the reason, differences in body image perceptions have been identified between the sexes, with females more concerned about thinness and attractiveness and males more concerned about body strength.

These differences in perceptions have important implications for eating behaviours, leading females more than males to attempt to control their weight through dieting and other means. Thus, the incidence of eating disorders is higher for females than males, peaking in the adolescent and early adult years. Eating disorders have implications for adolescent mental and physical health; indeed, anorexia nervosa has a mortality rate of about 10 per cent. The challenge for adolescents is to balance the cultural demands regarding attractiveness and their own physical wellbeing.

5   Sex and AIDS

5.1 INTRODUCTION

The teenage years coincide with an awakening of sexual identity. This is a rather complex process and is closely associated with the striving to achieve a personal identity. During this time, adolescents are discovering 'who they are' and questions about sexual identity form an important part of this process. The gradual awakening or unfolding of sexual identity (Sarrel and Sarrel 1981) incorporates several facets of sexuality. On one level, the teenager is developing physically, while another level involves psychological challenge, namely sexual interest in members of the same or opposite sex, sexual behaviour, sex drive, and sexual readiness (Miller and Dyk 1993). For many teenagers this sexual awakening can be an anxious and confusing time for, although adolescents may be physically ready to engage in sexual activity, they may not be emotionally ready to accept the associated consequences and responsibilities of such behaviour.

The spread of sexually transmitted diseases such as HIV/AIDS has raised the community's awareness about adolescent sexuality. Whereas previously concern focused on pregnancy prevention, it is now generally accepted that sexual activity during the teenage years has very important implications for health status, notably HIV infection. Evidence suggests that the number of teenagers infected with HIV is relatively small (Rosenthal and Moore 1991), although the gap between knowledge about HIV/AIDS and appropriate preventive behaviour is wide. Thus, it is possible that infection rates among teenagers could rise quite substantially unless safe-sex practices such as condom use are adopted on a more consistent basis.

This chapter will examine adolescent sexuality in the context of the HIV/AIDS epidemic. It will discuss adolescent sexual orientation and development as well as attitudes toward sex and the use of condoms. In addition, findings pertaining to the prediction of condom use among teenagers will also be discussed. We begin by discussing sexual development.

5.2 SEXUAL DEVELOPMENT

Implicit in sexual development is becoming aware of one's sexual *identity*, and sexual preference for most males and females is likely to be determined by the time they reach adolescence (Miller and Dyk 1993). Whereas only a relatively small minority of teenagers will grow up to be homosexual, most will probably come to view themselves as heterosexual.

Underlying the process of sexual identity is the striving for a personal identity (Erikson 1968). It is important that adolescents develop a personal identity, that is, that they come to a realisation of just who they are and, more importantly, come to accept themselves as someone unique – of value and worth. This is vital for later emotional health. As Newman and Newman (1988) explain, adolescents must learn to merge their past with their future aspirations while at the same time recognising their present characteristics, talents, and limitations.

Erikson (1968) suggested that adolescents live in a 'no-man's-land' and that they appear to be caught between childhood and adulthood. At the same time they must begin to explore their slowly awakening personal and sexual identities. To this end, they will in due course experiment with a range of different social behaviours that are an important learning experience on the road to identity formation. Simultaneously, however, they will also experience many social, parental, and peer pressures to conform to often conflicting norms.

The sexual unfolding or awakening process has been described by Sarrel and Sarrel (cited in Miller and Dyk 1993: 99–100) as follows:

- Individuals (particularly adolescents) must learn the facts about their genitals and understand the physical changes which occur within their body
- Teenagers need to overcome the guilt, shame, and fear about their sexual thoughts, fantasies, and behaviours. They must arrive at a level that they find comfortable and acceptable
- Adolescents must gradually disengage themselves from their tight emotional relationship with their parents and siblings. They must also begin to form a close attachment to an age-mate
- Adolescents must learn to distinguish between what they find erotically pleasing and displeasing. These attitudes need to be communicated to their partner

- Adolescents must be in a position to resolve conflict and confusion about their sexual orientation
- Individuals should be striving for a satisfying sexual life which is free of sexual dysfunction or compulsion
- It is important that one be aware of oneself as a sexual person as well as being aware of the value of sex in one's life. One must also be aware of various sexual options such as celibacy

This unfolding process begins with an awareness of physical changes in early adolescence and ends later with an awareness of oneself as a sexual being. This appears, at best, to be a theoretical model of sexual unfolding and there is no empirical evidence to suggest that it can be applied in its entirety to sexual identity formation during the adolescent years. Indeed, it is unlikely that all adolescents will function at the highest level by the time they reach late adolescence. It is not clear to what extent most 18 or 19 year olds view themselves as a sexual person or to what extent they are 'striving for a satisfying sexual life'. There are a number of reasons for this.

Firstly, teenagers are at different levels of cognitive maturity and some may not reach the final stage presented in the model until much later. Secondly, not all teenagers have the same opportunities or motivation to be as sexually active as the model may suggest. Finally, it is apparent that some individuals still grapple with sexual identity formation during the adult years, as manifested by those who 'change' or adopt a different sexual orientation.

Adolescents progress through various stages of autoerotic and socio-sexual behaviour (Katchadourian 1990). Autoerotic behaviour includes erotic fantasy, nocturnal orgasm, and masturbation. Some reports suggest that boys and girls in the United States begin masturbating in their early teen years, around 12 years of age, with 46 per cent of boys and 24 per cent of girls admitting to masturbation. Among a sample of Brazilian teenagers masturbation was found to be more common among males (97 per cent) than among females (36 per cent) (De Souza, De Almeida, Wagner *et al.* 1993). There are various stages of sociosexual behaviour which include petting, oral sex, and sexual intercourse. Thus, there is a steady progression from less intimate to more intimate forms of sexuality. Masturbation may be followed by light forms of petting, heavy petting, and then intercourse. These forms of behaviour are important components of sexual exploration and sexual identity formation.

Many reports suggest that adolescents appear to be experimenting with sex at an increasingly early age, a view that is borne out by the results of cross-cultural research. A study among Danish teenagers aged 16–20 years found that about one-third had experienced sexual intercourse by the time they were 16 years (Wielandt and Boldsen 1989). In a study among American teenagers, it was noted that, whereas 30 per cent of never-married females of 15–19 years of age had experienced sexual intercourse in 1971, by 1979 the figure was 50 per cent (Baker, Thalberg and Morrison 1988). In one Australian survey (Zubrick, Silburn, Garton et al. 1995), 21 per cent of teenagers reported having had sexual intercourse at 13 years of age or younger. Forty-three per cent reported having had sex by age 15 or 16 years.

In the United States, the mean age for first sexual experience in one heterogenous Californian sample was 13.3 years for males and 14 years for females. Almost half of this high school sample admitted to having had sexual relations (Leland and Barth 1992). These figures correspond quite closely to those reported from Brazil (De Souza et al. 1993) and Germany (Oswald and Pforr 1992). The Brazilian authors found that the mean age at first sexual intercourse for males and females was 13.7 years and 15.5 years respectively. Over one-fifth of boys had their first sexual experience with a prostitute. In a French study of over 4,000 adolescents it was found that 16 per cent and 4 per cent respectively of males and females younger than 13 years reported having had sexual relations. For those older than 18 years, 70 per cent (boys) and 44 per cent (girls) had had sexual intercourse (Choquet and Manfredi 1992).

When examining the sexual behaviour of older teenagers, it is not surprising that a different pattern emerges. One study of 19-year-old females in the United States noted that 73 per cent reported having had sexual intercourse (Dusek 1991). Racial differences have also been observed within some societies. In the United States, more black adolescents engage in their first sexual intercourse at a younger age than do their white counterparts (Rosenbaum and Kandel 1990; Zelnik and Kantner 1980). Table 5.1 shows the age at first intercourse by racial group and gender for almost 3,000 teenagers of different age groups in the United States. The table also gives the cumulative percentages, thereby showing the total proportion who had experienced sexual intercourse by the time they were 20 years of age. The highest proportion of sexual intercourse was found among black males, while the least sexually experienced teenagers in the sample were Hispanic females.

Perhaps somewhat surprisingly, a relatively large proportion of adolescents admit to engaging in oral sex. According to one report (e.g. Katchadourian 1990), 50 per cent of males and 41 per cent of females engaged in cunnilingus, while 44 per cent of males and 32 per cent of females engaged in fellatio. Boys are reported to enjoy these activities more than girls, with

Table 5.1 Age at first sexual intercourse by gender and racial group (US study)

| | Age in years | | | | | |
Group	< 14 %	15–16 %	17–18 %	19–20 %	Cum. %	Virgin %
White males	14.7	32.3	30.1	6.3	83.4	16.7
Black males	48.6	36.1	10.4	0.8	95.9	4.2
Hispanic males	18.0	35.0	30.5	3.4	86.9	13.1
White females	4.9	23.4	37.4	8.7	74.4	25.6
Black females	7.6	32.5	40.5	4.8	85.4	14.6
Hispanic females	2.2	27.2	20.8	12.8	63.0	36.9

Source: derived from Rosenbaum and Kandel 1990

both groups using oral sex as a substitute for sexual intercourse and as a pregnancy prevention measure.

Notwithstanding the social, moral, and health implications of sexual intercourse among teenagers, it remains a momentous psychological event for the adolescent. As such, it has the potential to elicit a range of quite diverse emotions, namely anxiety, pleasure, curiosity, or guilt (Darling and Davidson 1986). Katchadourian (1990: 335) describes the significance of this act as follows:

> The most important sexual milestone that heterosexual adolescents achieve is the initiation of sexual intercourse. Not only is coitus generally considered by heterosexuals to be the most satisfying of all sexual relations, but it also has the most significant personal and social consequences. Couples who engage in coitus cross a line that irreversibly alters the character of their relationship.

Social constructions of sexuality

In a recent detailed report on adolescent sexuality, Moore and Rosenthal (1993) discuss the nature of teenagers' social constructions of sexuality. Social constructions or discourses refer to the implicit *meanings* that people attach to events. If we are to understand adolescent sexual behaviour it is imperative that we examine adolescents' meanings or constructions thereof. This review will, of necessity, be brief, but interested readers may consult more detailed expositions elsewhere (e.g. Moore and Rosenthal

1993; Nix, Pasteur and Servance 1988; Kippax, Crawford, Waldby and Benton 1990).

Young men and women differ in their explanations for or the meanings they attach to sexuality and sexual intercourse. It is something of a simplification to think that young men 'prowl' around on the look-out for 'vulnerable' and 'attractive' females. Although such a view fits very neatly with our stereotypical images of male and female behaviour, the reality is somewhat more complicated. According to Moore and Rosenthal (1993), adolescents develop *scripts* of appropriate sexual behaviour by listening to their peers and, later, through their own experience. These scripts are important because not only do they have an influence on behaviour but they also have implications for health status.

It now seems to be generally accepted, for example, that young females show an interest in males in a *romantic* way, whereas males think of females in a *sexual* way (Harris and Liebert 1987). As Moore and Rosenthal (1993: 85) explain:

> girls have learned to link sexual intercourse with love and often rationalise their sexual behaviour by believing that they were carried away by love. . . . Male sexual scripts stress the satisfaction of their sexual desires.

This general sentiment is supported by the results of an empirical study among Italian adolescents (Zani 1991). Most of the females in this study had their first sexual experience with a male whom they had known for several months. Although some females reported disappointment with sexual intercourse, they appeared to find the continued *emotional* support from their boyfriends as more valuable. By contrast, boys tended to think of their first sexual experience as an *episode* devoid of any meaningful relationship. This episode served merely to demonstrate that they were normal men who had passed a crucial test.

Teenagers in less developed nations think about sex in similar terms. De Souza and colleagues (1993) in Brazil observed that girls in the southern regions of the country thought it very important that sexual intercourse occur within the context of *affection* for one's partner. Indeed, this view was endorsed by 94 per cent of the female respondents; but only by 63 per cent of the males.

Moore and Rosenthal (1993) note that a double standard characterises much of adolescent sexual behaviour and negotiation (see also Kippax *et al.* 1990). Some behaviours and negotiation strategies appear more acceptable for males than for females. The authors observed, for instance, that whereas a boy's reputation may be enhanced by frequent sexual triumphs, girls need to be less overt about their behaviour or sexual motivation. For instance, girls who 'sleep around' too frequently are viewed more negatively than boys who exhibit the same behaviour.

Male and female teenagers also use different scripts when deciding whether or not to use condoms. Recent evidence suggests that, should males insist on *not* using a condom during intercourse, females very often succumb to this pressure. One explanation is that some females believe that, by engaging in unprotected sexual intercourse, they are demonstrating the depth of their love for and commitment to their boyfriend (Gordon 1990), even though their behaviour could be described as risky.

Nix and her colleagues (1988) were interested in the sexual discourses of sexually active young black males in the United States. Their ages ranged from 13 to 20 years. Most of the boys tended to have negative attitudes toward condom use. The underlying scripts that shape behaviour are evident in one boy who expressed his views in the following terms (p. 748):

> Because for the X amount of minutes or hours you're going to be in a very uncomfortable stage and you're not going to really enjoy yourself. It stops the blood circulation for one. It won't be me that's using it, I'll tell you straight up. Now if she have enough pride to enjoy herself because she is going to be the one having the baby, I'm not going to be having it. I'm just going to be a participant. The woman should take the extra precautions of taking something to better protect herself.

This male seems to be diverting all responsibility for pregnancy or disease prevention on to his partner. For him the main concern is physical satisfaction. These sentiments were echoed by another male (Nix *et al.* 1988: 749):

> Me use contraceptives? Oh no! I can't put nothing on. I got to go bare back. I got to feel every motion of this. When we lay down, I want her to feel good. I want her to feel so good that the next time she sees me she's going to be knocking on my door.

Abstaining from sexual intercourse

Not all teenagers have engaged in sexual intercourse, although very few research programmes have been directed at explaining this behaviour. An exception is the report by Leland and Barth (1992) who studied over 1,000 Californian high school students. The respondents were asked to provide reasons for abstaining from intercourse and these have been summarised in Table 5.2. Most respondents were afraid of contracting sexually transmitted

Table 5.2 Reasons for not having sexual intercourse

Reason	Males %	Females %
Afraid of STDs/AIDS	30.7	40.1[1]
Not ready	40.3	71.4[2]
No boy/girlfriend	38.2	31.0
Values/religion	13.7	31.6[2]
Parents' wishes	11.6	37.7[2]
Other	15.0	29.3[2]

Notes: 1 $p < 0.05$ 2 $p < 0.01$

Source: derived from Leland and Barth 1992

diseases (STDs) or AIDS, with females showing more concern in this regard than males. Girls were far more likely than boys not to have had sex because of their religious or personal values, the wishes of their parents or because they felt that they were not yet ready for sex. No significant sex differences were noted for the reason 'No boy/girlfriend'.

Homosexual identity

It is now well established that many children and teenagers engage in 'sex play' with members of the same sex. As Katchadourian (1990) remarked, such behaviour is mainly exploratory in nature and very transient. For the great majority of these youngsters this behaviour is unlikely to lead to self-identification as a homosexual. However, most adult homosexuals trace the origins of their sexual identity to homosexual activity in the teenage years. Indeed, homosexual men are less likely to have experienced heterosexual intercourse as a teenager than heterosexual men. Thus, the adolescent period is an important time for the development of an adult homosexual identity, and Gordon and Gilgun (1987) argue that an adult homosexual identity is simply the continuation of an identity that was established during adolescence and, in some cases, childhood.

There are four biological theories that attempt to explain homosexual orientation, namely hormonal mechanisms, brain structure, neuropsychological function, and genetic factors. According to Bancroft (1994), empirical support for the first three views is somewhat equivocal. With respect to the role of genetic factors, he cites evidence based on twin studies suggesting that markers on the X chromosome may be implicated. The actual nature of the genotype is at this stage unclear, although it seems certain that psychosocial factors may also play a prominent role in the development of sexual orientation.

Reliable estimates indicate that between 20 and 30 per cent of adult males report having had at least one homosexual experience up to orgasm (Miller and Dyk 1993; Remafedi 1987). For the adolescent who feels sexually attracted to individuals of the same sex, this period of their life can be very disturbing and confusing. These teenagers live in a heterosexual world with heterosexual norms. They are expected to behave in a hetero-sexual way. Yet, they soon realise that somehow they are 'different' and do not fit with others' expectations. They have 'strange' and often unwelcome desires. As some authors have explained, homosexual teenagers soon learn to hide their true feelings, and become isolated and alienated from close friends and the peer group (Gordon and Gilgun 1987). Others wait for years, invariably in vain, in the hope that they will uncover their 'true' heterosexuality.

Garnets and Kimmel (1991) have provided some guidelines as to the developmental stages of homosexual identity formation. They distinguish between the following stages:

• Initial awareness of same-gender affectional-erotic feelings
• Initial same-gender sexual experience
• Self-identification as lesbian or gay
• Positive gay or lesbian identity

The authors suggest that the initial awareness of being erotically attracted to members of the same sex occurs in the early teenage years, as early as 12 years for some or as late as 16 years for others. Males tend to have these experiences before females. Self-identification of the self as homosexual precedes a positive identity as such by between three and six years on average. For some, this positive identity may occur only late in the adult years.

Gay youth and AIDS

Given their age and feelings of alienation, many gay youth are on the fringes not only of mainstream society, but also of the wider gay com-munity. This may therefore have a serious impact on their knowledge about HIV/AIDS and safe-sex practices (Millan and Ross 1987).

Evidence to date indicates that gay youth differ from older gay men as to the sources of their information about AIDS. Whereas the younger generation are more likely to obtain their information from television, radio, friends, gay venues (e.g. bars), and leaflets, older men rely more on newspapers for their AIDS information (Millan and Ross 1987). Notwithstanding their wider source of information, gay youth are still more likely than older men to report not having enough information about AIDS. This should be of serious concern to all health professionals and educators.

According to a study conducted by Millan and Ross (1987) among a sample of Australian gays, it would appear that few gay youth have changed their lifestyle or sexual habits in the face of the HIV/AIDS epidemic. Much more effort therefore needs to be put into ensuring that gay youth change their sexual habits and reduce their risky behaviour. Providing adequate information about HIV infection and safe-sex strategies appears to be just the first step in the fight against the disease. A bigger challenge is actually changing behaviour.

5.3 ATTITUDES TO SEX

First sexual intercourse

Reactions of teenagers to their first sexual intercourse appear somewhat mixed, with boys reporting more favourable attitudes. One report noted that, whereas 11 per cent of girls reported being 'sorry' for what they had done, 23 per cent said that they were 'glad'. For those who admitted to a subsequent sexual experience, 70 per cent of girls reported enjoying it a great deal (Katchadourian 1990). A study among older teenagers found that more males than females reported experiencing psychological and physiological satisfaction during their first sexual intercourse. Females were also more likely than males to experience guilt frequently or occasionally (see Table 5.3).

Sexual practices

Teenagers in the late twentieth century appear to have quite favourable attitudes toward different sexual practices. Furnham and Gunter (1989) conducted a survey among a large sample of over 2,000 British teenagers aged between 10 and 17 years. They found that almost half of the respondents felt that society should tolerate all types of sexual relationships and not just heterosexual ones. About 75 per cent of the sample approved of pre-marital sex. Only a relatively small number (about 20 per cent) believed that the main reason for sexual intercourse was to have children.

These tolerant attitudes are reflected in a study among American undergraduates (Wilson and Medora 1990). Generally, the students were in

Table 5.3 Reactions to sexual intercourse among teenagers

Reaction	Boys %	Girls %
Those feeling 'sorry'	1	11
Those feeling 'glad'	60	23
Enjoyed subsequent coitus	80	70
Psychological satisfaction	67.4	28.3
Physiological satisfaction	80.9	28.3
Experiencing guilt		
Never	59.6	43.6
Seldom	23.4	19.1
Occasionally	11.7	24.5
Frequently	3.2	7.3

Sources: derived from Darling and Davidson 1986; Katchadourian 1990

favour of pre-marital sex if the couple were in love or engaged. The respondents were also approving of oral sex, while they tended to disapprove of homosexuality and extra-marital sex. On all of the questions, however, males tended to have more tolerant attitudes than females.

Not only do some adolescents have tolerant attitudes toward sexual practice, but they also engage in a variety of sexual behaviours. Almost all university students report engaging in such activities as lip kissing and tongue kissing. A surprisingly large number also report having had their genitals orally stimulated (females, 88.7 per cent; males, 92.7 per cent). Nearly all (more than 95 per cent) report having touched their partner's genitals while clothed as well as while unclothed (Darling and Davidson 1986).

5.4 SEXUAL BEHAVIOUR AND CONDOMS

The findings reported above make it quite clear that many teenagers are engaging in sexual activity from an early age. Indeed, teenagers appear to be quite sophisticated and experienced in terms of their sexual practice. This has important health implications for adolescents. The more teenagers engage in casual sexual activity, the greater the risk of spreading infectious diseases. Safe-sex practices such as the use of condoms during intercourse reduce the risks of STDs such as HIV/AIDS. Thus, it is imperative that we understand teenagers' attitudes to condom use and the conditions likely to increase or militate against such behaviour.

Of course, condom use should not be viewed solely as a buffer against HIV infection. Important too are risks of pregnancy as well as other STDs. Female adolescents have relatively high rates of gonorrhea, cytomegalovirus, chlamydia cervicitis, and pelvic inflammation (Brooks-Gunn and Furstenberg 1989). However, these diseases are likely to be exacerbated not only by early sexual activity, but also by inconsistent condom use.

Condom use among sexually active teenagers appears to have increased somewhat over recent years. A report by Pleck, Sonenstein and Ku (1991) notes that condom use among teenage males more than doubled between 1979 and 1988, while its use doubled for 15–19-year-old females between 1982 and 1988. These authors also suggest that teenagers who became sexually active during the late 1980s were 110 per cent more likely to practise safe sex than were teenagers in the late 1970s. What is disturbing is the finding among many researchers that condom use seems to be inconsistent. Coupled with quite pervasive sexual experimentation and perceptions of invulnerability (see below), it is possible that STD infection rates among adolescents could rise quite dramatically.

Condoms: HIV knowledge versus behaviour

There is compelling evidence suggesting that safe-sex behaviour does not always match one's knowledge about the risks of infection. One Australian study among high school students found that, whereas 83 per cent of the respondents agreed that condoms help prevent the spread of STDs, 38 per cent also agreed that AIDS was something that they had not thought a lot about (Barling and Moore 1990). Some teenagers, therefore, appear to underestimate their own level of risk by preferring not to think too much about 'what would happen to me'.

This gap between sexual attitudes and sexual behaviour is also evident among older adolescents. Studying the beliefs and sexual behaviours of more than 600 university students, one research team found that more than half of the respondents had engaged in sexual intercourse. Of these, 25 per cent had had sex on a casual basis, while fewer than 10 per cent had experienced anal sex. However, more than 90 per cent of the respondents thought that they were unlikely or very unlikely to contract HIV. Not surprisingly, such perceptions of low risk were found to be translated into risky behaviour. For example, although nearly all believed that unprotected anal and vaginal sex with a casual partner incurred the risk of HIV infection, only 26 per cent had actually used a condom when having vaginal sex with a casual partner. For anal sex with a casual partner, the corresponding figure was a low 2 per cent. Thus, knowledge about safe-sex practices is in itself insufficient to direct individuals into taking appropriate preventive measures (Turtle, Ford, Habgood *et al.* 1989).

Turtle and her colleagues suggest several reasons for the disparity between knowledge and behaviour. On the one hand, it may be possible that adolescents view the use of condoms as embarrassing or as interfering with sexual pleasure. Thus, there are certain costs and benefits that are considered when deciding whether or not to use condoms (Pleck *et al.* 1991; see discussion below). On the other hand it is also likely that condom use may be determined by additional factors such as beliefs about the desirability of using condoms or subjective norms about condom use (see section 5.5). Other factors include perceptions of invulnerability and social constructions of the risks of HIV infection (see later).

It is also likely that the gap between AIDS knowledge and appropriate behaviour may be due to the fact that teenagers do not perceive themselves as vulnerable to HIV infection. One study among mostly black youth in an urban centre in the United States focused on the extent to which the following four factors predicted safe-sex behaviours including condom use (Zimet, Bunch, Anglin *et al.* 1992): knowledge about AIDS, beliefs and social anxiety about AIDS, and perception of risk from HIV infection.

The authors found that behaviour change was related to these factors as follows (Zimet *et al.* 1992). Males who reduced their frequency of sexual activity were more knowledgeable about AIDS than other males; females who reduced their number of partners were more knowledgeable than other females. Likewise, males who reported a decrease in frequency of sexual relations had more accurate beliefs than those males who did not, although just the opposite was the case for females, a finding the authors are at a loss to explain. Generally, males were more anxious than females about AIDS, but males who reported *no* changes in frequency were much more anxious than females. Teenagers who reduced their frequency of sexual activity perceived themselves to be more at risk of infection than those who did not reduce their frequency. More importantly, those who perceived themselves to be vulnerable to infection were more likely to use condoms than other teenagers (see also section 5.5).

A weakness of this research is that behaviour change was measured retrospectively rather than prospectively (Zimet *et al.* 1992). Nonetheless, the data suggest that the four factors that were included in the study are related, in a meaningful way, to various sexual behaviours.

HIV knowledge among some minority youth

Different groups of adolescents differ in their knowledge and beliefs about HIV/AIDS. Although studies using university students as respondents have shown relatively high levels of AIDS knowledge (e.g. Turtle *et al.* 1989; Wilson and Medora 1990), studies among some inner-city minority youth have raised doubts that correct AIDS knowledge is widespread. In fact, there appears to be a disturbing level of ignorance among some, but not all, of these adolescents. For example, research by St. Lawrence (1993) among youth who tend to frequent public health clinics and community-based teenage centres revealed that 63 per cent believed (incorrectly) that 'all sexually transmitted diseases can be cured'. She also found that 52 per cent believed that 'the AIDS virus doesn't go through unbroken skin', while 64 per cent believed that 'people who have the AIDS virus feel quite sick'. These findings suggest that some minority youth, particularly those in more run-down areas of large cities, are less knowledgeable about AIDS-related issues than one may normally assume. These adolescents are therefore placing their own health at some risk. Special educational programmes may therefore need to be directed at these groups of teenagers. No doubt the best venues for such education, in addition to community centres and health clinics, are the clubs, pubs, and bars that these youth tend to frequent.

Condoms: costs and benefits

Teenagers who use condoms during sexual intercourse believe that this practice helps reduce the spread of STDs. At the same time, however, a significant proportion readily admit that condom use leads to a reduction of sexual pleasure (Oswald and Pforr 1992). What is more, sexually experienced adolescents are more likely than less experienced ones to have negative attitudes toward condom use.

According to one view (Pleck *et al.* 1991), adolescents reason about condom use in terms of perceived costs and benefits. If the costs of condom use are perceived as being too high this is likely to lead to a reduction in safe-sex practices. Based on their study of over 2,000 male teenagers in the United States, Pleck and colleagues (1991) suggest that the following costs-benefits are relevant with respect to condom use:

- Preventing pregnancy: personal costs-benefits
  e.g. Concern about pregnancy increases condom use; belief that a female using the pill will reduce condom use
- Preventing pregnancy: normative belief
  e.g. The belief that males have a responsibility to reduce pregnancy increases condom use

- Avoiding AIDS
  e.g. A belief that it is important to avoid AIDS will increase condom use
- Partner expectations
  e.g. Requests by females raise condom use
- Embarrassment and reduction of pleasure
  e.g. Perception of not being embarrassed will increase condom use

Reasoning about risk and invulnerability

Some writers have argued quite cogently that adolescents cannot adequately reason about risk, chance, and probability. Gordon (1990) has referred to this as deficits in cognitive functioning or as 'global developmental delay'. It would seem that such teenagers do not properly evaluate the consequences of their behaviour, preferring instead to reason that just one act of unprotected sexual intercourse is unlikely to lead to pregnancy or a STD and is less risky than several such acts. (Although such views may be prevalent among some adolescents, they do not appear to be universal. For instance, the research by Zimet and colleagues (1992) referred to earlier is a case in point.)

Some minority teenagers in the United States tend to perceive themselves as being less at risk of HIV infection than teenagers from other racial groups (St. Lawrence 1993). One explanation for this is that some black youth may view AIDS as a disease afflicting white gay men. Such a perception has serious implications for their safe-sex practices, although it is not clear to what extent such perceptions are held by minority youth in countries such as Great Britain, Canada, Germany, or France, for example.

Following Elkind (1967), who coined the concept 'personal fable', some authors have suggested that adolescents employ cognitive egocentrism in their reasoning about risk. As Moore and Rosenthal (1991: 164) have explained, some teenagers believe:

> that one is special, unique, and invulnerable to the risks and hazards which beset other mortals. Adolescents are reported to be highly susceptible to this kind of thinking, that is, the illusion that although others may suffer the consequences of dangerous and risky actions they are somehow immune.

The authors found empirical support for this view based on an examination of adolescents' actual behaviour and their perceptions of risk. Although most respondents were knowledgeable about safe-sex practices and AIDS, this was not always reflected in their behaviour. Evidence suggested that those whose sexual behaviour could be described as risky were more likely to score low on their belief in control over the likelihood of contracting HIV. Moreover, those who perceived their risk of HIV infection as low were more likely to hold stereotypical views of a person with HIV/AIDS.

Although it is well recognised that HIV/AIDS is no longer a 'gay' disease and that, increasingly, heterosexual women are at risk of infection, Moore and Rosenthal (1991) found that females believed themselves to be *less* at risk of AIDS than did males. In fact, the authors found that females were taking greater risks with so-called 'regular' partners, believing them to be 'safe' or 'clean'. This may be due, in part, to how individuals mentally construct HIV infection, a topic to which we shall now turn.

Social constructions of the risks of HIV infection

Why is it that there is very little correspondence between sexual knowledge and safe-sex behaviour? Why do some adolescents appear impervious to messages about safe sex? One explanation is that they perceive themselves as invulnerable or they construct the risks of HIV infection in such a way that they minimise their chances of practising preventive behaviour.

This matter was recently investigated among university students in the United States (Williams, Kimble, Covell *et al.* 1992). Using focus group discussions, the researchers found that the respondents constructed theories about the risks of HIV infection that were likely to predict unsafe-sex practices. These constructions of reality were grouped into four categories which are shown in Table 5.4.

The first category, judgements of riskiness of sexual partners, suggests that one makes judgements about riskiness based on outward appearance or based on what one 'knows' about the other person. Hence, HIV positive people are thought to dress 'provocatively', while those whom we like are unlikely, in our view, to be HIV positive.

Table 5.4 Students' social constructions of the risks of HIV infection

---

1. Judgements of riskiness of sexual partners
2. Assessments of personal risk
3. Reasons for unsafe sex
4. Beliefs about condoms

Source: derived from Williams *et al.* 1992

The second category, assessments of personal risk, alludes to our earlier discussion of invulnerability. That is, respondents often thought of themselves as simply not being at risk. Common expressions were 'AIDS is not a problem on this campus', or 'I am not gay'. The third category, reasons for unsafe sex, generally attributes unsafe behaviour to factors beyond one's control. These include being affected by alcohol at the time, or being overcome by lust or passion. The final category, beliefs about condoms, is in line with the earlier discussion regarding costs and benefits of condom use. On the present occasion, respondents suggested that condoms tend to interfere with sex, are unpleasant to use, are inconvenient, and have undesirable implications such as suggesting that you do not trust your partner.

5.5 PREDICTING CONDOM USE

Thus far in this chapter we have reviewed the nature of sexual development, attitudes to sex, and sexual behaviour with specific reference to implications for health status. What is clear is that adolescents do not always use condoms during sexual intercourse, that is, their safe-sex behaviour is inconsistent. It is not surprising, therefore, that a rather large research literature has developed in order to identify the factors that best predict adolescents' intentions to use condoms. Some of this research will now be discussed.

Self-efficacy theory

Some research teams have concentrated their efforts on examining the role of self-efficacy in intention to use condoms. As Richard and Van der Pligt (1991) explained, self-efficacy is important as it reflects the extent to which individuals believe that they have some control over their motivation, behaviour, and social environment.

To what extent do adolescents feel in control during sexual encounters? How likely are they to withstand sexual advances by another? Evidence to date (Rosenthal, Moore and Flynn 1991:82) suggests that males are less likely than females to:

- Be unable to refuse a sexual advance by the partner
- Be unable to reject an unwanted sexual advance from someone other than the partner
- Be unable to do something sexually which they don't feel comfortable about

Table 5.5 Predictions of intention to use condoms

Group	Best predictors
Sexually active males	Frequency of past use
	Talk with new partner[1]
	Enjoy sex using condoms[1]
Sexually active females	Frequency of past use
	Enjoy sex using condoms[1]
Never sexually active males	Convince partners to use condoms[1]
	Buy condoms[1]
Never sexually active females	Convince partner to use condoms[1]

Note: 1 measure of self-efficacy

Source: derived from Joffe and Radius 1993

Females, on the other hand, are more likely than males to:

- Be unable to put a condom on an erect penis
- Be unable to meet their own sexual needs through masturbation
- Be unable to carry condoms 'just in case'

In one study, Joffe and Radius (1993) examined the impact of several self-efficacy measures as well as previous experience with condoms on intention. Although they also included other independent variables such as the role of subjective norms, they found that self-efficacy was a consistent predictor among both sexually active and abstinent adolescents (see Table 5.5). Among the self-efficacy measures, 'talk with partner', 'enjoy sex with condoms', 'convince partner', and 'buy condoms' were significant predictors of intention.

The role of self-efficacy varies for adolescents in monogamous and non-monogamous groups. Although it is an important factor in explaining intention among those in monogamous relationships, an equally important factor would appear to be frequency of previous sexual intercourse. Indeed, Richard and Van der Pligt (1991) found that the more frequently couples had sexual intercourse, the *less* they were inclined to use condoms.

For those in non-monogamous relationships, self-efficacy was an important predictor for girls. Among boys intention was best predicted by such factors as affective reactions, age at first sexual intercourse, number of sexual partners, and age (Richard and Van der Pligt 1991). Thus, the researchers demonstrated interesting trends for their sample. Those in monogamous relationships appear less concerned about the spread of HIV and are therefore less likely to use condoms, whereas just the reverse applies to those in non-monogamous relationships. This may suggest that couples in monogamous relationships are more trusting of each other and believe that they need not protect themselves from AIDS (Rosenthal *et al.* 1991). Of course, this is a risky strategy given the long incubation period of HIV.

Self-efficacy plays different roles in predicting intention to use condoms among regular and casual partners (Rosenthal *et al.* 1991). Although the ability to 'say no' is an important predictor of safe-sex intention among casual partners of both sexes, it explains only a small amount of the variance. Other factors are likely to be important here such as general beliefs about sexuality, values, and subjective beliefs, to name a few. Among regular partners components of self-efficacy such as 'saying no', 'being assertive', as well as one's own sexual esteem are important in predicting intention to use condoms.

These results therefore demonstrate that self-efficacy is a multi-dimensional construct having differential effects for regular and casual partners. In other words, the perception of 'being in control' varies according to sexual circumstances and is also, no doubt, affected by subtle influences such as trust. Notwithstanding, results are unanimous in suggesting that higher levels of self-efficacy are more likely to increase intentions to practise safe sex. It is to be hoped that such intentions will lead to corresponding preventive behaviour.

Testing the theory of reasoned action

It was noted in Chapter 2 that social psychological models have been designed to enhance our understanding of health-related behaviours by uncovering those factors that are best able to predict behaviour. One such model is the theory of reasoned action (Ajzen and Fishbein 1980) and its extension, the theory of planned behaviour (Ajzen 1991). In its original form the theory proposes that behaviour can best be predicted by an intention to commit the behaviour. Intention is a function of attitude toward the behaviour as well as subjective norms. Each of these, in turn, has its own unique predictors (see Chapter 2 for a more detailed exposition). Thus, the theory would predict that condom use during intercourse is predicted by the intention to use condoms which, in turn, is predicted by attitudes toward the use of condoms as norms about using condoms.

Several research studies have been designed to test the validity of the model with respect to practising safe-sex behaviour (see Terry, Gallois and McCamish 1993b for reviews). A large majority of these studies have demonstrated some support for the model, although it is important to bear in mind that results are affected by the population under study as well as the way in which components of the model are operationalised.

One study sought to determine the relative merits of the theories of reasoned action and planned behaviour as applied to students' use of condoms during sexual intercourse (Nucifora, Gallois and Kashima 1993). Support was found for aspects of both theories. For example, it was noted that attitudes to condom use and subjective norms predicted intention to use a condom which, in turn, predicted behaviour. The influence of the belief-based measures of attitude and norm on intention were not mediated by the direct measures of attitude and norm, however.

Of some importance was the finding that intention as well as perceived control and actual control predicted condom use. This is in line with the theory of planned behaviour. Thus, the findings demonstrate that individuals are more likely to use a condom if they perceive or believe that they have some control over this behaviour. In this regard, therefore, perceived control is similar to self-efficacy, which was discussed earlier (Nucifora *et al.* 1993).

According to the results of another study (Chan and Fishbein 1993), the theory of reasoned action can be used to predict women's intentions to tell their partners to use condoms during sexual intercourse. As predicted on the basis of the model, attitudes to the behavioural act as well as perceived norms were found to predict intention. The authors extended the theory somewhat by showing that factors not incorporated in the model are also salient predictors. They found that 'gut' emotional reactions to the act (such as 'telling my partner to use a condom every time makes me feel delighted/disgusted') also predicted behaviour.

Further support for some of the underlying principles of the model is provided in a study by Boldero, Moore and Rosenthal (1992). Although the authors found intention to predict actual condom use, the impact of attitudes and norms was rather more limited. However, they found that the influence of intention to use a condom during intercourse was moderated by certain *contextual* factors. They found that sexual arousal, partner communication, and condom availability had an important influence on whether the intended behaviour was actually performed. These findings indicate that, notwithstanding one's attitudes and the influence of subjective norms in favour of condom use, other factors such as level of sexual arousal or the availability of condoms can override original intention.

Similar findings have been reported by Fisher (1984). As predicted by the theory of reasoned action, he found that attitudes and norms predict behaviour through intention, although respondents' emotional responses to sexuality should not be overlooked. He found that factors such as sexual information and sexual fantasy were co-predictors with intention, norms, and attitudes of safe-sex behaviour. Thus, the findings reviewed here (e.g. Boldero *et al.* 1992; Chan and Fishbein 1993; Fisher 1984) demonstrate that the theory of reasoned action is a useful tool for understanding adolescents' use of condoms during intercourse. However, the findings demonstrate quite clearly that elements not contained within the model have an important influence on ultimate behaviour. Very often, these elements are of a social or contextual nature.

5.6 SUMMARY

Adolescence is a period of sexual development. Although the sexual awakening process seems to occur quickly for some teenagers, for others it is a gradual unfolding happening. Nonetheless, for many adolescents this stage of the life span is one of sexual experimentation. In this chapter we saw that some teenagers are engaging in sexual intercourse as young as 12 years of age, while the great majority will have had sex by their late teens. Some will have had sex with prostitutes (De Souza *et al.* 1993), while many will be in non-monogamous relationships. Thus, the risks of HIV infection and the spread of other STDs are heightened.

The research literature to date indicates that most adolescents are knowledgeable about the risks imposed by engaging in unprotected sexual intercourse. However, fewer appear to be actually practising safe sex. One possible explanation could be that many do not perceive themselves as vulnerable to HIV infection. These are worrying findings for they have very serious implications for adolescent health. A major challenge which therefore faces health professionals and educators is how to persuade teenagers to translate their knowledge into appropriate safe-sex behaviour.

In an attempt to shed some light on the underlying processes of adolescent sexual behaviour, researchers have proposed theoretical models that seek to better explain sexual behaviour. These have shown some promise for they highlight some of the factors that play a demonstrable role in safe-sex behaviour. Although these models have the potential to be useful as a guide in shaping health education strategies, they tend to overlook the important part played by social factors in sexual negotiation. Thus, it is vital that researchers are aware of the role of sexual arousal, condom availability, and emotion as well as one's social constructions of sexuality in teenagers' reasoning about sex.

6 Substance use: alcohol, cigarettes, and other drugs

6.1 INTRODUCTION

This chapter will examine the social and psychological factors surrounding excessive or problematic substance use. In particular, we shall focus on cigarette smoking, alcohol, and drug use among adolescents. Some authors have suggested that substance use and abuse now form an important part of the lives of most teenagers and that many will experiment with substances such as alcohol and cigarettes (Irwin and Millstein 1991; Rice 1992). Moreover, not only do these substances have a potentially harmful effect on one's health, but they have also been shown to be implicated in a variety of risky and anti-social behaviours such as violent and non-violent crime, delinquency, and sexual promiscuity. In this light, therefore, substance abuse by teenagers takes on added significance.

It is important to bear in mind that substance use forms a normal part of adolescent development. That is, many adolescents who are striving to attain a sense of personal identity will at some time during their teenage years experiment with substances such as alcohol and cigarettes. Part of the search for an identity encompasses experimentation with new behaviours and ideas. As Brunswik (1991: 441) has explained, this striving for personal identity incorporates 'expanding the boundaries for exercising competency and control'.

Although it has been reported that some teenagers may misuse certain prescribed and over-the-counter drugs, or erogenic aids such as anabolic steroids (Hein 1991), those behaviours will not be discussed in this chapter. Rather, we are concerned here with the social psychological processes that lead some teenagers to *misuse* well-known substances like cigarettes, alcohol, and illicit drugs. It is to these and related issues that we now turn our attention.

6.2 PATTERNS OF SUBSTANCE USE

Adolescents progress through various stages of drug use, Kandel (1975) having suggested the following sequence:

- Beer or wine, or both
- Cigarettes or hard liquor
- Marijuana
- Other illicit drugs

In Kandel's view very few teenagers start with marijuana or illicit drugs; rather, they experiment first with the legal drugs such as beer and wine. Very few of these adolescents will progress to the final category of drug use. Of those who start with wine or beer, most will progress to spirits rather than cigarettes. Kandel (1975) also found in her study that no adolescent progressed from the first stage to illicit drugs without also experimenting with cigarettes or spirits. Finally, evidence suggests that marijuana use is crucial in identifying those who proceed to further illicit drug use. Kandel found that only 2–3 per cent of users of legal drugs proceeded to the illicit category *without* first trying marijuana.

More recently, Kandel and Yamaguchi (1993) confirmed that a drug such as crack is initiated after experience with marijuana. Moreover, important gender differences in the developmental progression of involvement with drugs were noted. Cigarettes were found to precede marijuana use among females, while alcohol use preceded marijuana use for males (even in the absence of cigarette usage). Cigarette smoking was found to be an important pathway to illicit drugs other than marijuana for males.

These views about the progression of drug use through various stages have been questioned by others. In one report (Mills and Noyes 1984), for example, it was argued that teenagers do not merely use previous stages as 'stepping stones', but that drug use is, in fact, cumulative. That is, individuals *expand* their repertoire of drug use by adding new drugs.

It is interesting to note that the patterns of alcohol and cigarette use among teenagers mirror quite closely those of the adult population. As with adults, more teenagers drink alcohol than smoke cigarettes. Moreover, gender differences in the use of these substances are similar to those among adults: more females than males smoke cigarettes, although males smoke more heavily, and more males than females drink alcohol, with females consuming less than males (Hill, Willcox, Gardner and Houston 1987).

Alcohol use

Alcohol is the preferred drug for most adolescents (Rice 1992). Some children are as young as 10 years of age when they experiment with alcohol for the first time. According to one Australian report (Wilks and Callan 1990), the mean age at the time of the first alcoholic drink for 16 year olds who drink is 10.6 years for males and 12.1 years for females. One study examined the drinking habits of over 20,000 Australian teenagers (Hill *et al.* 1987). The main results are displayed in Table 6.1 and indicate that alcohol consumption increases with age so that over 90 per cent of 17 year olds report having tried alcohol. Close to 50 per cent of 16 year olds consume alcohol on a regular basis in Australia (see also Wilks and Callan 1990).

Zeitlin and Swadi (1991) found that between 60 and 90 per cent of British teenagers drink regularly, while 10 per cent drink more than moderately, although the writers do not define just what they mean by 'moderate'. It is also not clear from the report what age group this information is based upon. Evidence from the United Kingdom supports Australian research regarding the age of onset of drinking. Based on a study of London teenagers, one report put the age of initiation at about 11 years (Zeitlin and Swadi 1991). More worrying is the apparent lowering of the age of initiation since the 1970s.

A report from the United States indicated that 56 per cent of teenagers of all races aged between 12 and 17 years had tried alcohol. About 25 per cent were classified as a current user (Rice 1992). Similar figures were obtained from a school-based clinic in New York state. Using a technique

Table 6.1 Alcohol consumption by Australian teenagers at school

		Age					
Drinking category	*Gender*	*12* *%*	*13* *%*	*14* *%*	*15* *%*	*16* *%*	*17* *%*
Drank in past year	M	64	70	76	84	89	91
	F	51	63	76	86	90	90
Drank in past month	M	33	40	46	58	65	73
	F	22	33	45	56	63	68
Drank in past week	M	23	29	33	44	52	56
	F	14	24	32	44	45	49

Source: adapted from Hill *et al.* 1987

known as randomised responses, it was estimated that 54 per cent of the high school respondents had used alcohol at least once in their lives, while 36 per cent had used alcohol within the past 3 months (Fisher, Kupferman and Lesser 1992).

One may be surprised that some teenagers report experimenting with alcohol when as young as 10 years. As Wilks and Callan (1990) suggest, one explanation for such behaviour may be that some parents see very little harm in their children taking alcohol. Indeed, parents may see this as preferable to using other drugs. It is also possible, of course, that those who first experimented with alcohol at an early age may have been altogether unsupervised by care-givers. A question that then arises is *why* some children are willing to experiment with alcohol. This will be discussed in more detail in section 6.4.

Most young adults have their first alcoholic drink in the home and they tend to begin drinking either out of curiosity or because parents or relatives offer them alcohol. Whereas between 40 and 50 per cent of teenagers report being offered their first drink by a family member, only about 4 per cent report that friends encouraged them to drink for the first time (Wilks and Callan 1990). Notwithstanding just how drinking behaviour is initiated, most young people tend to drink in the company of friends (56–64 per cent) followed by relatives (33–43 per cent). Very few adolescents (up to 2 per cent) drink alone (Wilks and Callan 1990).

Alcohol consumption is also a problem for some adolescents in university or college. It has been estimated in the United States that between 90 and 92 per cent of university students have used alcohol over the past year, while 7 per cent report using alcohol on a daily basis. This latter figure is worrying, the authors suggesting that daily intake of alcohol is related to personal injury, missing classes, poorer academic performance, unplanned pregnancy, and so forth (Werner and Greene 1992).

On the basis of a study on one American campus, Werner and Greene (1992) concluded that up to one-third of first-year students are at risk from a drinking problem. They found that frequency of drinking did not differ between the sexes, but that males were more inclined to engage in binge drinking than were females. It is important to bear in mind, however, that estimates of problem drinking in a university setting may be slightly exaggerated, and that one needs to consider the *social contexts* of the drinking behaviour (see also Bush 1990). Some authors (e.g. Werner and Greene 1992: 491) have argued as follows:

> Any evaluation of college students' drinking patterns needs to consider the social environment and situational factors involved in college

students' decisions about drinking. . . . Approaches that utilize an understanding of students' beliefs, expectations, and motivations may be more useful.

Cross-cultural differences

Wilks and his colleagues (Wilks and Callan 1990; Wilks, Callan and Forsyth 1985) have uncovered some important cross-cultural trends in adolescent drinking patterns. In one study, they compared the attitudes of teenagers in Australia, the USA, and Papua New Guinea. They found that all groups reported that alcohol increased one's level of happiness, enjoyment, sociability, and relaxation. Very few reported drinking because they liked the taste of alcohol or because they wanted to meet new friends (see Table 6.2).

Papua New Guinean teenagers more than those from the other two cultures rated financial costs and ensuing family problems as major disadvantages of drinking. They also tended to view alcohol use as leading to general trouble, arguing, and fighting. The Australian and American students, however, tended to be concerned about the physical side-effects of too much alcohol, such as addiction, vomiting, and hangover. They were also more concerned about the risks of motor car accidents.

It would also seem that some teenagers underestimate the negative side-effects of alcohol consumption. One survey among Australians indicated that teenagers are not opposed to drinking and driving and that, in fact, they tend to admire those who can drive after having consumed some alcohol. These teenagers argue that they can drive safely if they just use their 'common sense' (Wilks and Callan 1990).

Recent research has examined cross-cultural differences in risk factors for drinking among Polish and German adolescents (Silbereisen, Noack and Schonpflug 1994). These authors conducted a two-year longitudinal study of teenagers aged between 11 and 17 years of age and were particularly interested in some of the social or contextual factors that may predispose some youth to drink alcohol.

The authors found that Polish students tended to drink less than their German counterparts. There was little variation *within* cultural groups between students in different educational tracks. It was also observed that changes in drinking behaviour among German youth were best predicted by romantic friendships. That is, the larger the gap between actual and desired state on this dimension, the more likely teenagers would misuse alcohol. By contrast, drinking among Polish youth was best predicted by membership of cliques. That is, those who were part of a small group of friends were

Table 6.2 Attitudes toward alcohol consumption in different cultural groups

	Papua New Guinea %	USA %	Australia %
Advantages			
Happiness and enjoyment	28.5	43	29.5
To be sociable	22	19.5	43
Relaxing	3.5	26.5	45.5
To escape or forget problems	14.5	17.5	10
Meet new friends	14.5	5	5
Reduces inhibitions	12	8	6
Like the taste	4	14	1
Gain weight	9.5	0.5	0
Disadvantages			
Financial cost	36.5	4	14
Family problems	32	7.5	9.5
General sickness over time	14	20	19.5
Car accidents	12.5	19.5	25.5
Causing general trouble	16.5	9.5	9.5
Arguing, fighting	18.5	4.5	5
Mental deterioration	9.5	6	5.5
Hangover	0.5	8	15
Addiction	0.5	14	12.5
Vomiting	4	15.5	11
Loss of mental control	15	12.5	7.5

Source: derived from Wilks and Callan 1990

more likely to increase their alcohol use. Thus, it is evident that different cultural groups have different risk factors for alcohol use. It is likely that the groups differ with respect to the timing or importance placed on romantic relationships and that these cultural factors are important in explaining shifts in drinking behaviour (Silbereisen *et al.* 1994).

Cigarette smoking

According to some writers (e.g. Gliksman, Dwyer, Wlodarczyk and Pierce 1989), adult patterns of cigarette smoking are reasonably well established by age 15 years. This fact is rather disquieting as cigarette smoking has been shown to be related to cardiovascular disease and lung cancer (Hill *et al.* 1990).

Attitudes toward smoking change quite markedly over the age-span 9 to 15 years. Whereas about 83 per cent of boys aged 9 think that it is very important *not* to smoke, only 62 per cent of 15 year olds think so. Among girls the comparable figures are 89 and 55 per cent respectively. Almost one-quarter of teenagers aged 14 to 19 years think that it is fine to smoke provided you know 'how to use it'. About one-fifth think that smoking is not at all dangerous. Only slightly more than 10 per cent view cigarette smoking as too dangerous to try (Department of Community Services and Health, Australia 1990).

Several large-scale surveys of the current smoking status of young people have been conducted over recent years (e.g. Byrne, Byrne and Reinhart 1993; Glicksman *et al.* 1989; Hill *et al.* 1987). Table 6.3 shows that children as young as 9 years report having smoked at least one cigarette in the seven days prior to the survey. More males than females smoked in the two youngest age groups, although this pattern was reversed for the older age groups. By age 17 years, up to 30 per cent of teenagers were classified as regular smokers.

Adolescents perceive distinct costs and benefits involved in cigarette smoking (Urberg and Robbins 1981). The costs are mainly health-related, while the benefits are mainly of a social nature (see Table 6.4). For many teenagers, smoking helps them feel part of the group or they think that it is something 'to do' when feeling nervous. Smoking also symbolises a sense of 'being adult' or being able to do as one pleases.

Table 6.3 Smoking patterns among teenagers in Australia

Study	Gender	Age								
		9 %	10 %	11 %	12 %	13 %	14 %	15 %	16 %	17 %
Glicksman *et al.* 1987	M	2.9	2.3	2.8	5.2	12.4	17.2	26.0		
	F	0.4	1.2	3.0	7.5	15.6	23.7	32.4		
Hill *et al.* 1989	M				10	17	24	29	29	27
	F				8	18	29	34	34	30
Byrne *et al.* 1993	M				6.8	10.4	12.6	22.5	21.8	23.5
	F				4.7	13.2	24.5	26.9	27.9	31.8

Table 6.4 Perceived costs and benefits of cigarette smoking among teenagers

Costs	Benefits
Against the law	Girls like boys who smoke
Friends dislike it	Feel part of the gang
Causes cancer	Makes parents mad
Against religion	Something to do when nervous
Can kill one	Shows you can do what you want
Hurts running	
Hurts in athletics	
Can get hooked	

Source: derived from Urberg and Robbins 1981

There are two notable characteristics regarding cigarette smoking. In the first instance, more females than males tend to smoke, although not all surveys support this finding. For example, a large-scale study in Western Australia found that, among older teenagers, more males (37 per cent) than females (31 per cent) smoked. The reverse was true in rural areas of the state: 54 per cent of female as opposed to 44 per cent of male teenagers smoked (Zubrick *et al.* 1995). The second feature is the fact that cigarette smoking ranks second to alcohol consumption among youth (Green 1979). This is noteworthy as young cigarette smokers are also more likely to experiment with a range of other substances (Green 1979).

Cross-cultural differences

Silbereisen and colleagues (1994) recently investigated the cross-cultural differences in smoking among Polish and German adolescents. According to their evidence, Polish youth smoke less than German youth. Among both groups, moreover, students in higher educational streams were found to smoke less than students in the lower streams. The authors also found that the best predictor of smoking behaviour for both cultural groups was self-esteem and this factor took on importance at different times for the two cultural groups. For the German sample self-esteem took on importance at a younger age.

Use of other drugs

In this section we shall consider some of the major illicit drugs such as cocaine, heroin, and marijuana. There are various categories of illicit drugs and Sullivan and Thompson (1994) refer to the following:

- Narcotics (e.g. opium, morphine, heroin, methadone, codeine)
- Stimulants (e.g. cocaine, amphetamines)
- Hallucinogens (e.g. LSD)
- Cannabis (e.g. marijuana, hashish)
- Depressants (e.g. barbiturates, tranquillisers)

These drugs, like alcohol, are referred to as psychoactive drugs. However, whereas alcohol is socially acceptable, the drugs referred to above are not. The drugs in the categories shown above cause toxicity and Organic Brain Syndrome which includes confusion, disorientation, and reduced intellectual functioning (Sullivan and Thompson 1994). All, except the narcotics, can have psychotic effects.

According to some researchers, drugs such as cocaine, heroin, and marijuana are used less frequently than alcohol or cigarettes. Regular use of cocaine by teenagers in the United States increased from around 2 per cent in 1975 to 7 per cent in 1986 (Swisher 1991) and declined to 1.9 per cent in 1990 (Sullivan and Thompson 1994). Other writers (e.g. Newcomb and Bentler 1991a) report that 16.9 per cent of high school students in the US have used cocaine at least once, while 0.4 per cent report using the drug on a regular basis. According to these authors, more Hispanic teenagers than white in the US use cocaine (6.7 per cent vs. 5.5 per cent), followed by black teenagers (2.9 per cent).

Use of some drugs such as cocaine should be viewed with alarm given their severe psychological and physiological effects. For those who 'snort' cocaine, an irritated nasal passageway or even a destroyed mucous membrane of the nose is quite likely. Extended use of this drug leads to a paranoid-type reaction, manic states, severe depression, or panic states (Sullivan and Thompson 1994). Cocaine is now available in varied forms referred to as 'free-base' and is sold on the streets as 'crack', 'rock', or 'coca paste' (Newcomb and Bentler 1991a). These forms of the drug can be smoked or taken intravenously, and are very addictive. While crack has the potential to accelerate the heart rate quite rapidly, intravenous use of the drug raises the risk of HIV infection.

Fewer teenagers use marijuana than alcohol. One survey in the United States found that 33–50 per cent of adults had smoked marijuana at least once and some authors report that marijuana use is now lower than during the mid-1970s (Sullivan and Thompson 1994). A large survey among Australian teenagers (Zubrick *et al.* 1995) found that 7 per cent reported having smoked marijuana by age 13 years, while 34 per cent of 15–16 year olds had. Although outlawed in many industrialised nations, it is legal in some states (e.g. Australian Capital Territory) to grow marijuana for private consumption. This suggests that there is some debate as to the effects of decriminalising marijuana use. Some writers (e.g. Yamaguchi and Kandel 1984; Kandel 1975; Kandel and Yamaguchi 1993) attribute a unique role to marijuana use in that users of the other 'hard' illicit drugs tend also to have first experimented with marijuana.

Teenagers who use alcohol and cigarettes are more at risk of experimentation with marijuana. Of interest are the behavioural and attitudinal predictors of marijuana use for both sexes. Friends' use of the drug is a strong influence for both sexes. Among males, however, involvement in delinquent activities and the belief that marijuana use is not harmful are also significant predictors of teenagers' decisions to use this drug. Those youth who use marijuana are more likely to be disaffected in a general sense. They are also more likely to be absent from school and hence to perform below their potential at academic pursuits. They tend not to be religious, while they tend to engage in delinquent and vandal acts, and to be aggressive (Kandel 1982).

Heroin use appears to be very low. In the United States, for example, only 0.7 per cent of 12 to 17 year olds reported ever using the drug. Narcotics such as heroin can produce the following effects (Sullivan and Thompson 1994: 362):

> drowsiness, mood changes, euphoria, and reduced mental functioning with high doses. They also depress the central nervous system and heart activity. . . . They are also highly addictive, with physical dependence developing very quickly.

Social judgements of substance use

Teenagers believe that regular use of drugs such as cocaine and marijuana is much more harmful than regular use of alcohol (82.2 per cent, 71.3 per cent, and 39.1 per cent, respectively). The perceived harmful effects if used only once or twice are proportionately lower (33.5 per cent, 15.1 per cent, and 4.6 per cent, respectively). Whereas 68 per cent of adolescents believe that most of their friends use alcohol, only 18.2 per cent and 6.2 per cent respectively believe that most of their friends use marijuana and cocaine (Swisher 1991).

The more adolescents use drugs, the more likely they are to view drug use as less harmful (Nucci, Guerra and Lee 1991). In one study, students in their final years of high school were asked to provide information about their use of various substances and then to give their views about the perceived effects of drug use. The authors found that low-drug-use respondents rated drug use as more wrong than did those who used drugs more frequently. Moreover, high-drug-users, more than low-drug-users, viewed this sort of behaviour as a *personal* issue. By contrast, low-drug-users viewed parents and the law as having legitimate authority in regulating their behaviour. Thus, for high-drug-users, such behaviour is viewed in personal terms, and as being *their* decision (Nucci *et al.* 1991).

Substance abuse among minority groups

To a large extent, substance abuse by young black males in the large metropolitan centres of the United States fulfils an economic function (Brunswik 1991). Many of these youth are poorly educated, face bleak employment prospects, and are alienated from society. As Brunswik suggests, the drug economy is one of the few options left to these teenagers.

Young black males tend to use illicit substances to a much greater degree than do comparable samples of other youth in the United States. Brunswik (1991) has reported that, according to one survey, 92 per cent of blacks in young adulthood reported ever using marijuana compared to 77 per cent of males in a state-wide sample. Young black males report substance abuse from an early age, with 20 per cent having tried alcohol by the time they are 10 years of age. By age 11 years, 10 per cent are reported to have tried marijuana. The sequence for drug use among black males is alcohol, inhalants, marijuana, heroin, cocaine, and psychedelics (Brunswik 1988). Heroin appears to be the drug that is used most frequently.

6.3 SYNDROME OF PROBLEM BEHAVIOUR

Are teenagers who use illicit substances also likely to engage in other unacceptable forms of behaviour? Jessor and his colleagues (Donovan and Jessor 1985; Donovan, Jessor and Costa 1988; Jessor 1984; Jessor and Jessor 1977) have proposed that a single general factor is able to account for much of adolescent problem behaviour (see also Chapter 1). More specifically, they have argued that behaviours such as illicit drug use, problem drinking, delinquency, and sexual promiscuity form a general syndrome of problem behaviour. In support of this view, it has been found that problem behaviours tend to be significantly related in many different adolescent samples. Not surprisingly, a single index of problem behaviours is also found to correlate negatively with social-conforming behaviours such as attendance at religious ceremonies (Donovan and Jessor 1985; see also research by Farrell, Danish and Howard 1992).

In one of the most thorough longitudinal studies conducted among adolescents in the United States (Jessor and Jessor 1977), respondents were followed up from junior high school into early adulthood. The authors also surveyed college students in the first year of study until age 30 years. For both groups, there was compelling evidence that showed that problem behaviours are significantly related and can be explained by a common underlying factor which the authors referred to as *unconventionality* (Donovan and Jessor 1985). Research with other samples found this common factor to be observable across gender, socio-economic, and ethnic groups, while further analyses suggested that the results should not be attributed to cohort effects (Donovan, Jessor and Costa 1988). In other words, *unconventionality* was not peculiar to teenagers who lived in the 1960s and 1970s.

It would appear that some behaviours are more determined than others by *unconventionality*. The behaviours below (each of which has important implications for one's health) can be rank-ordered from those that are most to those that are least determined by *unconventionality* as follows (Donovan, Jessor and Costa 1988):

- Number of times drunk
- Marijuana use
- General deviance
- Sexual experience

The research by Jessor and his associates is embedded within a conceptual framework referred to as Problem-Behaviour Theory (Jessor *et al.* 1991). As was noted in the first chapter, this theory is concerned with the relationships between three domains, namely the personality system, the perceived environment system, and the behaviour system. It is suggested that these are important in explaining problem behaviour and that the various components of each will have differential effects upon such behaviours as smoking and promiscuity.

It is worth noting that fundamental to Problem-Behaviour Theory is the view that behaviour is a function of the interaction between the person and the environment (Jessor *et al.* 1991). As such, this approach is firmly based upon the earlier pioneering ideas of Kurt Lewin (1890–1947). Although Jessor and many others have identified personality and social factors that are related to substance abuse in adolescents, some writers (e.g. Bush 1990) question whether this approach is relevant for people like adolescents who are in the 'transition years'. Bush provides two reasons for his view. Firstly, factors indicative of drinking in the teenage years, such as the quest for independence from parents, are natural developmental phenomena. Secondly, he argues that drinking should be defined by the social context or environment within which it takes place and that to ignore this detracts from one's understanding of why adolescents drink alcohol (see also Werner and Greene 1992).

Another weakness of Jessor's approach is that he fails to make clear just how or to what extent various personality and environmental factors lead some teenagers to engage in problem behaviours including substance abuse. That is, what are the processes by which these factors become important antecedents of substance abuse? This task has been left to other researchers and will be reviewed below.

6.4 THEORETICAL PERSPECTIVES

It is now well established that different psychological processes underpin the various stages of addictive behaviour (e.g. Gorsuch and Butler 1976; Marlatt, Baer, Donovan and Kivlahan 1988; Rauch and Huba 1991). The following two stages will be discussed in this chapter:

- Initiation of drug use
- Maintenance of drug use

Initiation of drug use

Included in this section are research studies which have examined the processes by which some teenagers are initiated into a culture of substance use. This research can be grouped into two main categories (Marlatt *et al.* 1988), namely one's genetic make-up and certain psycho social factors.

Genetic predispositions

The underlying argument here is that some teenagers have a genetic pre-disposition to begin substance use, although some argue too that herit-ability *interacts* with certain environmental factors resulting in substance use. In order to examine these different effects, researchers have resorted to twin studies, studies of half-siblings, and studies of adopted children (Adityanjee and Murray 1991).

Most, but not all, of the studies of identical and fraternal twins suggest a strong genetic influence on alcoholism. One review of research conducted from 1960 to 1987 concluded that the concordance rate for alcoholism in identical twins was much higher than that for fraternal twins (Adityanjee and Murray 1991). Another review of some of this literature (Crabbe, McSwigan and Belknap 1985) reported the results of a study of 16,000 male twins who were classified for the prevalence and concordance for alcoholism, alcoholic psychosis, liver cirrhosis, and pancreatitis. The concordance rates for all diseases except pancreatitis were found to be twice as high among identical twins, suggesting strong genetic influence. Studies of half-siblings and adoptees, which are important in disentangling environmental and genetic influences, have also suggested strong genetic effects on alcohol abuse (Adityanjee and Murray 1991).

There also appear to be distinct physiological differences between alcoholics and non-alcoholics. For instance, Marlatt and colleagues (1988) report that children of alcoholics have an initial tolerance for ethanol as well as decreased EEG alpha rhythms compared to control groups. Sons of alcoholics also tend to show poorer verbal intellectual performance and other neuropsychological differences. In summary, there is evidence to suggest that genetic and physiological factors may predispose some teenagers to begin substance use.

Psychosocial predictors

Several psychosocial factors have been shown to be implicated in the initiation of substance use. These include peer drug use, parental drug use, parental sociopathy, poor self-esteem, stress, and lack of social conformity (Green 1979; Marlatt *et al.* 1988).

Many studies have examined the influences of parents and the peer group on teenagers' drug use. Kandel (1990) has provided convincing evidence as to the important determining role that peer drug behaviour plays in initial substance use. In her research she also assessed the extent to which peer drug behaviour interacts with the adolescent's involvement with the peer group. Kandel found that whether teenagers are active members of the peer group or not, those with friends who do not smoke marijuana hold similar attitudes and beliefs about a range of issues such as the use of other drugs and quality of interaction with parents. However, those teenagers who are very actively involved in the peer group and who have friends who smoke marijuana, are themselves more likely to use marijuana and other illicit drugs than are those teenagers with low peer involvement who have marijuana-smoking friends.

The important effect that friends have on the smoking behaviour of others has also been noted in other research (Urberg and Robbins 1981). Studying the responses of mainly white young Americans, the authors noted that boys who have friends who smoke are more likely to see benefits in smoking compared to boys who do not have friends who smoke. That is, boys who have friends who smoke tend to disregard and minimise the health risks associated with smoking, viewing it as a coping mechanism.

For girls, on the other hand, smoking is a sign of rebellion, independence, and autonomy. As the authors (Urberg and Robbins 1981: 359) explain:

> It may be a signal to parents and others that the girl considers herself capable of making up her own mind about what she will do now.

Teenagers are more likely to engage in substance use if their parents do. All types of drugs are likely to be initiated in this fashion: cigarettes, barbiturates, tranquillisers, and alcohol (Green 1979). Learning theorists posit that teenagers simply model their own behaviour on that of their parents.

One longitudinal study of over 3,000 teenagers examined the interactive effects of personality factors and perceptions of others' smoking on their smoking patterns (Collins, Sussman, Rauch *et al.* 1987). Two factors were seen as important in predicting the initiation of cigarette smoking, namely risk-taking/rebelliousness and perceived smoking prevalence. The authors noted that the extent to which significant others are perceived to smoke was an important predictor, together with risk-taking, in the decision to start smoking.

A series of several detailed research studies by J. Brook and her colleagues (see Brook and Brook 1990) has uncovered several domains of variables that determine drug use. These domains are:

- *Childhood factors*
    Child's personality
    Family factors
- *Parent personality and drug use*
    Conventionality
    Control of emotion
    Parent drug use
    Intrapsychic functioning
- *Marital harmony*
- *Adolescent personality*
    Conventionality
    Control of emotion
    Sibling relations
    Inter-personal relatedness
    Intrapsychic functioning
- *Parent-adolescent relations*
    Mutual attachment
- *Peer system*

Huba and Bentler (1982) have also proposed a domain model of drug initiation and use. As with other domain approaches such as the one described above, they incorporate psychosocial factors into their model, yet go further by including genetic and biological considerations as well. They are of the view that biological, intra-personal, inter-personal, and socio-cultural factors interact in explaining drug behaviour. They suggest that some domains might exert more influence on particular individuals, while other domains might be more important at particular stages of drug use.

Brook and her colleagues have shown that peers have an important influence on the frequency and timing of drug use, whereas family and personality factors are more likely to determine the individual's stage of drug use (Brook and Brook 1990). Thus, family and peer factors interact in determining drug use. It is argued that the family, in particular the teenager's attachment to mother and father, acts as a protective factor which shields the adolescent from participation in the drug culture. By internalising parental norms and values, and by living in a family that is characterised by emotional warmth and in which the channels of communication between members are open, adolescents are less likely to be initiated into drug use. Teenagers who do not use drugs or alcohol are more likely to be on good terms with their parents. Very often drug use is found in homes where one parent is absent or in homes where marital separation has occurred (Green 1979).

Of added importance are sibling relationships in which older siblings can play a powerful role in the substance use of younger brothers and sisters. For instance, younger brothers may model their behaviour on that of the older brother. If both brothers have a positive attitude to deviance, such unconventional attitudes might easily be manifest in drug use (Brook and Brook 1990).

Personality factors which have been identified in the initiation of drug use are a positive attitude toward deviancy, low self-esteem, being low on social conformity, sensation-seeking (Gorsuch and Butler 1976), emotional distress, and aggression/acting out (Brook and Brook 1990). These do not act in isolation and it is possible for personality factors to combine with certain social and familial factors. For example, peer modelling and a particular constellation of family factors may combine with certain individual factors, such as rejection of social norms or sensation-seeking, which may then lead to substance use.

Winefield and her colleagues (Winefield, Winefield, Tiggemann and Goldney 1989) investigated the role of personality factors in alcohol and cigarette use in a longitudinal study with 19 year olds. It was found that those who initiated smoking at age 19 were much more likely to feel hopeless prior to initiation than were students who did not begin smoking. Males who started to drink reported more hopelessness, although females reported less hopelessness and healthier self-esteem.

When the authors compared smokers with non-smokers, and drinkers with non-drinkers, other noteworthy trends were observed. For example, smokers were more externally controlled than non-smokers, a finding that has important implications for health education programmes. The authors (Winefield *et al.* 1989: 1071) explain:

> anti-smoking messages should seek to boost perceptions of personal control and efficacy ('taking control via freeing oneself from cigarettes'), rather than to threaten eventual punishment (illness) for continued deviance.

Of further interest was the observation that moderate drinking was found to be associated with healthy adjustment among young people, especially among female drinkers. Non-drinkers felt more hopeless, externally controlled, and alienated than moderate drinkers, suggesting that moderate drinking is viewed as perhaps more socially acceptable than either heavy drinking or total abstinence (Winefield *et al.* 1989).

Are inter-personal factors more or less important than intra-personal factors in determining substance use? This question was recently posed by Flannery and associates (Flannery, Vazsonyi, Torquati and Fridrich 1994). It was found that, for both males and females of either Caucasian or Hispanic origin, inter-personal rather than intra-personal factors were important predictors of substance use. In particular, perceived susceptibility to peer pressure and whether or not they had a close friend who used a substance were crucial factors. The authors argue that the findings have important implications for education and intervention programmes and stress the following points. Firstly, practitioners should assist teenagers to learn skills that will assist them to solve peer-related problems. Secondly, they need to learn to select friends in a responsible manner. Thirdly, teenagers need to develop strategies that help them cope with peer pressure (Flannery *et al.* 1994).

Finally, etiological factors may differ for different racial and ethnic groups. O'Donnell and Clayton (1979) found that determinants of marijuana use differed for black and white youth in the United States (see also Brunswik 1988). Whereas family influence acted as an important buffer for the white sample, peer influences and early deviant behaviour were much more important predictors of marijuana use among the black teenagers. These findings suggest that, even within one society, the dynamics of drug use vary for different ethnic or cultural groups.

Biological and personality factors

There has been some debate over recent years as to whether there are biological markers that can assist one in differentiating alcoholics from non-alcoholics. Some have argued, for instance, that alcoholics have lower platelet monoamine oxidase (MAO) activity compared to non-alcoholics (see Mezzich, Tarter, Moss, Yao, Hsich and Kirisci 1994). Some authors have also shown that MAO activity is related to certain personality traits (such as sensation-seeking) which may be suggestive of the fact that biological factors underscore the relationship between alcohol abuse and personality.

Some studies that have examined these issues have yielded equivocal results. Recently, Mezzich and colleagues (1994) compared the MAO activity of female adolescent alcohol abusers with a control group. They also checked for differences in personality such as wellbeing, social closeness, stress reaction, harm avoidance, positive affectivity, negative affectivity, alienation, and aggression, to name only some. The researchers found that there were no significant differences between the two adolescent groups on MAO activity, although MAO activity was related to negative affectivity for the alcoholic group only. The authors concluded that MAO activity by itself may not explain alcohol abuse among this sample. However, it may lead to alcohol abuse in combination with certain personality traits such as a difficult affective temperament.

Maintenance of drug use

This section will briefly review those studies that have assessed the relationships between actual substance use and certain psychosocial factors. Not surprisingly, there is a great deal of overlap between theories of initiation and theories of maintenance.

Pharmacological effects

It is now well documented that individuals build up a tolerance for a drug. Littleton (1991) explains that nerve cells within the brain compensate for the presence of a drug by adapting to its presence and therefore allowing normal function. This is referred to as drug tolerance. When the drug is withdrawn or withheld, however, brain function is altered which results in a craving for the drug. Cocaine, for example, is metabolised very quickly by the liver, resulting in 'rebound depression' (Newcomb and Bentler 1991a) associated with falling blood levels of cocaine. As a consequence, users are driven to cocaine again to relieve this depression.

Some adolescents maintain substance use because of the mood-enhancing properties of the drug (Marlatt *et al.* 1988). Hallucinogens such as LSD have their own peculiar psychological and emotional effects which may explain continued use. LSD causes auditory and visual illusions and time distortions. Some of these are experienced as 'consciousness-expanding' (Newcomb and Bentler 1991b), which may encourage individuals to continue using the drug. LSD can also result in mood changes which can be euphoric, although some effects might be quite fearful leading to depression. Thus, in many instances when drugs have a 'positive' or rewarding effect for the user, the drug behaviour is maintained by traditional learning processes. That is, the euphoric state or enhanced mood acts as a stimulus which induces the teenager to repeat the behaviour.

Psychosocial factors

Many studies have noted that particular personality and attitudinal factors are related to substance use. These include personal motivations, low self-esteem, impulsivity, sensation-seeking, negative attitudes toward authority figures, high depression, acting out behaviour (Marlatt *et al.* 1988), less responsibility, and rebelliousness (Brook, Gordon and Brook 1987).

Personal motivations are important in explaining why some continue to use drugs. For example, adolescents who smoke have clear reasons for so doing. In an Australian study, it was observed that teenagers smoke so as to be *socially acceptable* (e.g. 'I feel confident'; 'My friends smoke'; 'It allows me to feel part of the crowd'), because it provides them with *pleasure* (e.g. 'It is enjoyable'; 'It relaxes me'), and because of *addiction* or *habitual needs* (e.g. 'I find it difficult to quit') (Ho 1994).

These motivations for smoking as identified by Ho have close links with expectancy factors identified by Marlatt and his colleagues (1988). These authors suggested that individuals have beliefs or expectancies that certain drugs will have specific behavioural or mood effects that make these drugs more desirable to use. The authors identified two forms of expectancies, namely *outcome* expectancies and beliefs in *self-efficacy*. Thus, a teenager might use alcohol because he or she believes that it will help them to relax, or because they believe that it will help them feel more confident.

In similar vein, adolescents have certain *expectancies* about the effects of drinking alcohol and it would seem that such expectations are related to actual behaviour (Christiansen and Goldman 1983). These authors identified the following alcohol expectancies:

- Leads to a positive transformation
- Enhances or impedes social behaviour

- Improves one's cognitive or motor abilities
- Produces sexual enhancement
- Leads to deteriorated cognitive and behavioural functions
- Increases arousal
- Promotes relaxation and tension reduction

The authors found that adolescents' expectations about drinking were related to their actual drinking behaviour. Thus, for example, problem and frequent drinkers tended to expect altered social behaviour (e.g. 'parties become more fun') and enhanced cognitive and motor functions (e.g. 'one understands things better'). The authors stress that these findings do not detract from the importance of other psycho social predictors such as the role of peers or personality factors. Rather, expectancies probably interact with such factors in maintaining and predicting alcohol use among adolescents.

Many studies have examined the role of personality factors. Research findings indicate that factors such as extraversion and neuroticism may be implicated in the maintenance of substance use. Some writers (e.g. Cherry and Kiernan 1976) have also noted that personality factors differentiate users of different intensity. It has been found, for instance, that cigarette smokers who inhale deeply are more neurotic than smokers who inhale only superficially. Moreover, male smokers appear to be more extraverted than female smokers.

Male smokers are more 'toughminded' than female smokers (Heaven 1989). In addition, differences have been noted between those who smoke every day and those who smoke less frequently. The research by Heaven (1989) found the regular smokers to be most toughminded (see Table 6.5). Although it is not clear why this factor was not an important predictor among the female smokers, that it was for males is not altogether surprising. Some writers (e.g. Eysenck and Eysenck 1975: 11) have noted that toughminded types are also likely to engage in sensation-seeking activities and so-called 'arousal jags'. Perhaps cigarette smoking is viewed by some adolescents as an 'arousal jag'.

Other researchers have examined the role of the family in maintaining substance use among teenagers. For instance, Brook and her colleagues (Brook *et al.* 1987) have shown that father characteristics have additive effects with the teenager's personality in predicting substance use. They argue that child-rearing practices are important in shaping the adolescent's drug-using behaviour. In particular, the nature of the bond between parent and teenager as well as the emotional warmth and responsiveness of the parent are crucial factors. The authors also found that the nature of attachment was more important in predicting drug behaviour than factors such as parental control.

Table 6.5 Mean scores of smokers and non-smokers on toughmindedness

Males	Mean	Standard deviation
I smoke every day	5.35	3.09
I smoke occasionally	3.60	1.77
I do not smoke now	3.74	2.46
	$F(2,105) = 3.30, p < 0.04$	

Source: adapted from Heaven 1989

Evidence also suggests that adolescent drug users undergoing treatment for their drug use differ significantly from others in their perceptions of their family of origin (Searight, Manley, Binder *et al.* 1991). Those undergoing treatment view their families as being deficient in communication skills and respect for personal boundaries. Thus, these families appear to be enmeshed so that teenagers are overly indulged and over-protected. These families also seem unable to express their emotions adequately as well as being emotionally distant or lacking in emotional warmth. In conclusion, the authors (Searight *et al.* 1991: 79) note that:

> The findings of the current study highlight the adolescent substance abuser as a symbol for a family that has not been able to manage the delicate balance between autonomy and intimacy.

6.5 SUMMARY

Large numbers of adolescents are experimenting with substances such as cigarettes, alcohol, and other drugs. A large proportion of contemporary teenagers have smoked or used alcohol at least once in their lives. Of course, this is a natural part of adolescent development and the striving to achieve personal identity. Some teenagers use substances to excess, however, and for these individuals their behaviour can have serious negative effects on their health status.

Not many teenagers progress to use illicit substances such as cocaine or heroin. These drugs have severe effects on health and are associated with a subculture of violence and other problem behaviours. Some writers have suggested that an important link in the progression to these drugs is marijuana use. It has been shown that most teenagers who use drugs such as cocaine or heroin have first experimented with marijuana.

Several theoretical explanations for drug initiation and use have been proposed. These explanations cover a wide spectrum and include biological and physiological factors, the role of individual differences, and social influences. Prominent among the social influences are peer groups and family processes. According to some authors there is evidence to suggest that these affect drug-using behaviour in quite unique ways. The literature also suggests that the best buffer against drug use is an emotionally warm and affectionate family. It would seem that a family that is characterised by open channels of communication and mutual respect for others is likely to produce teenagers who are disinclined to use drugs to excess.

7 Mental health: schizophrenia, depression, and suicide

7.1 INTRODUCTION

A surprising number of teenagers suffer emotional and mental dysfunction. Of added importance is the fact that such turmoil is very often carried over into adulthood with serious implications for adjustment during the post-adolescent years. The mental health of children and adolescents has tended to be a neglected topic, and it is only recently that researchers have begun to examine mental health issues among younger people (Kazdin 1993). Therefore, the view that teenagers will simply eventually outgrow their mental health problems has lost credence.

This chapter will examine schizophrenia, depression, and suicide in adolescents. Depression is very often linked to suicide which itself is a leading cause of death among youth, particularly males. In many cases of suicide, warning signs are present and so it is imperative that one fully understands its antecedents. Although schizophrenia affects only a small proportion of the adult population, it is a debilitating disorder that can have its genesis during the teenage years. There is much ignorance about schizo-phrenia in the public domain and most people would be unaware of its nature or etiology. Like depression it has links with suicide. These dis-orders have been selected for discussion because they highlight very clearly how day-to-day functioning and wellbeing in individuals can be impaired by mental dysfunction. It is therefore appropriate that professionals and parents fully understand the extent, nature, and etiology of these behaviours. By increasing our understanding of schizophrenia, depression, and suicide we shall be able, where appropriate, to enhance our intervention.

In this chapter we shall discuss theories and antecedents of these behaviours as well as the individual difference factors deemed to be asso-ciated with them. We begin by examining schizophrenia.

7.2 SCHIZOPHRENIA

Schizophrenia is a psychiatric disorder that can appear during adolescence and early adulthood. Many years ago it was referred to as *dementia praecox*, or insanity of youth (Erlenmeyer-Kimling and Cornblatt 1991) and implied an early degeneration or decline of mental function (Westermeyer 1993). Today schizophrenia is viewed as a psychotic state in which individuals suffer from disordered thinking. It is estimated to affect about 1 per cent of the adult population (Erlenmeyer-Kimling and Cornblatt 1991).

Clinical symptoms

There is no one overall symptom that can be said to be typically characteristic of schizophrenia. As all authors indicate, there are several defining traits, some of which need to be present to effect a positive diagnosis (Westermeyer 1993). Davison and Neale (1994) provide the following outline of symptoms:

> *Positive symptoms*
>   Disorganised speech
>   Delusions
>   Hallucinations and disorders of perception
> *Negative symptoms*
>   Avolition (apathy or lack of energy)
>   Alogia (negative thought disorder)
>   Anhedonia (cannot experience pleasure)
>   Flat affect

Davison and Neale (1994) describe positive symptoms as 'excesses'. Disorganised speech is synonymous with thought disorder thus implying that the individual suffers from problems in both areas. For instance, language appears to be totally disjointed and incoherent. One sentence seems to bear very little relation to the next; one thought pattern unconnected to the following. The thought disorder of many schizophrenics is also apparent in that they suffer from delusions and appear to lack insight into their condition and the reasons for their hospitalisation. They appear not to comprehend the seriousness of their illness nor the extent of their dishevelled appearance. They therefore tend to misinterpret reality (Davison and Neale 1994).

These authors also note specific types of delusions. For instance, some schizophrenics suffer thought insertion, that is, the belief that alien thoughts have been inserted into their mind. Others suffer from thought broadcast, that is, they believe that their thoughts are well known to those around them. Thought withdrawal refers to the fact that some schizophrenics believe that their thoughts have been stolen from them.

Perhaps most notably, schizophrenics very often suffer from disorders of perception, such as hallucinations. They may therefore 'hear' their thoughts or hear voices inside them and engage in conversations with these 'others'. At other times, their body may feel unreal or 'depersonalised' or they may experience strange sounds, dazzling lights, strange smells, etc.

Negative symptoms are characterised as behavioural deficits by Davison and Neale (1994). In other words, schizophrenics appear to lack energy or motivation and are apathetic. Many seem incapable of experiencing any pleasure. When such lack of energy is taken to extremes, patients may present with an unkempt appearance. Some suffer from 'flat affect' or lack of emotion. As Davison and Neale (1994: 393) explain:

> [They] may stare vacantly, the muscles of the face flaccid, the eyes lifeless. When spoken to, he or she answers in a flat and toneless voice. . . . It is important to be clear that the concept of flat affect refers only to the outward expression of emotion and not to the patient's inner experience.

There are several other symptoms characteristic of the schizophrenic individual that fall outside the classifications just referred to. These include catatonia, catatonic immobility, waxy flexibility, inappropriate affect, and bizarre behaviour. They are summarised in Table 7.1.

Table 7.1 Symptoms of schizophrenia outside positive–negative scheme

Symptom	Description
Catatonia	Adopts strange facial expressions and strange bodily movements (e.g. rapid movement)
Catatonic immobility	Unusual postures are held for a long time
Waxy flexibility	One is able to move patient's limbs into strange positions Patient can maintain this position for long time
Inappropriate affect	Emotional responses to events are inappropriate
Bizarre behaviour	For example, collecting garbage, hoarding food, etc.

Source: derived from Davison and Neale 1994

Requirements for a positive diagnosis

According to some writers (e.g. Davison and Neale 1994), a positive diagnosis of schizophrenia is made after a 6-month period characterised by three phases. During the active phase at least two of the following need to be present, namely delusions, hallucinations, disorganised speech, disorganised or catatonic behaviour, and negative symptoms. Some of the following also need to be present either before or after the active phase: social withdrawal, flat affect, lack of initiative, vague speech, impairment of hygiene and appearance, odd beliefs, and disordered perceptions (Davison and Neale 1994: 396).

Gender differences

Westermeyer (1993) has provided useful information on gender differences in schizophrenia. He points out that, although it has always been assumed that gender differences are non-existent, it is now known that males have a higher incidence of schizophrenia than females. Moreover, hospital admissions for males with this disorder tend to be earlier than those for females, indicating that females have a later onset for schizophrenia. By contrast, there do not appear to be gender differences for other disturbances such as manic disorders.

There are a number of explanations for gender differences in age of onset. Some have suggested the following factors (Westermeyer 1993). In the first place, it has been found that dopamine levels tend to peak later in women. Secondly, it has also been suggested that levels of oestrogen in women affect the onset of schizophrenia, while another view holds that men experience stress earlier than do women, resulting in earlier onset of the disorder among men. However, this latter view is open to some dispute especially given the fact that gender roles are in a state of flux. It is therefore suggested that this explanation requires further experimental validation.

Schizophrenia and suicide

The suicide rate of schizophrenics is approximately 10 per cent (Westermeyer 1993). According to the results of one Swedish study, the suicide rate was more than 10 times that of the general population, while the overall mortality rate was twice that of a comparable general population sample.

The research literature suggests that there are three theories on suicide among schizophrenics. These are summarised in Westermeyer 1993. In the first instance, some schizophrenics initially have high expectations for themselves. Upon diagnosis, however, these hopes are dashed leading to possible suicide. Secondly, individuals may become increasingly frustrated with or depressed about their condition. They may suffer hopelessness and despair which could drive some to suicide. In the third instance, it is suggested that the period immediately following diagnosis is critical as this is the time when individuals have to accept the diagnosis and come to terms with their condition. This critical period lasts for about six to eight years, thus raising the risks of suicide among adolescent schizophrenics.

Antecedents of schizophrenia

Schizophrenia may be caused by genetic factors, biochemical factors, or stress (Erlenmeyer-Kimling and Cornblatt 1991; Davison and Neale 1994; Westermeyer 1993). Although each of these factors will be separately discussed, it is possible that some factors (e.g. stress and biochemical factors) may, in fact, interact in causing schizophrenia.

Studies of twins and children who have been adopted out are useful for examining the influence of heredity and the environment on personality, including schizophrenia. As twins share the same genetic material it is assumed that similarities in behaviour and personality are attributable to genetic influence. The same applies to biological parents and their children who have been adopted out. On the other hand, adoptive parents and their adopted children share the same environment with the result that any similarities found are believed to be due to environmental influences.

Genetic factors

There is evidence based on twin and adoption studies that schizophrenia may have a genetic basis. Indeed, the closer people are related, the higher their risks appear to be that if one develops schizophrenia the other is likely to as well. According to Gottesman and associates (cited in Davison and Neale 1994) the risk increases from 1 per cent for spouses to 44.30 per cent for identical twins. According to other reports (e.g. Kendler and Robinette 1983), the concordance rates for identical twins are 69 per cent, but only 13 per cent for fraternal twins. As Davison and Neale (1994) point out, these risks are less than 100 per cent, suggesting an important role for other causal factors such as environmental factors (see below).

Adoption studies have also added some support to the view that genetic factors are important. Numbers of studies have shown a closer match between schizophrenic children and their biological parents than between schizophrenic children and their adoptive parents.

Biochemical factors

Some evidence points to the role of birthing and associated factors in the development of schizophrenia. It is argued that pre-natal trauma, difficult birth or lack of oxygen during the birth process may lead to schizophrenia. In the case of twins where only one develops schizophrenia, it usually happens to be the one born second with a lower birth weight (Gray 1991).

According to another view, schizophrenia may be caused by too much dopamine activity in the nerve synapses. Support for this theory comes from the use of certain anti-psychotic drugs that reduce typical schizophrenic symptoms. These drugs also *decrease* the levels of dopamine in the synapses. It has also been found that drugs like cocaine have the potential to increase schizophrenia in patients due to the fact that they increase dopamine levels (Gray 1991).

Recent research results cited in Davison and Neale (1994) suggest that neural pathways in the brain that use dopamine as a neurotransmitter may do so to different degrees with differential effects. According to the authors, two pathways are crucial, namely the mesolimbic and mesocortical pathways. Both originate in the same basal region of the brain, with the mesocortical pathway ending in the prefrontal cortex. That these pathways have the potential to exert different influences on dopamine activity may explain the existence of positive and negative symptoms of schizophrenia.

Influence of stress

Two factors are relevant here, namely social class and the role of the family (Argyle 1994; Davison and Neale 1994; Westermeyer 1993).

Argyle (1994) has reported that schizophrenia is very strongly linked to social class and that people labelled 'working class' are five times more likely than those in other classes to be diagnosed as schizophrenic. Support for such a view is based on studies conducted in different cultures (Davison and Neale 1994).

There are two possible explanations for this view of the relationship between stress and schizophrenia, namely the *sociogenic* and *social-selection* theories. According to the first, being in the lowest social class is in itself so stressful that one develops schizophrenia. Argyle (1994) also adds that working-class people typically lack the personal resources to cope with stress thus exacerbating their situation. As he explains, they are low in internal control, self-esteem, and general coping ability, probably due to their earlier socialisation experiences including low levels of social support.

The second view posits that schizophrenia is so debilitating that the affected individuals cannot function adequately. As a consequence, they tend to drift into the run-down poverty-stricken areas of communities. Here it is easier to remain anonymous and hidden from scrutiny. This view is also referred to as the downward-drift theory.

Yet other writers have concentrated on the role of the family. According to this view, family function is crucial in explaining schizophrenia, although the results at this stage appear somewhat equivocal. Some authors have pointed to the role of the mother in inducing the disorder in her offspring, while others have suggested that faulty parent–child communication has the potential to lead to schizophrenia in children.

Although research data supports the role of each of these theories of schizophrenia, one must also entertain the possibility that some of them may interact in causing the disorder. As alluded to earlier, it is possible that continued stress may affect biochemical balance thus precipitating schizophrenia. This is a possible avenue for further research.

7.3 DEPRESSION

In the psychiatric literature, depression is referred to as a mood disorder (Carson, Butcher and Coleman 1988). Depression involves changes in one's mood or affect with these changes varying from individual to individual. For some, mood swings can be quite severe, marked, and noticeable.

The nature of depression

The literature dealing with the nature of *adult* depression highlights different classifications (American Psychiatric Association 1994). It is beyond the scope of this chapter to review all these types in detail. It is important to note, however, that they vary in their severity of mood swings and symptoms. In major depression, for example, there are very few, if any, elated phases and the individual can be severely depressed for up to two weeks, with adolescents being irritable rather than sad. Day-to-day functioning can be severely impeded and common symptoms can include overeating or poor appetite, sleeping problems, suicide ideation, feelings of worthlessness, and so forth (Cantwell and Baker 1991; Fleming, Offord and Boyle 1989).

Those who work in the area of adolescent depression tend to use a classificatory system that is based upon the adult version. In a recent review, Petersen and her colleagues (Petersen, Compas, Brooks-Gunn, Stemmler, Ey and Grant 1993) suggested the following:

- Depressed mood
- Depression syndromes
- Clinical depression

In depressed mood teenagers report having the 'blues' or report feeling sad and down. Such feelings are usually triggered by an external source, for example a bad grade at school or the break-up of a special relationship. The depressed mood may be quite brief (a day or so) or may extend for a much longer period. According to Petersen and colleagues (1993), other symptoms are also very often associated with depressed mood and these may include fear, guilt, anger, contempt, disgust, anxiety, or social withdrawal.

Aspects of adolescent depression can be viewed as part of a wide range of related problems that form part of a behavioural syndrome (Petersen *et al.* 1993). Several research studies have suggested that depression co-exists along with anxiety, feelings of loneliness, a fear of doing bad things, and a fear of being unloved. Additional components can also include a feeling that others might be out to 'get' you, feelings of worthlessness, nervousness, guilt, etc.

Clinical depression coincides with major depression and dysthymia in adults. To be diagnosed with major depression, a teenager must have experienced five or more of the following over a two-week period (Petersen *et al.* 1993: 156):

- Depressed mood or irritable mood most of the day
- Decreased interest in pleasurable activities
- Changes in weight or perhaps failure to make necessary weight gains in adolescence
- Sleep problems
- Psychomotor agitation or retardation
- Fatigue or loss of energy
- Feelings of worthlessness or abnormal amount of guilt
- Reduced concentration and decision-making ability
- Repeated suicidal ideation attempts, or plans of suicide

For a teenager to be diagnosed with a dysthymic disorder, evidence of a depressed or irritable mood needs to be present for nearly every day for almost a year. In addition, at least two of the following need also to be present (Petersen *et al.* 1993: 156):

- Eating problems
- Sleeping problems
- Lack of energy
- Low self-esteem

- Reduced concentration or decision-making ability
- Feelings of hopelessness

The incidence of depression

The incidence of depresssion among teenagers varies considerably from report to report. This may be due to the fact that authors use different definitions of 'depression' as well as the fact that they compare the results of different age groups. One review (Angold 1988) of some of this literature found the percentage of teenagers with a 'diagnosis' of depression to range from 0.14 per cent to 49 per cent.

When discussing depression among teenagers it is important to consider the age of the respondents as well as the measure of depression. Studies of older teenagers with the Beck Depression Inventory have suggested that one can expect to find that about 5.4 per cent will report being sad or miserable, while crying is reported by up to 10.6 per cent of respondents. Table 7.2 presents the incidence of selected symptoms of depression among teenagers aged between 11 and 18 years. The data are based on two studies cited by Angold (1988).

The symptoms reported in Table 7.2 are mild and, for most adolescents, will be of a temporary nature. With respect to clinical depression, however, some authors suggest that 4.7 per cent of teenagers suffer from major depression, while about 3.3 per cent suffer from dysthymic disorder (Kashani, Carlson and Beck *et al.* 1987). Some researchers have also

Table 7.2 Percentage incidence of selected depressive symptoms

Symptom	Study 1	Study 2
Sad/miserable	5.4	2.9
Crying	10.6	7.5
Low appetite	8.3	5.3
Irritable	14.3	8.9
Hopeless/pessimistic	6.1	2.6
Feels failure	11.1	4.9
Dislikes self	5.9	7.5
Indecisive	7.2	3.7
Deserves punishment	11.8	–

Source: derived from Angold 1988

reported a threefold increase in depression from pre-adolescence to adolescence (Fleming, Offord and Boyle 1989). Of course, this may simply reflect the fact that older teenagers are better able to verbalise their true feelings more accurately.

Of some importance are the many findings that suggest that females tend to be more depressed than their male counterparts (e.g. Fleming *et al.* 1989; Petersen, Sarigiani and Kennedy 1991). An important review of the many studies in this area confirmed this position, further pointing out that this trend persists into adulthood (Petersen *et al.* 1993).

Not all research supports this view, however. One study (Reinherz, Giaconia, Pakiz *et al.* 1993) observed that females were much more likely than males to meet the lifetime criteria for major depression and also to suffer from an early onset of depression. However, after age 15 years males were more likely than females to experience *later* onset of depression. In a study of Canadian youth, Fleming and her colleagues (1989) found that females more than males reported less severe forms of depression, such as depressed mood, although no sex differences were observed in the incidence of more severe forms of depression. The authors (Fleming *et al.* 1989: 652) therefore concluded that:

> [This] suggests that perhaps female adolescents are more likely than males to report depressive symptoms, but no more likely than males to have a clinical syndrome of depression.

If it is true that females tend to be more depressed than males, how then is one to explain this? According to some (e.g. Petersen *et al.* 1993) there is, in fact, a *true* gender difference in depression. Some authors have suggested that the sexes differ in their responses to depression with females pondering over their state much more than males. This only serves to heighten their negative mood.

Some have referred to this state as 'rumination' (Nolen-Hoeksema 1991) and it is suggested that females are more attentive to their mood and emotional experiences. As a consequence, they tend to *focus* much more on their mood and various symptoms than men do. This activity can often result in increases in current depressive mood and heightened negative self-evaluations. This is likely to result in an increase in helplessness (Compas, Orosan and Grant 1993). Traditionally, males have been socialised not to focus on their moods or emotions, but rather to focus on other tasks or activities. As a result, males generally have lower levels of depressive affect (Compas *et al.* 1993).

It is possible that early maturing girls may develop a negative body image which could be associated with higher levels of depression. An accompanying experience of stress exacerbates this predisposition (Petersen *et al.* 1991). Other explanations include differences in hormonal activity or a negative cognitive set (Rutter 1986). For example, it is possible that hormonal changes may trigger depression in girls, but not in boys. It has also been suggested that girls are more likely to attribute negative events to an internal stable disposition, thus raising negative mood.

Factors associated with depression

In this section we shall briefly review some of the psychosocial factors that have been shown to be associated with depression in adolescents. Research evidence suggests that a wide variety of such factors are implicated.

Many studies have examined the role of the family in the etiology of adolescent depression with findings suggesting that parent–child relationship problems or family dysfunction are salient and key factors. There is evidence to suggest that several within-family relationships are crucial in predicting depression. These include mother–child and father–child relationships, parents' spousal relationship, and sibling relationships (Puig-Antich, Kaufman, Ryan *et al.* 1993).

This is in line with an earlier report suggesting a link between teenagers' perceptions of their parents and depression scores. It has been argued that warm, communicative, and caring parents instil confidence, mastery, and high self-esteem in their children. A perception of parents as overprotective, however, appears to be linked to low levels of mastery and higher levels of depression (Avison and McAlpine 1992).

Adolescent self-esteem appears to a large extent dependent upon parenting style and, together, they act as antecedents for depression. In one study it was found that parental rejection, rather than factors such as family conflict or family religiosity, was important in determining adolescent depression (Robertson and Simons 1989). More specifically, parental rejection was found to predict depression in those homes where parents failed to nurture adolescents' self-esteem by providing a warm and caring family environment. Thus, family dynamics can influence adolescent depression through adolescent self-esteem.

In a noteworthy longitudinal study among 385 teenagers spanning 14 years, a group of researchers examined the effects of a wide range of psycho social factors on depression at 18 years of age (Reinherz *et al.* 1993). The authors were able to trace the impact of childhood events on adolescent depression. Table 7.3 highlights some noticeable similarities and differences in risk for the two sexes. Among both boys and girls a poor perception of the child's role in the family at 9 years of age as well as a perception

Table 7.3 Predictors of depression at age 18 years

Males

Before age 6 years	Neonatal health problems
	Serious illness and hospitalisation
Age 5 years	Rated as having problems with dependence by mother
Age 9 years	Poor perception of his role within the family
	Poor perception of his popularity
Age 10–15 years	Experienced increased family arguments and family violence
	Remarriage of a parent
Age 15 years	Self-rated anxiety
	Mother-rated anxiety

Females

Birth	Family structure; 3rd or later in birth order
	Mother > 30 years of age; Father > 35 years of age
	Three or more siblings
Age 9 years	Poor perception of role within the family
	Poor perception of popularity
	Low self-esteem
	Self-rated anxiety
Age 10–15 years	Onset of health problems
Before age 15 years	Death of a parent
	Pregnancy

Source: derived from Reinherz *et al.* 1993

of being unpopular were found to be important predictors of depression at 18 years of age. Among girls, but not boys, the death of a parent was an important antecedent of depression as was the family structure at the time of birth. For boys, health problems after birth were found to be related to depression at age 18 years, although this was not the case for girls.

Other writers have examined the effects of cognitions on depression. In this regard, social self-appraisal and self-esteem appear to be especially important. One research study concluded that, although depressed adolescents are capable of correctly assessing inter-personal problems and can appreciate the perspectives of others, they tend to formulate faulty strategies to deal with social problems (Marton, Connolly, Kutcher and Korenblum 1993). Moreover, their situation seems to be aggravated by their low self-esteem and low social self-confidence rendering them socially dysfunctional. As Marton and colleagues (1993: 742–743) explain:

> Such negative self-evaluation may affect the social behavior of these youngsters rendering them more hesitant, more negative, and more passive . . . these youngsters are not deficient in their cognitive social problem-solving skills . . . nor in their social understanding. . . . Their cognitive social skill deficits are in the area of attributions and self-appraisal.

Adolescents differentiate various domains of self-esteem, and their evaluation of these appears to be linked to depression. Evidence indicates that those who have low self-perceptions on domains such as their romantic appeal are more likely to be depressed. There does not appear to be a link between depression and self-evaluation on scholastic, athletic, or job domains (King, Naylor, Segal *et al.* 1993). As the authors explain, domains such as romantic appeal, close friendship, and social acceptance are important in terms of adolescent developmental tasks that need to be completed. These domains form part of a 'self-schema' (King *et al.* 1993: 749) which itself plays an important role in determining healthy emotional adjustment.

Stress has also been linked to depression. Adolescents are susceptible to various stressors such as biological changes, social changes (e.g. relocating), school transitions, parental separation or divorce, and gender-role expectations (Gore, Aseltine and Colton 1992). As we noted earlier, family processes are important in understanding depression. Gore and associates (1992) have suggested that family processes and socio-economic factors have the ability to act as buffers against the negative effects of stress thereby reducing the likelihood of depression.

7.4 SUICIDE

Suicide is a leading cause of death among adolescents (McClure 1986). Sometimes suicide may follow upon a *single* external stressor such as the death of a loved one or the break-up of a special relationship. There are also 'copy cat' suicides in which some teenagers are driven to emulate the suicide of someone known to them or a character in a film. Yet others are the result of years of psychological anguish and feelings of hopelessness. For these teenagers, therefore, suicide seems to be the only way out of a situation that appears to them to be desperate and from which there seems to be little escape.

The incidence of suicide and suicide ideation

Data from Australia show that a surprisingly large number of teenagers think about suicide (Zubrick *et al.* 1995). Among 12–14 year olds, for instance, 11.5 per cent sometimes or often think about suicide. However, among 15–16 year olds, 23.5 per cent sometimes or often think about suicide.

Lester (1988) has recently summarised the changes in suicide rates for 15 to 24 year olds in several countries from 1970–1980. Table 7.4 lists those countries that have recorded sharp increases in their youth suicide rate. Thus, countries such as Thailand, Switzerland, Norway, Scotland, and New Zealand, to name a few, had increases of more than 50 per cent. However, countries like Venezuela, Gautemala, and Chile had significant reductions in their youth suicide rate over the same period of time.

Data from countries such as the United States and Australia indicate that more adolescent males than females commit suicide. Moreover, the annual rates for these two countries are quite similar. In 1990, for instance, the suicide rate for Australian females aged between 15 and 24 years was 4 per 100,000 population, while the corresponding figure in the United States in 1989 was 4.2. Among Australian males in 1990 there were 27 youth suicides per 100,000 population for 15–24 year olds. The United States rates for 1989 were 21.9 (Australian Bureau of Statistics 1991; Rice 1992).

Table 7.4 Countries showing significant increases in the youth suicide rate 1970–1980

Country	1970	% change by 1980
Canada	10.2	+50.0
Finland	14.7	+60.5
France	7.0	+52.9
Israel	3.7	+64.9
Netherlands	4.0	+50.0
New Zealand	8.0	+73.7
Norway	3.7	+224.3
Spain	1.4	+92.9
Switzerland	13.0	+80.0
Thailand	7.2	+77.8
United Kingdom (Scotland)	5.8	+65.5

Source: derived from Lester 1988

Older adolescents are more likely to commit suicide than younger teenagers. The following rates have been noted for the age groups 10–14 years, 15–19 years, and 20–24 years in the United States (Bingham, Bennion, Openshaw and Adams 1994): 12.2, 101.6, and 193.2 per 100,000 population respectively. There are also important racial differences in suicide rate. This is particularly evident in the United States as shown by the following figures for 1988 (Rice 1992: 299). The suicide rate is per 100,000 at-risk population:

Black females	2.2
Black males	9.7
White females	4.8
White males	19.6

Bingham and colleagues (1994) noted that white and other non-African teenagers in the United States are much more at risk of suicide than black (African) American youth. They quote the following rates: 110.2, 131.9, and 64.9 per 100,000 population respectively. Moreover, whites and other groups were more likely to commit suicide by hanging, using gases, and firearms. There are also differences in suicide rates across different native American groups. Figures cited recently (Rice 1992) show that the rate for Navajo Indians is 12 per 100,000, while for some Apache groups it is 43 per 100,000.

It is not entirely clear why some countries have witnessed sharp rises or falls in their youth suicide rate, nor is it clear why there are racial and ethnic differences within a country. There are several different factors that could play a role, such as economic and other social conditions at a given time (e.g. high levels of unemployment or feelings of alienation among some minority groups). Cultural norms regarding suicide might also be an important factor. That is, suicide might be much less acceptable among some ethnic groups than others.

Suicide attempts

According to some estimates (see Garland and Zigler 1993) the rate of suicide attempts is about 50 to 200 times higher than that of completed suicides. In the United States, females attempt suicide three times more frequently than do males who, in turn, complete suicide four times more often than females. These estimates are borne out by Australian data. In Western Australia during 1985, 14-year-old girls attempting suicide were admitted at the rate of 270 per 100,000 at-risk population. For boys, however, the figure was 70 per 100,000 (Mason 1990).

Method of suicide

Teenage boys and girls differ in their preferred method of suicide. Nonetheless, completed suicides by both genders are achieved most frequently by firearms, followed by hanging and gassing (Garland and Zigler 1993). In the United States, boys tend to use violent means such as firearms and hanging, while girls are more likely to use non-violent means like gassing and the ingestion of substances. In Finland, one research team found that males were more likely to resort to firearms (45 per cent), hanging (27 per cent), and drugs (5 per cent). Females were more likely to commit suicide by drug use (33 per cent) and hanging (33 per cent) (Marttunen, Aro and Lonnqvist 1992).

McClure (1986) recorded changes in the method of youth suicide in England and Wales between 1970–1974 and 1980–1984. Poisoning by solids or liquids decreased for males and females. However, suicide by hanging, strangulation, and suffocation increased for both sexes over the time period: for males it rose from 7.9 per cent to 13.4 per cent, while for females the incidence rose from 1.6 per cent to 2.1 per cent. Suicide by firearms and explosives increased for males from 1.9 per cent to 5.4 per cent.

According to Garland and Zigler (1993) these gender differences in method of suicide can be explained by an interaction of several factors, notably biological, intra-psychic, social, and cultural. They point out that males tend to be more aggressive, impulsive, and violent than females, traits which are reflected in the preferred method of suicide.

Factors associated with suicide

Researchers have identified several factors associated with suicide. These include drug and alcohol abuse, previous suicide attempt, psychiatric problems, family history of suicidal behaviour, and the availability of a firearm (Garland and Zigler 1993). Other factors are family discord, sexual, physical and emotional abuse, school and peer problems, unemployment, poverty/homelessness, and the loss of a relationship (Mason 1990).

Using the *psychological autopsy* method to examine the events surrounding teenage suicides in Finland over a one-year period, support was found for the influence of several inter-personal stressors (Marttunen, Aro and Lonnqvist 1993). The stressors included relationship problems, inter-personal conflict, and general stressors such as disciplinary or legal problems, school problems, unemployment, financial problems, and family discord, etc.

It is very difficult to distinguish psychologically between suicidal and depressed adolescents. This certainly was the conclusion reached following a study among Dutch adolescents (De Wilde, Kienhorst, Diekstra and Wolters 1993). The traits that best characterised the 'normal' adolescents in that study were having strong social support, family cohesion, and an attitude of hopefulness. Suicidal and depressed teenagers, however, were more likely to be characterised by a range of negative feelings and traits, such as anxiety, feelings of insufficiency, being distrustful of other people, having low family cohesion, believing that most matters were beyond their control, and having low self-esteem.

Not surprisingly, the likelihood that an adolescent will commit suicide is a function of the number of risk factors the teenager is exposed to (Lewinsohn, Rohde and Seeley 1993). According to these authors, suicide is very rarely just an isolated event. Rather, it is one of several other psychopathological events. The probability of a suicide attempt in relation to risk is shown in Table 7.5.

Lewinsohn and colleagues (1993) were able to identify a number of risk factors for suicide after controlling for *current* depression. These were female gender, other psychopathologies besides depression, maladaptive cognitive patterns, lack of personal resources to cope with the social environment, low family support, and academic difficulties. Thus, the presence of one or more of these factors was found to substantially increase the risks of attempted suicide among some teenagers.

In similar vein, Lester (1987) has proposed a subcultural view of youth suicide. He points out that youth suicide is part of a subculture with its own values, customs, and attitudes, and identified the following as constituting the suicidal subculture (Lester 1987: 320): heavy drug involvement,

Table 7.5 Probability of suicide attempts as a function of number of risk factors

Probability of suicide	*Number of risk factors*
1%	Zero and one factor
3%	2 factors
8%	3 factors
17%	4 factors
29%	5 factors
65%	6 factors
69%	7 or more factors

Source: derived from Lewinsohn *et al.* 1993

difficult relations with parents (e.g. resentment or indifference), poor self-image (e.g. feelings of worthlessness), shyness, and a dependency on one person or a small number of peers.

It is not unusual to find that adolescents who contemplate suicide have poor skills in dealing with social problems. It appears that this may be due to what is referred to as cognitive distortion and attributional style. There is evidence to suggest that, compared to other teenagers, suicide attempters approach a social problem in a way that is likely to result in their using faulty decision-making strategies, thus usually generating unsuccessful solutions (Sadowski and Kelley 1993). The authors also noticed that suicide attempters tend to respond to problems rather emotionally using maladaptive cognitive strategies pertaining to expectancies, commitments, and explanations for events. These results therefore led Sadowski and Kelley (1993: 125) to conclude that:

> It is possible that maladaptive attributions, expectancies, and commitments may lead suicide attempters to inaccurately assess environmental circumstances and view suicide as the only option. Moreover, their deficits in problem orientation may exacerbate their specific skill deficits in later problem-solving steps.

Suicide attempters are not an homogenous group. Borst and Noam (1993) have reasoned that girls attempting suicide can be differentiated in terms of their level of ego development and that attempters can be grouped according to their level of social and cognitive development. They distinguish between preconformist and conformist developmental levels. Preconformist types are least mature and can be described as impulsive with very little awareness of their inner self. Those functioning at conformist levels are socially and cognitively more mature, have more self-awareness, and consider the feelings of others.

In their research, Borst and Noam (1993) found that preconformist suicide attempters differed markedly from so-called conformist attempters. The researchers labelled the first group *angry-defiant*; they were at risk of impulsive suicide, and were also angry and aggressive. These teenagers directed their aggression at others as well as at themselves. It was found that they lacked the ability to think abstractly and, in Piagetian terms, would be functioning at the concrete-operational stage (Borst and Noam 1993). By contrast, conformist attempters were found not to blame others for their situation. They tended to use various defence mechanisms to explain their situation and were labelled by the authors as self-blaming.

Preventing suicide

There are different strategies for helping prevent youth suicide – including therapeutic interventions and educational programmes – and these will be briefly reviewed here.

Therapeutic interventions

The research conducted by Borst and Noam (1993) and referred to earlier identified angry-defiant and self-blaming suicide attempters. The authors suggest that these groups require different therapeutic approaches for suicide prevention. They are of the opinion that angry-defiant types are very successful at alienating those around them, including those who would be of some assistance to them. Very often, these teenagers find therapy or clinical intervention too intrusive. It is vital that, during therapy, these teenagers are taught how to take another's perspective. They require much group work as well as the support of their peers, because they regard adults as 'authority figures' (Borst and Noam 1993).

Self-blaming suicide attempters require a quite different therapeutic approach. Although they also need support from others, they tend to find insight-oriented therapy more useful (Borst and Noam 1993). They gain much from one-to-one therapy as it helps them feel less alone and less self-blaming.

Educational programmes

School-based educational programmes are useful in that they teach teenagers how to identify those at risk of suicide. Included in these programmes are the following aims: to heighten students' awareness of the problem, to help them recognise clinical features, to provide students with information about mental health resources, and to improve teenagers' coping abilities (Garland and Zigler 1993; Shafer, Garland, Gould, Fisher and Trautman 1988: 680). In the course of these programmes suicide is viewed not as an illness, but as a reaction to stress. Thus, educators attempt to remove from suicide the stigma of mental illness in order to encourage those students who may feel suicidal to seek professional help (Garland and Zigler 1993).

Sometimes, however, these programmes may also have the opposite effect, possibly leading adolescents to view suicide as a relatively acceptable and common act (Garland and Zigler 1993). As the authors explain (p. 175):

students may closely identify with the problems portrayed by the case examples and may come to see suicide as the logical solution to their problems.

Other strategies

It is possible to help reduce the incidence of youth suicide by more effectively controlling the availability of firearms and by being sensitive to the influence of the media (Garland and Zigler 1993). In support of the first strategy, the authors cite evidence from those states in the USA where stricter gun control appears to be associated with lower suicide rates. Thus, there is a link between weapon availability and suicide. To bolster their argument, the authors cite evidence from the United Kingdom showing that suicide by carbon monoxide poisoning was reduced following a reduction of that substance in domestic gas.

Publicity about suicide has the potential to increase the suicide rate. The media therefore have a duty to report suicide in a way which is not likely to lead to an increase in suicide rates. This is a delicate and sensitive issue and opinion may differ as to the best method of achieving this aim – short of total censorship.

7.5 SUMMARY

It is no longer held to be true that adolescents are simply in a 'transition' phase of life and that they will outgrow mental dysfunction. Rather, mental and emotional disturbance have important implications for the later adjustment of the individual.

This chapter briefly reviewed the nature of schizophrenia, depression, and suicide. We noted that schizophrenia can have its onset during the adolescent years and is more likely to affect males than females. There are several views as to its etiology, but genetic, biochemical balance, and stress factors are deemed to be the most likely. Whatever the cause, schizophrenic teenagers, or those thought to be at risk, require immediate and professional care.

Depression and suicide are linked and data indicate a worrying rise in teenage suicide levels in some countries. It is not clear why some countries should show such significant increases in their youth suicide rate and why most of the increases have occurred in the highly industrialised nations. Nonetheless, it is important that we understand the factors associated with suicide so that appropriate prevention strategies can be implemented. In this regard, it is essential that we take note of the varied strategies for preventing suicide that are at our disposal. These range from professional (e.g. therapeutic intervention and educational programmes) to policy input (e.g. limiting the availability of firearms).

8 Lifestyle, exercise, and diet

8.1 INTRODUCTION

Throughout this book we have discussed those behaviours that place the adolescent at risk of becoming ill. In our review, we covered a wide variety of different behaviours and examined the risks involved in drug and alcohol misuse, the problems associated with eating disorders, depression, suicide, and schizophrenia as well as sex and the risks of sexually transmitted diseases such as HIV. We also examined the nature of stress and the coping mechanisms that some employ to deal with stressful events. To some extent each of these issues is concerned with *lifestyle*, which can be defined as those behaviours that affect one's health status (Bruhn 1988). In this chapter, we shall pay closer attention to the concept of lifestyle and discuss the importance of exercise and a healthy diet to adolescent health.

It is probably true to say that teenagers in the late twentieth century are at greatest risk of leading an unhealthy lifestyle. Some behaviours appear quite commonplace, are taken for granted, and are not associated with risk. These include hours of passive television watching or the consumption of large quantities of fast foods, or the practice in some communities of introducing teenagers to alcohol at a relatively young age. A recent review by Harris (1991), for example, reminds us that many degenerative diseases start during the teenage years. In the United States, for example, 42 per cent of youth have elevated cholesterol, while obesity increased alarmingly (54 per cent) in the short space of 20 years among children aged 6–11 years. It is quite likely that these figures and trends are mirrored in other industrial-ised nations. Thus, it is suggested in this chapter that it is important that parents, educators, and professionals be knowledgeable about how lifestyle can affect one's health and the different ways in which lifestyle can be improved. We begin this chapter by reviewing the concept of lifestyle before discussing the importance of exercise and fitness.

8.2 THE CONCEPT OF LIFESTYLE

According to Bruhn (1988: 71), lifestyle refers to an individual's 'philosophy of life' and usually incorporates one's values, beliefs, attitudes, and behaviours. One can acquire a lifestyle in all sorts of different ways: by watching and learning from others (see Chapter 2, the section on control of reinforcement), through information provided by different media, and through life changes (Bruhn 1988). For instance, parents who smoke cigarettes or drink alcohol or eat unhealthy food are likely to instil similar values or behaviours in their children who will come to view such behaviour as acceptable. Or it is possible that a glossy advertisement in which cigarette smoking is linked to a glamorous lifestyle might entice someone to begin smoking.

It is possible to list several illness *lifestyles* (Bruhn 1988). These may include the following, to mention just a few: minimal self-care activities, risk-seeking health behaviour, external locus of control (see below; see also Chapter 2), low self-esteem, as well as the perception that one's behaviour is difficult to change or that change itself is not worth it. It is possible that an individual who puts his or her health at risk may manifest one (but rarely all) of the lifestyles listed above.

Several factors may have an influence on one's lifestyle. These are environmental, cultural, group, and personal factors (Bruhn 1988). Included among the environmental influences are public policies such as the type and availability of health services, noise, pollution, pesticides in our food, and the quality of our food and water. An example of this sort of influence has been noted by Hetzel and McMichael (1987) who cite lifestyle changes occurring among traditional hunter/gatherer people. Among some Australian Aboriginal groups, for instance, cardiovascular disease and obesity have increased markedly due to the adoption by these groups of a western diet.

Among the cultural factors are the values and goals of the society in which we live. Thus, a society that is prepared to educate its youth about the dangers of unsafe sex and how HIV is spread is more likely to help stem the spread of the virus than a society that does not educate its citizens about HIV. Likewise, rural communities and some less industrialised nations may not have adequate access to proper sanitation and may thus be more at risk of infectious diseases.

Group factors refer mainly to the family unit (Bruhn 1988). According to this view, lifestyle may in part reflect the socio-economic status of the family, which determines the level and type of medical care that the family can afford. Also important are the often quite subtle messages about health that parents convey to their children. Finally, personal factors refer to those factors that are unique to the individual and which determine lifestyle and, hence, health behaviour. Included here are attitudes about health-related matters (see, for example, next section) and personality factors such as psychoticism, personal control, and optimism (see below).

As adolescents develop their own lifestyle, they are likely to be strongly influenced by their family and friends (Hetzel and McMichael 1987). Peer groups serve an important function in that they provide a context for sociable behaviour and are a source of companionship. They also facilitate the achievement of identity (Heaven 1994). Very often, teenagers look to their peer group for advice about acceptable behaviour and lifestyle. It has been well documented that teenagers experience peer pressure to engage in various activities that could have implications for health. In one study (Brown, Clasen and Eicher 1986), teenagers were asked to list the peer pressure they experienced. Among the categories that they nominated were drug and alcohol use and sexual intercourse. Thus, teenagers can be pressured into adopting certain lifestyles that could have detrimental effects on their health.

8.3 EXERCISE AND FITNESS

All teenagers need regular physical activity. There is much evidence, for instance, that regular participation in sport yields immense physical and psychological benefits. Unfortunately, many youth (just like their parents) lead sedentary lives. That such a lifestyle is likely to be maintained as an adult is supported by recent surveys that suggest that only a small proportion of adults actually engage in exercise on a regular basis. For example, one survey of adults conducted in the United States showed that 70 per cent felt that they should exercise more. Similar trends emerged from Australia and Canada (Hetzel and McMichael 1987).

Some reports have argued that as children enter the teenage years, they are increasingly at risk of coronary heart disease (Hetzel and McMichael 1987). The reason appears quite straightforward: fitness levels actually decrease during the teenage years. At the same time cholesterol levels in the blood tend to show an increase, as do levels of obesity, thus placing the individual at risk of disease. As these authors point out, the best time to learn new habits, including those of being physically fit and exercising regularly, are during childhood and the early teenage years.

Harris (1991: 324–325) has defined physical fitness as follows:

a state of optimal physical well-being that suggests that one has the ability to move with efficiency and the capacity to sustain effort over a long period of time without undue fatigue.

According to Harris (1991), most definitions of physical fitness comprise the following elements: muscular strength, endurance, cardiovascular-respiratory capacity, body composition, and flexibility. Thus, those individuals who more regularly engage in physical activity will have cardio-respiratory capacities that are greater than those who are less physically active. She also points out that physically fit adolescents will show greater flexibility in movement of segments around joints and in the elasticity of body ligaments.

As alluded to earlier, there are several benefits of fitness. One view holds that, in order to generate energy, one must actually use energy and that this will result in an increase in vigour and vitality (Harris 1991). Some of the physical advantages of fitness are the following (Donatelle, Davis and Hoover 1991: 347; Harris 1991: 326):

- heart works more efficiently; pumps more blood per stroke and beats at a reduced rate
- Reduces cholesterol levels by increasing lipo-proteins
- Lowers and regulates blood pressure
- Reduces risks of obesity
- There is a greater resistance to illness through a stronger immune system
- Improved oxygen uptake
- Increased metabolic rate
- Increased longevity

Table 8.1 lists some of the psychological benefits that flow from physical fitness. These include such features as feeling more positive about oneself, reducing depression (see Chapter 7), helping to reduce hostile behaviour in oneself and so forth. Thus, as Harris (1991) has argued, there are many benefits to being physically active. Indeed, she stresses that one cannot afford *not* to exercise. It is as though physical exercise remains the only constant factor in the teenager's world, which is subject to biological, emotional, and cognitive change. Regular exercise also has some discernible physical benefits. These are, for instance, the reduction of obesity and body fat and a reduction of glucose intolerance. Exercise also helps reduce one's heart rate, one's blood pressure, and one's vulnerability to dysrhythmias (Insel, Roth, Rollins *et al.* 1991).

Physical fitness has several associated dimensions and each of these is important for one's overall level of health. In this regard, Payne and Hahn (1986) have listed emotional, social, intellectual, and spiritual dimensions, and it is clear that they overlap to some extent with the advantages listed in Table 8.1. Being physically fit can provide an emotional 'lift' that reduces the impact of stress on one's life, helps one feel good about oneself, and

Table 8.1 Psychological benefits of regular physical activity

1. Acts as an energising force.
2. Relief from tension and anxiety.
3. Helps to strengthen the body's ability to cope with stress.
4. Counteracts hostile behaviour.
5. Helps clean the mind – improves concentration and memory.
6. Encourages a positive self-image and helps improve self-confidence.
7. Contributes to feelings of exhilaration and physical wellbeing.
8. Helps improve sleeping patterns.
9. Helps alleviate depression and anxiety.

Source: Harris 1991

imbues one with a sense of achievement and accomplishment. As these authors point out, physical activity is a *natural* way of helping your body rid itself of unspent energy.

Physical activity provides one with numerous social advantages. For all youth, games and organised sport at school or local club level provide valuable opportunities for working with others as part of a team and also provide many occasions for social interaction, social skills development, sharing, and listening.

Physical fitness also has positive effects on mental activity. Payne and Hahn (1986) are of the view that young people appear to be much more mentally alert after exercise and seem able to study much more efficiently. Finally, physical exercise can broaden one's spiritual dimension by providing one with opportunities to serve others.

8.4 DIET AND HEALTH

In Chapter 4 we discussed the extent to which eating disorders such as anorexia nervosa and bulimia affect one's mental and physical health. In this section we shall discuss a related problem, namely the problem of poor nutrition.

There is at least one compelling reason for adolescents to maintain a healthy *and* balanced diet and that is because of the *growth spurt*. Each of us undergoes enormous physical and biological changes during puberty and adolescence. Thus, for example, skeletal and muscle parts undergo change and one begins to mature sexually. Some changes are quite noticeable and include hair growth, fat composition, weight gain, and height gain. There are sex differences, however, with boys tending to gain more muscle than girls who, in turn, gain more fat (Williams and Worthington-Roberts 1992).

Some changes are hormonal in nature. For instance, during late adulthood and early adolescence there is a rapid increase in the presence of three types of hormones that are important for sexual development. These are gonadotropins (which have a stimulating effect on the testes and ovaries), gonadal steroids (these initiate and maintain masculine body changes in males and females), and adrenal androgens (causing masculine-like changes in the male or female body) (Susman and Dorn 1991).

Contemporary adolescents face nutritional problems that differ in important ways from those faced by teenagers several generations ago (Freedland and Dwyer 1991). Whereas problems earlier centred around undernutrition or vitamin deficiencies, today many adolescents face problems that are the result of inappropriate diets and diet imbalances.

The availability of fast food outlets in most of the industrialised west, particularly in the United States, has dramatically altered the eating patterns of large sections of the population. Little time is spent on food preparation. Whereas a generation ago most families would sit down to a meal of vegetables and meat, dinner time has now become a much more hurried affair with less time for the purchase of balanced meals (including fresh fruit and vegetables) and their preparation. TV dinners and processed foods seem to have become the norm in many homes. In one recent Australian survey of 12–16 year olds conducted in Western Australia, 45 per cent reported eating potato chips and crisps the day prior to the survey, 29 per cent consumed foods such as hamburgers and meat pies the day before the survey, and about 73 per cent reported having consumed such foodstuffs as ice cream, doughnuts, and biscuits (Zubrick *et al.* 1995).

How can we, as a community, wean our young people off fast food, most of which has a high fat and sodium content? Recently, the United States government proposed specific goals for promoting awareness of good eating habits in young children and youth. Some of these goals are (Freedland and Dwyer 1991):

- 75 per cent of the population should know the main dietary factors that are linked to heart disease
- schools should offer healthy food in their lunch programmes. There should be no snack foods available on school campuses
- schools should teach core concepts of health education

It is important that teenagers follow a balanced and healthy diet containing the basic nutrients identified as vital for optimal health. There is evidence to show that diets lacking in certain basic nutrients could retard physical growth or even delay the development of sexual maturity (Johnson, Johnson, Wang *et al.* 1994). Essential nutrients fall into two categories, namely those that supply the body with energy or calories (proteins, fats, and carbohydrates), and those that are non-caloric in nature. This latter group, which includes vitamins, minerals, fibre, and water, is essential for the utilisation of energy (Dickman 1988).

Protein

Dietary protein is commonly found in red meats, poultry, fish, and dairy products and is an essential ingredient for the development of bone, muscle, skin, and blood (Donatelle *et al.* 1991). Proteins are made up of amino acids and are integral to the production of antibodies, enzymes, and hormones. The daily recommended dose of protein is about 0.8 gm per kilogramme of body weight (Freedland and Dwyer 1991) or 7 to 8 per cent of total energy intake (Williams and Worthington-Roberts 1992). Although such a requirement can quite easily be met, it is suggested, for example, that care should be taken in selecting lean cuts of meat thus limiting one's intake of calories and fatty substances.

Dietary fat

It might come as a surprise to learn that a moderate intake of fat is necessary. Donatelle and colleagues (1991) indicate that fat intake is required for a range of functions such as skin and hair maintenance, body temperature maintenance, and cell functioning. Overconsumption of fat, however, is problematic with the excess fat being stored in the blood stream in the form of *triglyceride*. This is often deposited in the body, giving an individual an 'overweight' appearance. Some fat excess also circulates in the blood in the form of cholesterol, forming plaque on the interior lining of the arteries. This can lead to atherosclerosis (Donatelle *et al.* 1991; Gagliano, Emans and Woods 1993).

Adolescents should be encouraged to cut down on their intake of excess calories, cholesterol, and saturated fats. A daily intake of 300 mg of cholesterol has been recommended for adolescents (Freedland and Dwyer 1991). Researchers have found that cholesterol levels in adolescence are predictive of adult cholesterol levels, hence the necessity for young people to moderate their intake of fatty and high-cholesterol foods (Gagliano *et al.* 1993).

Saturated fats are derived from animal sources and differ from unsaturated fats in their chemical structure. Whereas saturated fats are unable to hold more hydrogen atoms in their chemical structure, unsaturated fats can. Unsaturated fats can be further differentiated as polyunsaturated or monounsaturated fats. The former are derived mainly from vegetable oils, while the latter are derived from peanut and olive oils (Payne and Hahn 1986). There is presently some debate as to the relative benefits of these two forms of unsaturated fats. Currently the view is that monounsaturated fats are more beneficial to one's health (Donatelle *et al.*1991).

Screening for cholesterol levels among adolescents

Because atherosclerosis is a major cause of death among adults (Gagliano *et al.* 1993), it has been recommended that adolescents be screened for this disease, especially those with a family history of elevated cholesterol. Recently, researchers have begun to question whether family history is a valid predictor of an adolescent's cholesterol level. It would appear not.

A recent study by Gagliano and associates (1993) found that even in those teenagers with abnormal eating and fasting patterns, family history was a weak predictor. They found the best predictor to be sex, with female teenagers having higher cholesterol levels than males. Notwithstanding, sex of respondent explained less than 3 per cent of the variance. The authors also found that systolic blood pressure was a significant predictor. The authors concluded their study by supporting the views of earlier writers who have suggested that by concentrating only on family history among those aged between 12 and 21 years of age, one could miss about 38–53 per cent of those with elevated levels of cholesterol.

In conclusion, it is important to reiterate that high cholesterol among teenagers has serious implications for adolescent health. Gagliano and colleagues (1993: 107) explain as follows:

Adolescence is a time of developing independence, including in such areas as nutrition and health care. After adolescence a man may not seek routine health care until he is 40 years, and a woman may address only her gynaecological needs. Thus, screening for hypercholesterolemia assumes added importance. Detecting a potential problem during adolescence may promote a prudent diet, exercise, and regular medical care during early adulthood when an improvement in risk factors may have an effect on one's life expectancy.

Carbohydrates

Carbohydrates, which are found in all plants, are produced from carbon dioxide and water through a process of photosynthesis (Hetzel and McMichael 1987). There are three main forms of carbohydrates: sugars, starches, and dietary fibre, and each source is essential for the production of energy (Payne and Hahn 1986). It is important to note that some authors (e.g. Dickman 1988) regard dietary fibre as a non-caloric nutrient not included in discussions of carbohydrates. For the sake of simplicity, we shall follow the lead of Hetzel and McMichael (1987) and include it here.

Adolescents, on average, consume an enormous amount of snack food that is typically quite high in sugar content. Most of their sugar supply comes from cold drinks and ice cream, sweets and pastries. Not only do these substances tend to be bad for one's teeth, but they are also implicated in obesity, behavioural disorders, diabetes mellitus, and cardiovascular disease (Payne and Hahn 1986). Thus, instead of snacking on biscuits and other such foodstuffs, we should rather be encouraging teenagers to snack on fresh fruit and nuts.

The perception of being hungry is linked to blood glucose concentration levels. When blood glucose is low, one tends to feel hungry. Snack foods that contain refined carbohydrates and sugars are quickly digested and relatively quickly absorbed leading to a rapid increase in blood sugar content and a large increase in insulin levels (Dickman 1988). This is usually followed by a rapid fall in blood glucose levels to fasting level so that the individual feels hungry, sometimes very shortly after the previous meal. This may lead to more snacking and, if this sort of eating pattern is perpetuated, obesity may result. Should a meal contain other nutritional elements in addition to carbohydrates, however, food is more slowly digested and absorbed and it may be some hours before the individual feels ready for the next meal (Dickman 1988).

Dietary fibre serves as an important laxative and natural sources of fibre are much more beneficial in this regard than fibre supplements. Fibre is also important in safeguarding against colon cancer, diabetes, and cardiovascular diseases (Dickman 1988). Essential are wholegrain cereals and breads, and high-fibre vegetables such as broccoli. The alleged benefit of some fibrous foodstuffs (e.g. wheat bran) is the topic of current debate, according to Dickman (1988). Current recommendations for daily intake of dietary fibre for adolescents are 15 gms per day (Freedland and Dwyer 1986).

Vitamins

We need only small doses of vitamins, yet they are essential for our everyday physiological functioning. They differ from other substances such as fats or proteins in that they do not serve the structural elements of our bodies (Payne and Hahn 1986). Rather, they assist in the action of enzymes (a natural substance that speeds up chemical reactions) so that the body is better able to use nutrients that are already present. There are two types of vitamins, namely water-soluble types (e.g. the B complex ones and vitamin C) and fat-soluble types (vitamins A, D, E, and K).

An excess in the body of the first type is easily dealt with because the body is able to eliminate what is not required. An excess of the second type, however, is usually stored in the body's tissue and can lead to a condition called *hypervitaminosis* (Payne and Hahn 1986). This condition gives rise to deficiencies or complications such as night blindness, rickets, bruising, and prolonged coagulation time. The different types of vitamins together with their main sources as well as their benefits are shown in Table 8.2. Readers who desire more complete information regarding the various benefits, and consequences of vitamin deficiency, should consult more detailed sources such as Payne and Hahn (1986) and Donatelle *et al.* (1991).

Minerals

Minerals are important materials that aid a wide range of physiological processes. There are many different minerals including calcium, copper, chlorine, zinc, sodium, iodine, iron, manganese, selenium, to name a few. Minerals are responsible for a wide range of different physiological processes from bone ossification to the acidity of stomach content to skeletal development and so forth.

Minerals are found in the human body as inorganic compounds, but their only source is through the diet. Therefore, a diet lacking in certain minerals could have serious consequences for one's health. However, some diets contain concentrations of certain minerals and it is vital that their intake be moderated. For example, it has been suggested that the sodium intake for adolescents should be between 900 and 2,700 mg per day. Fast food is particularly high in added salt (Freedland and Dwyer 1991) and is one reason why teenagers should cut down on their intake of fast foods.

The recommended daily allowance of iron for adolescent girls who menstruate is about 18mg per day, while boys require slightly less, namely 10mg per day (Freedland and Dwyer 1991). Pregnant girls require an even higher daily dose. Although boys require less iron than girls, they do need iron for the build-up of muscle. Meat, fish, or poultry are particularly good sources of iron as are fortified cereals and soybeans. Because skeletal growth is particularly rapid during the early teenage years, adolescents require calcium which is necessary for reducing the risks of developing osteoporosis (Freedland and Dwyer 1991).

To conclude this section, it is important to note that adolescents require a balanced intake of all essential minerals. Indeed, it is quite possible that

Table 8.2 Major vitamins, food sources, and benefits

Vitamin	Food source	Benefits
Fat soluble		
A	e.g. Liver, eggs, milk; orange, yellow, and green vegetables	e.g. Night vision, sperm production, bone growth, mucus gland secretion
D	e.g. Egg-yolk, fish-liver oil, sunlight	e.g. Bone growth, neuromuscular activity
E	e.g. Vegetable oils, cereals, leafy green vegetables	e.g. Antioxidation of unsaturated fatty acids
K	e.g. Dark-green leafy vegetables, tomatoes, liver, eggs	e.g. Synthesis of blood clotting factors in liver
Water soluble		
B1	e.g. Enriched bread and cereals, kidney, peas	e.g. Nervous system synaptic functioning
B2	e.g. Liver, yogurt, milk, cheese, almonds, broccoli	Energy release from glucose and fatty acids, adrenal cortical activity, red blood cell formation
B3	e.g. Liver, meat, poultry, peanut butter	e.g. Protein and fat synthesis
B6	e.g. Chicken, fish, whole-grain cereal, bananas, avocados	e.g. Foetal nervous system function, neurotransmitter synthesis
B12	e.g. Liver, kidneys, eggs, dairy products	e.g. Growth and function of nervous system, red blood cell formation
Folic acid	e.g. Oranges, asparagus, broccoli, meat, fish, poultry, eggs	e.g. Red blood cell formation, foetal development
C	e.g. Liver, lemons, broccoli, strawberries, spinach	e.g. Tooth development, collagen formation, neurotransmitter synthesis, absorption of iron and calcium

Source: derived from Donatelle *et al.* 1991; Payne and Hahn 1986

the minerals discussed here interact or combine and work in unison as they influence adolescent health.

Water

Water is an essential nutrient responsible for the transportation not only of other nutrients, but also waste products. Although one can survive for some length of time without food, one would soon die of dehydration without water (Payne and Hahn 1986). Fifty to 60 per cent of our body weight is water. It is a significant component of our blood and it is responsible for ensuring that the body's cells are maintained in working order. The average person requires about one litre of water per day (Hetzel and McMichael 1987). It might be, however, that adolescents require more, particularly those who consume more fast food.

8.5 ATTITUDES TO FOOD AND NUTRITION

Adolescents seem to be aware that the typical teenage diet is a poor one. In-depth discussions with groups of adolescents reveal that young people admit to skipping meals, eating unbalanced meals, and consuming far too many snacks (Story and Resnick 1986). Indeed, some of the most popular foods cited by (US) teenagers are fast foods, meat with fried or baked potatoes, and fizzy drinks. Indeed, adolescents even use the term 'junk food' to describe some of the foods they like the most. Included, for example, are foods that are high in sugar, fat, and calorie content, and foodstuffs high in additives and low in nutritional value including sweets, potato chips, fizzy drinks, biscuits, cakes, and pizza (Story and Resnick 1986: 190). Junk food is also seen as being unhealthy and used in contrast to terms such as nutritious, good, and healthy (Chapman and Maclean 1993).

Teenagers think of junk food and healthy food in quite different sorts of ways. In-depth discussions have revealed that teenagers are fully aware of the additives and preservatives in junk food yet they associate this food with convenience, being affordable, and tasting good, but also with being fattening and causing pimples. The social constructions of healthy food are quite dissimilar, namely staying at home, meals, parents, and being concerned about one's appearance (Chapman and Maclean 1993).

One must be concerned about the view expressed by some teenagers that they simply do not have the time to follow a balanced diet, or the view that balanced meals are not readily available as evidenced by what one normally finds in vending machines. Students are aware that they must improve their diet and volunteer the following ways:

• They should follow a balanced diet
• They should plan their meal times better. For example, they should eat more meals with their family

Adolescents perceive certain barriers to improving their nutrient intake (Story and Resnick 1986). These are lack of time, the view that eating properly is inconvenient, and the lack of a sense of urgency. These perceptions seem to be an integral part of family life in the 1990s, for many youth noted the busy and often conflicting schedules of different family members. As some remarked (Story and Resnick 1986: 190):

We don't have time – too many pressures

and

there's a lot more than food that's really important to us.

How are attitudes toward diet and nutritional issues shaped? As alluded to earlier, teenagers absorb parental values about a wide range of important health issues and so family experience is vital. Interestingly, some evidence suggests that this might be the case for males, but not for females. One Australian study (Baghurst and McMichael 1980) among army recruits and university students found family influences to be more important than school experiences or magazines and newspapers among males while among females the dominant socialisation agent was the school. This was followed by family and magazines and newspapers. Television images were seen to be less important than magazines and newspapers for both recruits and students.

More recently strong arguments have been made about the important effects that television programmes and advertisements have in shaping attitudes toward health issues as well as health behaviours (e.g. Wallack and Dorfman 1992). These writers note, for instance, that those individuals who watch more television are more likely to believe in the healing powers of medication than to adopt healthy behaviours.

Wallack and Dorfman (1992) conducted a content analysis of twenty hours of television selected randomly over a three-week period in the United States. Of the commercial time, 31 per cent contained some health-related message. Food and beverages made up 40 per cent of all health messages in advertisements. Some of the key concepts that comprised these were the following: low cholesterol or fat, balanced diet, Lean Cuisine. Some focused on inpatient drug treatment programmes or dealt with issues such as stress at work or occupational health and safety, while others dealt with issues related to diagnosis for breast cancer. Yet other advertisements dealt with specific drugs or medication for particular ailments. One category was labelled Public Service Announcements and included messages about cancers, AIDS, drug use, hunger, heart disease, child abuse and so forth.

Wallack and Dorfman (1992) concluded that advertisements that deal with food and beverages rarely point out what is nutritious about a product with the exception of focusing on 'low cholesterol' or 'low fat', etc. As they argue, most advertisements seem less concerned about providing information that could be regarded as useful for the consumer. Rather there appears to be more concern for 'positioning' the product as 'healthy'.

Predicting the nutrient intake of adolescents

We noted at the beginning of this section on diet and health that a balanced diet is vital for ensuring adequate health. Indeed, some researchers have attempted to ascertain the predictors of balanced nutrient intake among teenagers. Are there easily identifiable groups of teenagers who are more likely than not to have balanced nutrient intakes? Research by Johnson and colleagues (1994) investigated this issue among a sample of almost 1,000 teenagers in the United States who were aged between 11 and 18 years. There were slightly more females than males. A large majority of the sample (79 per cent) were white, 14 per cent were black, while the rest comprised other racial or ethnic groups.

The authors made use of self-reported data. Respondents were asked to recall their dietary intake over a 24-hour period which was then followed by a two-day record of their actual food intake. The respondents' nutrient intakes were averaged across the three days and then compared with established standards issued by the National Research Council in the United States. Finally, the authors determined the nutrient adequacy ratio, that is, the nutrient intake as a function of nutrient allowance.

The researchers found that, overall, diets for males and females were too high in total fat content, saturated fat content, sodium, and cholesterol

Table 8.3 Underconsumption of nutrients by adolescents

Males	Females
Vitamin A	Vitamin A
Vitamin E	Vitamin E
Calcium	Calcium
	Phosphorus
Magnesium	Magnesium
	Iron
Zinc	Zinc

Source: derived from Johnson *et al.* 1994

(males only). Moreover, diets were lacking in certain other nutrients as determined by the nutrient adequacy ratios as listed in Table 8.3. The authors also found that there were significant differences between various groups of respondents as a function of racial origin and region of residence. For instance, blacks tended to consume more cholesterol and salt than did whites. Those living in the southern regions were also much more likely to consume significantly less vitamin A, calcium, magnesium, and phosphorus than those adolescents living in other regions of the United States.

It is difficult to explain these discrepancies and one must conclude that values and educational levels may be partly responsible for these findings. The United States, an affluent nation, exhibits marked differences in nutrient consumption as a function of regional, racial, and gender background. This begs the question: what may the discrepancies be like in other less affluent and less industrialised nations?

Many teenagers today appear to enjoy eating a variety of fast foods. Although such food is quick to purchase and does not require any preparation time (think of university students who may be pressured for time), it does have distinct disadvantages, being low on essential nutrients. It is now known that many fast food varieties lack the following (Williams and Worthington-Roberts 1992: 294):

- *Calcium, riboflavin, vitamin A* Drinking milk or milk shakes may be a good source of these minerals. However, many teenagers seem to prefer cold [sweetened and/or fizzy] drinks
- *Folate, fibre* Few sources of these nutrients in most fast foods.
- *Fat* Many meals have a high fat content
- *Sodium* Many meals have a high salt content
- *Energy* Too much energy (calories) provided relative to the amount of nutrients

8.6 PSYCHOLOGICAL PREDICTORS OF HEALTHY LIFESTYLE

Although some of the studies we have reviewed thus far suggest that socio-economic factors and racial origin may be important determinants of certain aspects of lifestyle such as nutrient intake, another body of literature has identified several personality traits said to be linked to healthy lifestyle and preventive behaviours. In this section, therefore, it is appropriate that we review some of those relevant individual difference factors. We begin by examining three related concepts, namely self-efficacy, self-esteem, and locus of control.

Self-efficacy refers to an individual belief that he or she *can* lead a healthy lifestyle or the belief that one *can* change behaviours that are unhealthy. Thus, this concept is strongly linked to a sense of empowerment and suggests that individuals have the skills or knowledge to change undesirable behaviour (Williams and Worthington-Roberts 1992). We shall return to this concept again a little later in this section. Self-esteem, or the regard in which one holds oneself, is also important in understanding lifestyle and health-related behaviours. For example, evidence suggests that a link exists between this factor and quality of diet among 15-year-old females. It was found that those girls who feel good about themselves are likely to follow a healthy diet. Low self-esteem, on the other hand, is likely to be related to a poor diet (Newell, Hammig, Jurich and Johnson 1990).

Another important factor is locus of control. This factor was discussed in some detail in Chapter 2 where its importance as a predictor of healthy lifestyle was noted. In short, we observed that those who feel that they are in control of their life events are much more likely than other individuals to engage in health-promoting behaviours. Thus, so-called 'internals' are more likely than externals to exercise, eat a balanced and healthy diet, or undertake preventive and safety practices. For example, one study of food behaviour (Houts and Warland 1989) found that internals reported significantly more nutritious behaviour than did externals. Another study revealed that internals were more likely than externals to consume high fibre foods and less likely to consume refined sugar. This finding held for males as well as females. Moreover, a significant association was observed between external control and high cholesterol levels among males, but not for females (Falconer, Baghurst and Rump 1993).

Do findings such as those just reported have implications for behaviour modification programmes? Can one expect so-called 'internals' to be more successful at attempts to change their behaviour or complete a course of therapy? It would appear so. Balch and Ross (1975) reported that internals were more likely than externals to complete a weight reduction programme as well as more likely to complete it successfully.

More recent research (Steptoe, Wardle, Vinck *et al.* 1994) extended previous studies by examining not only the role of locus of control, but also optimism and personality dimensions as measured by the Eysenck Personality Questionnaire. The locus of control measure yielded three scores, namely internal beliefs, belief in the influence of powerful others (external), and the belief that events happen by chance (external). Health practices were measured by determining the extent to which certain health practices were observed. These included a wide range of behaviours such as red meat consumption, breast or testicle self-examination, alcohol consumption, tobacco consumption, and others.

The authors found no sex difference in the pattern of correlations between health practices and personality. Overall, health practices tended to be associated with being extroverted and optimistic. These respondents also tended to score high on a social desirability measure, but low on neuroticism, psychoticism, and a belief in chance factors. These patterns of association remained after controlling for the influence of social desirability. Based on these results, particularly those pertaining to the trait psychoticism, the authors were able to conclude that those who practise health enhancing behaviours are more likely to be described as responsible and conscientious and lacking in impulsivity.

A similar study was conducted by Falconer, Baghurst and Rump (1993) in Australia although with slightly different results. They found that the attitudes of males and females toward nutritional issues differed and that this may be attributable to personality factors. They found that among males, high psychoticism scores were negatively associated with complex carbohydrate density, while among females this personality variable was negatively related to protein density. With respect to the dimension neuroticism, the authors noted that it was negatively related to fibre density among males, but positively related to sugar density among females.

Although professionals and nutrition educators would seldom assess the personality of the client, these results suggest the important ways in which personality might affect one's attitudes and behaviours toward nutrition-related issues. Thus, it appears that different personality types have different attitudes toward different aspects of nutrition.

In Chapter 2 we discussed the value of the health belief model as a framework for understanding individuals' health-related behaviours. Not surprisingly, some studies have attempted to assess which elements of the model are best able to predict health behaviour. In one study (Schafer, Schafer, Bultena and Hoiberg 1993), the authors were interested in the links between attitudes and behaviours concerning food safety and the health belief model. The authors found that those who perceived unsafe food as a threat to the self were high on a measure of self-efficacy and health motivation, and were much more likely than other respondents to engage in food safety behaviour. Thus, the findings support the view that elements of the health belief model can be used to predict health-enhancing behaviours.

That self-efficacy was found to be related to healthy behaviours is of some significance, according to the researchers (Schafer *et al.* 1993). For instance, one may be concerned about one's health, yet believe that one is unable to do much about it (be low in self-efficacy). Thus, healthy behaviours are likely to be impeded by one's belief about oneself or one's feelings of efficacy.

Research findings such as these have important practical implications. For example, by understanding the motivations for individual behaviour one can improve the educational programmes that are on offer. In this regard, knowing the self-efficacy level of participants could be useful. As the authors (Schafer *et al.* 1993: 22) explain:

> Before professionals attempt to change health behaviors . . . they would be well-advised to examine how many in the potential audience believe the threat can be modified by personal action, and which audience members feel capable (self-efficacious) of carrying out the recommended actions.

8.7 CHANGING LIFESTYLE

Is it possible to change lifestyle? Can one alter a teenager's beliefs and values regarding nutrition or exercise? Are some strategies for change better than others? In this section, we shall review some of the work that has been conducted in this regard.

When considering changing attitudes and behaviours related to nutrition, it is likely that school-based programmes and the media will be among the most effective methods. Some writers are of the opinion that the media may play the most effective role in producing changes to lifestyle. In this respect, television and teenage magazines seem particularly successful. Evidence also suggests that the media may be more influential among older than younger teenagers (Guillen and Barr 1994).

Magazines that are devoted to the adolescent female market very often cover nutrition-related issues in topics and advertisements. According to Guillen and Barr (1994), they tend to discuss weight loss plans and nutrition information (vitamins, fibre, and fat). These authors conducted a content analysis of advertisements in a particular teenage magazine in the United States between 1970 and 1990. They found that most of the advertisements (about 25 per cent) were concerned with diet camps or 'health farms', while many others (approximately 12 per cent) dealt with food or drink, their main aim being to facilitate weight loss in the reader. Almost 9 per cent dealt with sweets and snacks, while only about 3 per cent focused on fruit. Beverages covered almost 6 per cent of advertisements.

Lifestyle can also be changed through education. It is therefore important that physical education programmes be introduced into high schools where this is not already the case. Indeed, such programmes appear quite common at the primary school level, at least in most Australian states. One study of the benefits of an exercise programme among 10-year-old children in Adelaide, South Australia, found significant falls in recorded body fat among those children who participated in the programme (Hetzel and McMichael 1987). The changes were evident after a 14-week programme occurring every day of the school week, with little apparent accompanying disadvantages. It is important that similar programmes be trialled among high school students or that teenagers be given the opportunities at school to participate in a wide variety of different sports.

Of course, it is conceivable that some adolescents may be resistant to exercise programmes offered at school, particularly if he or she does not place a high priority on health, is generally in good health, or has a negative attitude to the teacher in charge of the programme (Bruhn 1988). It is therefore essential that education accompany the exercise and that teenagers be reminded of the value of a healthy body and how exercise can facilitate this goal. Thus, those who work with adolescents need to have particular skills so as to increase their success rate. Included in this skills base are knowledge of teenagers' physical and psychological development, knowledge of their habits and lifestyles, and effective communication skills (Williams and Worthington-Roberts 1992).

It is also desirable that schools educate children about nutrition. Research evidence has shown that many young people need more education in this regard. For instance, although some may be aware that fibre is good for one, many appear unsure about which foods actually contain fibre (Resnicow and Reinhardt 1991). Moreover, professionals engaged in attempting to change teenagers' dietary habits should not lose sight of the family of which the teenager is a part. Some adolescents might be willing to change their lifestyle, yet reside in homes where parents' values are at odds with the new goals that their children have set for themselves. The influence of the family, especially on the health behaviours, attitudes, and knowledge of younger and emotionally insecure adolescents, can be quite salient (Sallis and Nader 1988). Professionals should therefore be aware of the potential for family conflict that could arise when they attempt to change the lifestyle of an adolescent.

8.8 SUMMARY

It is important that young people are aware of the value to their health of exercise and diet. In this chapter we discussed aspects of exercise and diet and noted the importance of exercise and how necessary it is to have a balanced intake of all nutrients. Teenagers in the 1990s lead more sedentary lives than young people of any other generation and so exercise and a healthy diet take on added importance. Many young people seem to move between school desk, sitting room, and movie theatre and need to be encouraged (and provided with the opportunity) to lead a more active life.

Teenagers can be alerted to these issues through a variety of means, notably the media and education programmes at school. Some research studies have shown that, although some products that are advertised in magazines and on television are claimed to be 'healthy', more needs to be done to explain to young consumers just what it is about the product that makes it preferable to other similar products. As it has been shown that many adult diseases (e.g. heart disease) sometimes originate in the teenage years, manufacturers have an added responsibility to ensure that they promote their products in ways that are ethically and morally responsible.

Health professionals should recognise that success in changing lifestyle attitudes and behaviours among young people depends, to some extent, on several individual difference factors. In this chapter we discussed the importance of self-efficacy, self-esteem, locus of control, and other personality factors such extroversion and psychoticism. We noted, for instance, that unless individuals feel that they are *capable* of changing their behaviour, that is, unless they feel efficacious, it is unlikely that attempts at change will meet with success. Unfortunately, the role of individual difference factors in lifestyle change appears to be often neglected in educational programmes.

9 Concluding comments

9.1 INTRODUCTION

This book has offered a psychological perspective on adolescent health and accentuated the role of individual differences. By adopting such an approach it is acknowledged that the medical model is sometimes inadequate for understanding illness and that one also needs to entertain other possible causal factors such as personality variables. As was indicated earlier, the boundaries between health and illness are not always clearly defined and so, in order to better understand illness, it is sometimes necessary to include the individual *as well as* the illness. Thus, in our review we noted the extent to which individual personality traits are implicated in many health behaviours such as body image, eating disorders, substance abuse, coping with stress, suicide, lifestyle, and so forth.

The second chapter of this volume was devoted to a discussion of psychological models that have been found useful in predicting various health behaviours. For instance, we reviewed research that indicated the importance of concepts such as internal locus of control and self-efficacy in explaining health-related behaviours. The point was also made that the use of drugs or alcohol by teenagers or the fact that an adolescent engages in unsafe sex signals a particular lifestyle or generalised pattern of behaviour. Two questions arise, therefore. Is it possible to change a negative lifestyle by focusing on the individual's personality? In what way can health professionals utilise individual differences so as to change those lifestyles that have negative implications for health?

This chapter will examine a central issue to changing a negative lifestyle, namely behaviour change through a perception of empowerment. It will conclude with a short discussion on improving health services for adolescents.

9.2 EMPOWERMENT

As Wallerstein (1992) has argued, empowerment is the opposite of power-lessness which is sometimes also referred to as alienation or learned help-lessness. Empowerment can be applied to psychological functioning, but also has implications for dealing with one's position in society (e.g. alienated minority youth).

Alienation or powerlessness can be likened to what McClosky and Schaar (1965) referred to as a 'state of mind' in which one accommodates poorly or not at all to social change. Such a state of mind is also characteristic of learned helplessness in which the individual may perceive control of the situation as being external, rather than internal, thus militating against adaptation to change. By contrast, those who are empowered are also likely to be self-efficacious, that is, they believe that they are competent and effective individuals (Myers 1989). Research has demonstrated that self-efficacy is related to several 'desirable' personality traits such as being more persistent, being less anxious and depressed, and being more successful academically (Myers 1989).

One way of assisting young people to kick a bad habit, change their lifestyle or help them cope with the daily struggle of living in a run-down inner-city ghetto is to raise their internal control, their self-efficacy and feelings of empowerment. How is one to achieve this? One way, according to Wallerstein (1992), is to raise the self-esteem of young people and assist them to challenge their perception of powerlessness. It is important not to underestimate the strong influences of the family, peer pressure, or societal influences, but empowerment can be achieved through improved self-concept and the development of critical thinking skills. Thus, there is an important role here for school teachers and health professionals in neighbourhood clinics and other community centres. If supportive networks are missing from the home, then we should provide sources of support in schools, health clinics and neighbourhood centres or those places where we encounter adolescents in our professional activities. Our function is to empower youth through innovative educational strategies.

As an example of imaginative thinking designed to assist teenagers in this regard, Cross (1994) recently proposed a novel way of creating awareness among teenagers of those behaviours that contribute toward health and illness. Adolescents complete a short 10-minute computerised questionnaire about a range of different topics related to their health (see Table 9.1). This is done anonymously and in an atmosphere of mutual trust between adolescent and counsellor. As this is a computerised inventory, results are immediately available to the adolescent, whereupon a dialogue

Table 9.1 Behavioural aspects covered by computerised inventory

Domain	Topics
Physical	Nutrition, exercise, recreational, sexuality
Emotional	Family relationships, humour, use of time
Social	Inter-personal, friends, activities, drugs, alcohol
Spiritual	Beliefs, purpose in life, death/suicide urges
Personal risk factors	Not wearing seat belt, smoking, swimming in unfamiliar places
Family and genetic risk factors	Hereditary diseases, dysfunctional families

Source: derived from Cross 1994

commences between student and counsellor. The *nature* of the dialogue is vital and professionals need to be skilled if they are to effect change in a teenager's approach to problems or to enhance self-efficacy, or to improve their coping skills.

Completion of this inventory by all students is now part of the school curriculum in one school district of Maine, USA. Cross (1994) reports that the use of this instrument has resulted in a dramatic increase in teenagers' willingness to discuss lifestyle issues and problems. In addition, students appear to be quite interested in this computerised approach to interviewing which they regard as more objective than the traditional method. Likewise, teachers are also approving and some have commented in the following terms (Cross 1994: 274):

It helps us to identify and address serious student problems; e.g. suicidal thoughts. Without this intervention we would learn of these problems much later. . . . The students are able to address serious issues much quicker and earlier in their stay.

One educational programme among Peruvian teenagers sought to empower them as 'sexual beings' (Caceres, Rosasco, Mandel and Hearst 1994). Part of the programme follows a conventional approach such as providing information about sexuality and AIDS. Other aspects, however, are more novel and deal with issues that are highly relevant for teenagers in Peru and are therefore culture specific. For example, one aspect that is discussed is the concept of 'machismo', namely the double standards that operate with respect to gender and sexual relations in many Latin American countries. Also discussed are attitudes to condoms, which is a highly sensitive issue in Catholic Peru. Not only are there strong religious views about condom use in Peruvian culture, but men who use condoms have not been regarded as 'machismo'. Thus, part of the empowerment strategy is to attempt to rid males and females of some of these social constructions surrounding sexuality and gender-specific roles (see, for instance, our earlier reference in Chapter 5 to the work of Moore and Rosenthal 1993 on social constructions of sexuality). Finally, the educational strategy includes a segment on attitudes toward people with HIV/AIDS. The authors (Caceres *et al.* 1994) reason that such negative stereotypes are simply a mechanism that some teenagers use to deny personal risk.

9.3 IMPROVING HEALTH SERVICES FOR ADOLESCENTS

The extent to which communities are able to provide adequate health services for adolescents is dependent on many factors not least of which are those external to the health professionals themselves. Included are such factors as the level of government funding or funding and commitment from local health authorities, as well as specific cultural factors. Thus, the following comments will be qualified by impediments at the local level.

The United States has set a fine example whereby school clinics now function on many school campuses. As 'health education' already forms an integral part of many school curricula, school clinics (at least on larger campuses) should be viewed as a natural extension of classroom activities. Rather than some parents perhaps viewing these clinics as a licence for promiscuity ('They will only provide our children with condoms'), clinics should instead be seen as a place where adolescents can discuss health and related concerns in private and in confidence with trained professionals. Authorities can help allay the fears of parents by funding Health and Guidance Clinics. Should this prove to be too costly, it might be more appropriate to fund clinics across the city to which all youth would have access.

Professionals working in these settings need special skills to deal with their client population. It is important that teenagers be made to feel accepted for who they are. Not only do professionals need specific training in core knowledge (e.g. medical training, counselling skills, etc.), but they also need to be skilled in effective communication as well as the ability to enhance self-esteem and facilitate empowerment in young people.

We must ensure that some of the major impediments to adolescents obtaining good health care are overcome. These are financing, appropriateness of service, and accessibility (Klerman 1991). What is good adolescent health worth? Should we leave the provision of health care for young people to the private sector, or should the community-at-large be responsible for its cost? The care that we do provide needs to be not only appropriate, but also accessible. Thus, it is important that we locate our services in places that have good rail, bus, and road connections.

Daniel (1991) has explained the magnitude of the task that confronts professionals who work with teenagers as follows (p. 452):

> It is the responsibility of all professionals, regardless of level of education or training, to continue to learn during their years of activity. New information is available from a variety of sources and must be added to information already known and used. Keeping current in one's own discipline is not enough: it is necessary to be aware of changes in other disciplines that relate to adolescence. It is likely that the problems of adolescents will continue to become more complex and require services from even more disciplines than at the present time.

We echo these sentiments. Providing adequate health care to adolescents in the late 1990s will require high levels of commitment on the part of the community, as well as dedication and on-going training on the part of professionals. These are indeed necessary if we are to meet the increasingly complex health needs of adolescents.

References

Abramson, L., Seligman, M. and Teasdale, J. (1978) 'Learned helplessness in humans: Critique and reformulation', *Journal of Abnormal Psychology* 87: 49–74.

Adityanjee and Murray, R. (1991) 'The role of genetic predisposition in alcoholism', in I. Glass (Ed.) *The international handbook of addiction behaviour*, London: Routledge.

Ahmad, S., Waller, G. and Verduyn, C. (1994) 'Eating attitudes and body satisfaction among Asian and Caucasian adolescents', *Journal of Adolescence* 17: 461–470.

Ajzen, I. (1991) 'The theory of planned behavior', *Organizational Behavior and Human Decision Processes* 50: 179–211.

Ajzen, I. and Fishbein, M. (1980) *Understanding attitudes and predicting social behavior*, Englewood Cliffs, N.J.: Prentice-Hall.

Ajzen, I. and Madden, T. (1986) 'Prediction of goal-directed behavior: Attitudes, intentions, and perceived behavioral control', *Journal of Experimental Social Psychology* 22: 453–474.

Altshuler, J. and Ruble, D. (1989) 'Developmental changes in children's awareness of strategies for coping with uncontrollable stress', *Child Development* 60: 1337–1349.

American Psychiatric Association (1994) *Diagnostic and statistical manual of mental disorders* (4th edn.), Washington, D.C.: American Psychiatric Association.

Angold, A. (1988) 'Childhood and adolescent depression 1: Epidemiological and aetiological aspects', *British Journal of Psychiatry* 152: 601–617.

Argyle, M. (1994) *The psychology of social class*, London: Routledge.

Attie, I. and Brooks-Gunn, J. (1989) 'Development of eating problems in adolescent girls: A longitudinal study', *Developmental Psychology* 25: 70–79.

Australian Bureau of Statistics (1991) *Causes of death: Australia 1990* (Catalogue No. 3303.0), Canberra: Government Printer.

Avison, W. and McAlpine, D. (1992) 'Gender differences in symptoms of depression among adolescents', *Journal of Health and Social Behavior* 33: 77–96.

Baghurst, K. and McMichael, A. (1980) 'Nutrition knowledge and dietary intake in young Australian populations', *Community Health Studies* 4: 207–214.

Baker, S., Thalberg, S. and Morrison, D. (1988) 'Parents' behavioural norms as predictors of adolescent sexual activity and contraceptive use', *Adolescence* 23: 265–282.

Balch, P. and Ross, A. (1975) 'Predicting success in weight reduction as a function of locus of control: A unidimensional and multidimensional approach', *Journal of Consulting and Clinical Psychology* 43: 119.

Balogun, J., Okonofua, F. and Balogun, A. (1992) 'An appraisal of body image among Nigerian university students', *Perceptual and Motor Skills* 75: 832–834.

Bancroft, J. (1994) 'Homosexual orientation: The search for a biological basis', *British Journal of Psychiatry* 164: 437–440.

Band, E. and Weisz, J. (1988) 'How to feel better when it feels bad: Children's perspectives on coping with everyday stress', *Developmental Psychology* 24: 247–253.

Barber, B. and Eccles, J. (1992) 'Long-term influence of divorce and single parenting on adolescent family- and work-related values, behaviors and aspirations', *Psychological Bulletin* 111: 108–126.

Barling, N. and Moore, S. (1990) 'Adolescents' attitudes towards AIDS precautions and intention to use condoms', *Psychological Reports* 67: 883–890.

Baron, R. and Byrne, D. (1994) *Social psychology: Understanding human interaction*, Boston: Allyn and Bacon.

Becker, M. (1974) 'The health belief model and sick role behavior', *Health Education Monographs* 2: 409–419.

Benthin, A., Slovic, P. and Severson, H. (1993) 'A psychometric study of adolescent risk perception', *Journal of Adolescence* 16: 153–168.

Beyth-Marom, R., Austin, L., Fischhoff, B., Palmgren, C. and Jacobs-Quadrel, M. (1993) 'Perceived consequences of risky behaviors: Adults and adolescents', *Developmental Psychology* 29: 549–563.

Bingham, C., Bennion, L., Openshaw, D. and Adams, G. (1994) 'An analysis of age, gender and racial differences in recent national trends of youth suicide', *Journal of Adolescence* 17: 53–71.

Boldero, J., Moore, S. and Rosenthal, D. (1992) 'Intention, context, and safe sex: Australian adolescents' responses to AIDS', *Journal of Applied Social Psychology* 22: 1374–1396.

Borst, S. and Noam, G. (1993) 'Developmental psychopathology in suicidal and nonsuicidal adolescent girls', *Journal of the American Academy of Child and Adolescent Psychiatry* 32: 501–508.

Brannon, L. and Feist, J. (1992) *Health psychology: An introduction to behavior and health*, Belmont, California: Wadsworth Publishing Company.

Brenner, D. and Hinsdale, G. (1978) 'Body build stereotypes and self-identification in three age groups of females', *Adolescence* 13: 551–561.

Brook, D. and Brook, J. (1990) 'The etiology and consequences of adolescent drug use', in R. Watson (Ed.) *Drug and alcohol abuse prevention*, Clifton, N.J.: Humana Press.

Brook, J., Gordon, A. and Brook, D. (1987) 'Fathers and daughters: Their relationship and personality characteristics associated with the daughter's smoking behavior', *Journal of Genetic Psychology* 148: 31–44.

Brooks-Gunn, J. (1991) 'How stressful is the transition to adolescence for girls?', in M. Colten and S. Gore (Eds) *Adolescent stress: Causes and consequences*, New York: Aldine de Gruyter.

Brooks-Gunn, J. and Furstenberg, F. (1989) 'Adolescent sexual behavior', *American Psychologist* 44: 249–257.

Brown, B., Clasen, D. and Eicher, S. (1986) 'Perceptions of peer pressure, peer conformity dispositions, and self-reported behavior among adolescents', *Developmental Psychology* 22: 521–530.

Bruhn, J. (1988) 'Life-style and health behavior', in D. Gochman (Ed.) *Health behavior: Emerging research perspectives*, New York: Plenum Press.

Brunswik, A. (1991) 'Health and substance use in adolescence: Ethnic and gender perspectives', in R. Lerner, A. Petersen and J. Brooks-Gunn (Eds) *Encyclopedia of Adolescence, Vol 1*, New York: Garland Press.

Bryant, F. and Yarnold, P. (1990) 'The impact of Type A behavior on subjective life quality: Bad for the heart, good for the soul?', *Journal of Social Behavior and Personality* 5: 369–404.

Burbach, D. and Peterson, L. (1986) 'Children's concepts of physical illness: A review and critique of the cognitive-developmental literature', *Health Psychology* 5: 307–325.

Bush, R. (1990) 'The social context of young men's and women's drinking: A psycho-social developmental perspective', in P. Heaven and V. Callan (Eds) *Adolescence: An Australian perspective*, Sydney: Harcourt Brace Jovanovich.

Byrne, D., Byrne, A. and Reinhart, M. (1993) 'Psychosocial correlates of adolescent cigarette smoking: Personality or environment', *Australian Journal of Psychology* 45: 87–95.

Byrne, D., Reinhart, M. and Heaven, P. (1989) 'Type A behaviour and the authoritarian personality', *British Journal of Medical Psychology* 62: 163–172.

Caceres, C., Rosasco, A., Mandel, J. and Hearst, N. (1994) 'Evaluating a school-based intervention for STD/AIDS prevention in Peru', *Journal of Adolescent Health* 15: 582–591.

Campbell, J. (1975) 'Illness is a point of view: The development of children's concepts of illness', *Child Development* 46: 92–100.

Cantwell, D. and Baker, L. (1991) 'Manifestations of depressive affect in adolescence', *Journal of Youth and Adolescence* 20: 121–133.

Carson, R., Butcher, J. and Coleman, J. (1988) *Abnormal psychology and modern life* (8th edn.), Glenview, Ill.: Scott, Foresman & Co.

Cauce, A., Hannan, K. and Sargeant, M. (1992) 'Life stress, social support, and locus of control during early adolescence: Interactive effects', *American Journal of Community Psychology* 20: 787–798.

Chan, D. and Fishbein, M. (1993) 'Determinants of college women's intentions to tell their partners to use condoms', *Journal of Applied Social Psychology* 23: 1455–1470.

Chapman, G. and Maclean, H. (1993) 'Junk food and "healthy food": Meanings of food in adolescent women's culture', *Journal of Nutrition Education* 25: 108–113.

Cherry, N. and Kiernan, K. (1976) 'Personality scores and smoking behaviour: A longitudinal study', *British Journal of Preventive and Social Medicine* 30: 123–131.

Choquet, M. and Manfredi, R. (1992) 'Sexual intercourse, contraception, and risk-taking behavior among unselected French adolescents aged 11–20 years', *Journal of Adolescent Health* 13: 623–630.

Christiansen, B. and Goldman, M. (1983) 'Alcohol-related expectancies versus demographic/background variables in the prediction of adolescent drinking', *Journal of Consulting and Clinical Psychology* 51: 249–257.

Cohen, R., Brownell, K. and Felix, M. (1990) 'Age and sex differences in health habits and beliefs of schoolchildren', *Health Psychology* 9: 208–224.

Coleman, J. (1992) 'Current views of the adolescent process', in J. Coleman (Ed.) *The school years: Current issues in the socialization of young people* (2nd edn.), London: Routledge.

Collins, L., Sussman, S., Rauch, J., Dent, C., Johnson, C., Hansen, W. and Flay, B. (1987) 'Psychosocial predictors of young adolescent cigarette smoking: A sixteen-month, three-wave longitudinal study', *Journal of Applied Social Psychology* 17: 554–573.

Colten, M. and Gore, S. (Eds) (1991) *Adolescent stress: Causes and consequences*, New York: Aldine de Gruyter.

Compas, B. (1987) 'Coping with stress during childhood and adolescence', *Psycho- logical Bulletin* 101: 393–403.

Compas, B. and Wagner, B. (1991) 'Psychosocial stress during adolescence: Intra-personal and interpersonal processes', in M. Colten and S. Gore (Eds) *Adolescent stress: Causes and consequences*, New York: Aldine de Gruyter.

Compas, B., Malcarne, V. and Fondacaro, K. (1988) 'Coping with stressful events in older children and young adolescents', *Journal of Consulting and Clinical Psychology* 56: 405–411.

Compas, B., Howell, D., Phares, V., Williams, R. and Giunta, C. (1989) 'Risk factors for emotional/behavioral problems in young adolescents: A prospective analysis of adolescent and parental stress and symptoms', *Journal of Consulting and Clinical Psychology* 57: 732–740.

Compas, B., Orosan, P. and Grant, K. (1993) 'Adolescent stress and coping: implications for psychopathology during adolescence', *Journal of Adolescence* 16: 331–349.

Conger, J. and Petersen, A. (1984) *Adolescence and youth: Psychological development in a changing world* (3rd edn.), New York: Harper & Row.

Crabbe, J., McSwigan, J. and Belknap, J. (1985) 'The role of genetics in substance abuse', in M. Galizio and S. Maisto (Eds) *Determinants of substance abuse treatment: Biological, psychological, and environmental factors*, New York: Plenum.

Crawford, J., Turtle, A. and Kippax, S. (1990) 'Student-favoured strategies for AIDS avoidance', *Australian Journal of Psychology* 42: 123–137.

Cross, H. (1994) 'An adolescent health system and lifestyle guidance system', *Adolescence* 29: 267–277.

Daniel, W. (1991) 'Health care, training in adolescence', in R. Lerner, A. Petersen and J. Brooks-Gunn (Eds) *Encyclopedia of adolescence, Vol. 1*, New York: Garland Press.

Darling, C. and Davidson, J. (1986) 'Coitally active university students: Sexual behaviors, concerns, and challenges', *Adolescence* 21: 403–418.

Davies, E. and Furnham, A. (1986a) 'Body satisfaction in adolescent girls', *British Journal of Medical Psychology* 59: 279–287.

Davies, E. and Furnham, A. (1986b) 'The dieting and body shape concerns of adolescent females', *Journal of Child Psychology and Psychiatry* 27: 417–428.

Davison, G. and Neale, J. (1994) *Abnormal Psychology* (7th edn.), New York: John Wiley & Sons.

Deisher, R. and Rogers, W. (1991) 'The medical care of street youth', *Journal of Adolescent Health* 12: 500–503.

Department of Community Services and Health (1990) *Tobacco in Australia: A summary of related statistics*, Canberra: Australian Government Publishing Service.

Department of Employment, Education & Training (1991) *1989 Australian Youth Survey – First results*, Canberra: Australian Government Publishing Service.

Desmond, S., Price, J., Gray, N. and O'Connell, K. (1986) 'The etiology of adolescents' perceptions of their weight', *Journal of Youth and Adolescence* 15: 461–474.

De Souza, R., De Almeida, A., Wagner, M., Zimerman, I., De Almeida, S., Caleffi, A. and Puperi, F. (1993) 'A study of the sexual behavior of teenagers in South Brazil', *Journal of Adolescent Health* 14: 336–339.

De Wilde, E., Kienhorst, I., Diekstra, R. and Wolters, W. (1993) 'The specificity of psychological characteristics of adolescent suicide attempters', *Journal of the American Academy of Child and Adolescent Psychiatry* 32: 51–59.

Dickman, S. (1988) *Pathways to wellness*, Champaign, Illinois: Life Enhancement Publications.

Dielman, T., Leech, S., Becker, M., Rosenstock, I., Horvath, W. and Radius, S. (1980) 'Dimensions of children's health beliefs', *Health Education Quarterly* 7: 219–238.

Donatelle, R., Davis, L. and Hoover, C. (1991) *Access to Health* (2nd edn.), Englewood Cliffs, N.J.: Prentice-Hall.

Donovan, J. and Jessor, R. (1985) 'Structure of problem behavior in adolescence and young adulthood', *Journal of Consulting and Clinical Psychology* 53: 890–904.

Donovan, J., Jessor, R. and Costa, F. (1988) 'Syndrome of problem behavior in adolescence: A replication', *Journal of Consulting and Clinical Psychology* 56: 762–765.

Downey, G. and Coyne, J. (1990) 'Children of depressed parents: An integrative review', *Psychological Bulletin* 108: 50–76.

Dusek, J. (1991) *Adolescent development and behaviour* (2nd edn.), Englewood Cliffs, N.J.: Prentice-Hall.

Eagleston, J., Kirmil-Gray, K., Thoresen, C., Wiedenfeld, S., Bracke, P., Heft, L. and Arnow, B. (1986) 'Physical health correlates of Type A behavior in children and adolescents', *Journal of Behavioral Medicine* 47: 341–362.

Egger, G. (1986) 'Health promotion', in N. King and A. Remenyi (Eds) *Health care: A behavioural approach*, Sydney: Grune & Stratton.

Elkind, D. (1967) 'Egocentrism in adolescence', *Child Development* 38: 1025–1034.

Engel, G. (1977) 'The need for a new medical model: A challenge for biomedicine', *Science* 196: 129–136.

English, A. (1991) 'Runaway and street youth at risk for HIV infection: Legal and ethical issues in access to care', *Journal of Adolescent Health* 12: 504–510.

Erikson, E. (1968) *Identity: Youth and crisis*, New York: W.W. Norton & Co.

Erlenmeyer-Kimling, L. and Cornblatt, B. (1991) 'Schizophrenia in adolescence and young adulthood, antecedents/predictors of', in R. Lerner, A. Petersen and J. Brooks-Gunn (Eds) *Encyclopedia of adolescence, Vol. 2*, New York: Garland Press.

Eysenck, H. and Eysenck, S. (1975) *Manual of the Eysenck Personality Questionnaire*, London: Hodder & Stoughton.

Falconer, H., Baghurst, K. and Rump, E. (1993) 'Nutrient intakes in relation to health-related aspects of personality', *Journal of Nutrition Education* 25: 307–319.

Farrell, A., Danish, S. and Howard, C. (1992) 'Relationship between drug use and other person behaviors in urban adolescents', *Journal of Consulting and Clinical Psychology* 60: 705–712.

Fisher, C. and Brone, R. (1991) 'Eating disorders in adolescence', in R. Lerner, A. Petersen and J. Brooks-Gunn (Eds) *Encyclopedia of adolescence, Vol. 1*, New York: Garland Press.

Fisher, M., Kupferman, L. and Lesser, M. (1992) 'Substance use in a school-based clinic population: Use of the randomized response technique to estimate prevalence', *Journal of Adolescent Health* 13: 281–285.

Fisher, W. (1984) 'Predicting contraceptive behavior among university men: The role of emotions and behavioral intentions', *Journal of Applied Social Psychology* 14: 104–123.

Flannery, D., Vazsonyi, A., Torquati, J. and Fridrich, A. (1994) 'Ethnic and gender differences in risk for early adolescent substance use', *Journal of Youth and Adolescence* 23: 195–213.

Fleming, J., Offord, D. and Boyle, M. (1989) 'Prevalence of childhood and adolescent depression in the community: Ontario child health study', *British Journal of Psychiatry* 155: 647–654.

Freedland, J. and Dwyer, J. (1991) 'Nutrition in adolescent girls', in R. Lerner, A. Petersen and J. Brooks-Gunn (Eds), *Encyclopedia of adolescence, Vol. 2*, New York: Garland Press.

Fromme, K. and Rivet, K. (1994) 'Young adults' coping style as a predictor of their alcohol use and response to daily events', *Journal of Youth and Adolescence* 23: 85–97.

Frydenberg, E. and Lewis, R. (1993) 'Boys play sports and girls turn to others: Age, gender and ethnicity as determinants of coping', *Journal of Adolescence* 16: 253–266.

Furnham, A. and Baguma, P. (1994) 'Cross-cultural differences in the evaluation of male and female body shapes', *International Journal of Eating Disorders* 15: 81–89.

Furnham A. and Greaves, N. (1994) 'Gender and locus of control correlates of body image dissatisfaction', *European Journal of Personality* 8: 183–200.

Furnham, A. and Gunter, B. (1989) *The anatomy of adolescence: Young people's social attitudes in Britain*, London: Routledge.

Furnham, A. and Radley, S. (1989) 'Sex differences in the perception of male and female body shapes', *Personality and Individual Differences* 10: 653–662.

Furnham, A. and Stacey, B. (1991) *Young people's understanding of society*, London: Routledge.

Furnham, A. and Steele, H. (1993) 'Measuring locus of control: A critique of general, children's, health- and work-related locus of control questionnaires', *British Journal of Psychology* 84: 443–479.

Gagliano, N., Emans, S. and Woods, E. (1993) 'Cholesterol screening in the adolescent', *Journal of Adolescent Health* 14: 104–108.

Garfinkel, P. and Garner, D. (1982) *Anorexia nervosa: A multidimensional perspective*, New York: Brunner/Mazel.

Garland, A. and Zigler, E. (1993) 'Adolescent suicide prevention: Current research and social policy implications', *American Psychologist* 48: 169–182.

Garnets, L. and Kimmel, D. (1991) 'Lesbian and gay male dimensions in the psychological study of human diversity', in J. Goodchilds (Ed.) *Psychological perspectives on human diversity in America: Master lectures*, Washington, D.C.: American Psychological Association.

Gibbs, J. (1988) 'The new morbidity: Homicide, suicide, accidents, and life-threatening behaviors', in J. Gibbs, A. Brunswik, M. Connor, R. Dembo, T. Larsen, R. Reed and B. Solomon (Eds) *Young, black, and male in America: An endangered species*, New York: Auburn House.

Gitter, A., Lomranz, J., Saxe, L. and Bar-Tal, D. (1983) 'Perception of female physique characteristics by American and Israeli students', *Journal of Social Psychology* 121: 7–13.

Glicksman, M., Dwyer, T., Wlodarczyk, J. and Pierce, J. (1989) 'Cigarette smoking in Australian schoolchildren', *Medical Journal of Australia* 150: 81–84.

Gochman, D. (1971) 'Some correlates of children's health beliefs and potential health behavior', *Journal of Health and Social Behavior* 12: 148–154.

Gochman, D. (1988) 'Health behavior: Plural perspectives', in D. Gochman (Ed.) *Health behavior: Emerging research perspectives*, New York: Plenum Press.

Gordon, D. (1990) 'Formal operation thinking: The role of cognitive-developmental processes in adolescent decision-making about pregnancy and contraception', *American Journal of Orthopsychiatry* 60: 346–356.

Gordon, S. and Gilgun, J. (1987) 'Adolescent sexuality', in V. Van Hasselt and M. Hersen (Eds) *Handbook of adolescent psychology*, New York: Oxford.

Gore, S., Aseltine, R. and Colton, M. (1992) 'Social structure, life stress and depressive symptoms in a high school-aged population', *Journal of Health and Social Behavior* 33: 97–113.

Gorsuch, R. and Butler, M. (1976) 'Initial drug abuse: A review of predisposing social psychological factors', *Psychological Bulletin* 83: 120–137.

Gray, P. (1991) *Psychology*, New York: Worth.

Green, J. (1979) 'Overview of adolescent drug use', in G. Beschner and A. Friedman (Eds) *Youth drug abuse: Problems, issues, and treatment*, Lexington, K.Y.: Lexington Books.

Guillen, E. and Barr, S. (1994) 'Nutrition, dieting, and fitness messages in a magazine for adolescent women, 1970–1990', *Journal of Adolescent Health* 15: 464–472.

Harris, D. (1991) 'Exercise and fitness during adolescence', in R. Lerner, A. Petersen and J. Brooks-Gunn (Eds) *Encyclopedia of adolescence, Vol. 1*, New York: Garland Press.

Harris, J. and Liebert, R. (1987) *The Child* (2nd edn.), Englewood Cliffs, N.J.: Prentice-Hall.

Hauser, S. and Bowlds, M. (1990) 'Stress, coping, and adaptation', in S. Feldman and G. Elliott (Eds) *At the threshold: The developing adolescent*, Cambridge, Massachusetts: Harvard University Press.

Heatherton, T. and Baumeister, R. (1991) 'Binge eating as escape from self-awareness', *Psychological Bulletin* 110: 86–108.

Heaven, P. (1989) 'Adolescent smoking, toughmindedness, and attitudes to authority', *Australian Psychologist* 24: 27–35.

Heaven, P. (1994) *Contemporary adolescence: A social psychological approach*, Melbourne: Macmillan.

Hein, K. (1991) 'Pharmacology, developmental', in R, Lerner, A. Petersen and J. Brooks-Gunn (Eds) *Encyclopedia of adolescence, Vol. 2*, New York: Garland Press.

Hergenhahn, B. (1988) *An introduction to theories of learning* (3rd edn.), Englewood Cliffs, N.J.: Prentice-Hall.

Hetzel, B. and McMichael, T. (1987) *The LS factor: Lifestyle and health*, Ringwood, Victoria: Penguin Books.

Hill, D., White, V., Pain, M. and Gardner, G. (1990) 'Tobacco and alcohol use among Australian secondary schoolchildren in 1987', *Medical Journal of Australia* 152: 124–130.

Hill, D., Willcox, S., Gardner, G. and Houston, J. (1987) 'Tobacco and alcohol use among Australian secondary schoolchildren', *Medical Journal of Australia* 146: 125–130.

Ho, R. (1994) 'Cigarette advertising and cigarette health warnings: What role do adolescents' motives for smoking play in their assessment?', *Australian Psychologist* 29: 49–56.

Hodgson, C., Feldman, W., Corber, S. and Quinn, A. (1986) 'Adolescent health needs II: Utilization of health care by adolescents', *Adolescence* 21: 383–390.

Hoffman, M., Levy-Shiff, R., Sohlberg, S. and Zarizki, J. (1992) 'The impact of stress and coping: Developmental changes in the transition to adolescence', *Journal of Youth and Adolescence* 21: 451–469.

Hoorens, V. and Buunk, B. (1993) 'Social comparison of health risks: Locus of control, the person-positivity bias, and unrealistic optimism', *Journal of Applied Social Psychology* 23: 291–302.

Houts, S. and Warland, R. (1989) 'Rotter's social learning theory of personality and dietary behavior', *Journal of Nutrition Education* 21: 172–179.

Huba, G. and Bentler, P. (1982) 'A developmental theory of drug use: Derivation and assessment of a causal modeling approach', in P. Baltes and O. Brim (Eds) *Life-span development and behavior*, Vol. 4, New York: Academic Press.

Houn, G. and Brown, L. (1988) *Fighting with food: Overcoming bulimia nervosa*, Sydney: University of New South Wales Press.

Insel, P., Roth, W., Rollins, L., Petersen, R. and Stone, T. (1991) *Core concepts in health* (Brief 6th edn.), Mountain View, California: Mayfield Publishing Company.

Irwin, C. and Millstein, S. (1991) 'Risk-taking behaviors during adolescence', in R. Lerner, A. Petersen and J. Brooks-Gunn (Eds) *Encyclopedia of adolescence, Vol. 2*, New York: Garland Press.

Irwin, C. and Orr, D. (1991) 'Health research in adolescence, future directions of', in R. Lerner, A. Petersen and J. Brooks-Gunn (Eds) *Encyclopedia of adolescence, Vol. 1*, New York: Garland Press.

Janz, N. and Becker, M. (1984) 'The health belief model: A decade later', *Health Education Quarterly* 11: 1–47.

Jessor, R. (1984) 'Adolescent development and behavioral health', in J. Matarazzo, S. Weiss, J. Herd, N. Miller and S. Weiss (Eds) *Behavioral health: A handbook of health enhancement and disease prevention*, New York: John Wiley & Sons.

Jessor, R. (1993) 'Successful adolescent development among youth in high-risk settings', *American Psychologist* 48: 117–126.

Jessor, R. and Jessor, S. (1977) *Problem behavior and psychosocial development: A longitudinal study of youth*, New York: Academic Press.

Jessor, R., Donovan, J. and Costa, F. (1991) *Beyond adolescence: Problem behaviour and young adult development*, Cambridge: Cambridge University Press.

Joffe, A. and Radius, S. (1993) 'Self-efficacy and intent to use condoms among entering college freshmen', *Journal of Adolescent Health* 14: 262–268.

Johnson, C. and Flach, A. (1985) 'Family characteristics of 105 patients with bulimia', *American Journal of Psychiatry* 142: 1321–1324.

Johnson, R., Johnson, D., Wang, M., Smiciklas-Wright, H. and Guthrie, H. (1994) 'Characterizing nutrient intakes of adolescents by sociodemographic factors', *Journal of Adolescent Health* 15: 149–154.

Kagan, J. (1991) 'Etiologies of adolescents at risk', *Journal of Adolescent Health* 12: 591–596.

Kandel, D. (1975) 'Stages in adolescent involvement in drug use', *Science* 190: 912–914.

Kandel, D. (1982) 'Epidemiological and psychosocial perspectives on adolescent drug use', *Journal of the American Academy of Child Psychiatry* 21: 328–347.

Kandel, D. (1990) 'On processes of peer influences in adolescent drug use: A developmental perspective', in R. Muuss (Ed.) *Adolescent behavior and society* (4th edn.), New York: McGraw-Hill.

Kandel, D. and Yamaguchi, K. (1993) 'From beer to crack: Developmental patterns of drug involvement', *American Journal of Public Health* 83: 851–855.

Kaplan, A. and Woodside, B. (1987) 'Biological aspects of anorexia nervosa and bulimia nervosa', *Journal of Consulting and Clinical Psychology* 55: 645–653.

Kashani, J., Carlson, G., Beck, N., Hoeper, E., Corcoran, C., McAllister, J., Fallahi, C., Rosenberg, T. and Reid, J. (1987) 'Depression, depressive symptoms, and depressed mood among a community sample of adolescents', *American Journal of Psychiatry* 144: 931–934.

Katchadourian, H. (1990) 'Sexuality', in S. Feldman and G. Elliott (Eds) *At the threshold: The developing adolescent*, Cambridge, Massachusetts: Harvard University Press.

Katzman, M. and Wolchik, S. (1984) 'Bulimia and binge eating in college women: A comparison of personality and behavioral characteristics', *Journal of Consulting and Clinical Psychology* 52: 423–428.

Kazdin, A. (1993) 'Adolescent mental health: Prevention and treatment programs', *American Psychologist* 48: 127–141.

Keitner, G. and Miller, I. (1990) 'Family functioning and major depression: An overview', *American Journal of Psychiatry* 147: 1128–1137.

Kendler, K. and Robinette, C. (1983) 'Schizophrenia in the National Academy of Sciences-National Research Council twin register: A 16-year update', *American Journal of Psychiatry* 140: 1551–1563.

Keys, A., Brozek, J., Henschel, A., Mickelsen, O. and Taylor, H. (1950) *The biology of human starvation (Vols. 1 and 2)*, Minneapolis: University of Minnesota Press.

King, C., Naylor, M., Segal, H., Evans, T. and Shain, B. (1993) 'Global self-worth, specific self-perceptions of competence, and depression in adolescents', *Journal of the American Academy of Child and Adolescent Psychiatry* 32: 745–752.

Kippax, S. and Crawford, J. (1993) 'Flaws in the theory of reasoned action', in

D. Terry, C. Gallois and M. McCamish (Eds) *The theory of reasoned action: Its application to AIDS-preventive behaviour*, Oxford: Pergamon Press.

Kippax, S., Crawford, J., Waldby, C. and Benton, P. (1990) 'Women negotiating heterosex: Implications for AIDS prevention', *Women's Studies International Forum* 13: 533–542.

Klerman, L. (1991) 'Health services for adolescents, barriers to', in R. Lerner, A. Petersen and J. Brooks-Gunn (Eds) *Encyclopedia of adolescence, Vol. 1*, New York: Garland Press.

Kliewer, W. (1991) 'Coping in middle childhood: Relations to competence, Type A behavior, monitoring, blunting, and locus of control', *Developmental Psychology* 27: 689–697.

Kovar, M. (1991) 'Health of adolescents in the United States: An overview', in R. Lerner, A. Petersen and J. Brooks-Gunn (Eds) *Encyclopedia of adolescence, Vol. 1*, New York: Garland Press.

Larson, R. and Asmussen, L. (1991) 'Anger, worry, and hurt in early adolescence: An enlarging world of negative emotions', in M. Colten and S. Gore (Eds) *Adolescent stress: Causes and consequences*, New York: Aldine de Gruyter.

Lau, R. (1988) 'Beliefs about control and health behavior', in D. Gochman (Ed.) *Health behavior: Emerging research perspectives*, New York: Plenum Press.

Lau, R., Quadrel, M. and Hartman, K. (1990) 'Development and change of young adults' preventive health beliefs and behavior: Influence from parents and peers', *Journal of Health and Social Behavior* 31: 240–259.

Lazarus, R. and Folkman, S. (1984) *Stress, appraisal and coping*, New York: Springer.

Lefcourt, H. (1976) *Locus of control: Current trends in theory and research*, Hillsdale, N.J.: Lawrence Erlbaum.

Lefebvre, C. (1992) 'Social marketing and health promotion', in R. Bunton and G. Macdonald (Eds) *Health promotion: disciplines and diversity*, London: Routledge.

Leland, N. and Barth, R. (1992) 'Gender differences in knowledge, intentions, and behaviors concerning pregnancy and sexually transmitted disease prevention among adolescents', *Journal of Adolescent Health* 13: 589–599.

Leon, G. (1990) *Case histories of psychopathology* (4th edn.), Boston: Allyn and Bacon.

Lerner, R., Iwawaki, S., Chihara, T. and Sorell, G. (1980) 'Self-concept, self-esteem, and body attitudes among Japanese male and female adolescents', *Child Development* 51: 847–855.

Lester, D. (1987) 'A subcultural theory of teenage suicide', *Adolescence* 22: 317–320.

Lester, D. (1988) 'Youth suicide: A cross-cultural perspective', *Adolescence* 23: 953–958.

Levinson, R., Powell, B. and Steelman, L. (1986) 'Social location, significant others and body image among adolescents', *Social Psychology Quarterly* 49: 330–337.

Lewinsohn, P., Rohde, P. and Seeley, J. (1993) 'Psychosocial characteristics of adolescents with a history of suicide attempt', *Journal of the American Academy of Child and Adolescent Psychiatry* 32: 60–68.

Liebert, R. and Spiegler, M. (1990) *Personality: Strategies and issues*, Pacific Grove: Brooks/Cole.

184 Adolescent health

Litt, I. (1991) 'Eating disorders, medical complications of', in R. Lerner, A. Petersen and J. Brooks-Gunn (Eds) *Encyclopedia of adolescence, Vol. 1*, New York: Garland Press.

Littleton, J. (1991) 'Drug dependence as pharmacological adaptation', in I. Glass (Ed.) *The international handbook of addiction behaviour*, London: Routledge.

Luna, G. (1991) 'Street youth: Adaptation and survival in the AIDS decade', *Journal of Adolescent Health* 12: 511–514.

McClosky, H. and Schaar, J. (1965) 'Psychological dimensions of anomie', *American Sociological Review* 30: 14–40.

McClure, G. (1986) 'Recent changes in suicide among adolescents in England and Wales', *Journal of Adolescence* 9: 135–143.

Macdonald, G. (1992) 'Communication theory and health promotion', in R. Bunton and G. Macdonald (Eds) *Health promotion: disciplines and diversity*, London: Routledge.

Marlatt, G., Baer, J., Donovan, D. and Kivlahan, D. (1988) 'Addictive behaviors: Etiology and treatment', *Annual Review of Psychology* 39: 223–252.

Marton, P., Connolly, J., Kutcher, S. and Korenblum, M. (1993) 'Cognitive social skills and social self-appraisal in depressed adolescents', *Journal of the American Academy of Child and Adolescent Psychiatry* 32: 739–744.

Marttunen, M., Aro, H. and Lonnqvist, J. (1992) 'Adolescent suicide: Endpoint of long-term difficulties', *Journal of the American Academy of Child and Adolescent Psychiatry* 31: 649–654.

Marttunen, M., Aro, H. and Lonnqvist, J. (1993) 'Precipitant stressors in adolescent suicide', *Journal of the American Academy of Child and Adolescent Psychiatry* 32: 1178–1183.

Mason, G. (1990) *Youth suicide in Australia: Prevention strategies*, Canberra: Government Printer.

Matthews, K. and Jennings, R. (1984) 'Cardiovascular responses of boys exhibiting the Type A behavior pattern', *Psychosomatic Medicine* 46: 484–497.

Matthews, K. and Siegel, J. (1982) 'The Type A behavior pattern in children and adolescents: Assessment, development, and associated coronary-risk', in A. Baum and J. Singer (Eds) *Handbook of psychology and health, Vol. 2: Issues in child health and adolescent health*, Hillsdale, N.J.: Lawrence Erlbaum.

Mechanic, D. (1991) 'Adolescents at risk: new directions', *Journal of Adolescent Health* 12: 638–643.

Mezzich, A., Tarter, R., Moss, H., Yao, J., Hsieh, Y. and Kirisci, L. (1994) 'Platelet monoamine oxidase activity and temperament and personality in adolescent female substance abusers', *Personality and Individual Differences* 16: 417–424.

Millan, G. and Ross, M. (1987) 'AIDS and gay youth: Attitudes and lifestyle modifications in young male homosexuals', *Community Health Studies* 11: 50–53.

Miller, B. and Dyk, P. (1993) 'Sexuality', in P. Tolan and B. Cohler (Eds) *Handbook of clinical research and practice with adolescents*, New York: John Wiley & Sons.

Mills, C. and Noyes, H. (1984) 'Patterns and correlates of initial and subsequent drug use among adolescents', *Journal of Consulting and Clinical Psychology* 52: 231–243.

Millstein, S. (1991) 'Health beliefs', in R. Lerner, A. Petersen and J. Brooks-Gunn (Eds) *Encyclopedia of adolescence, Vol. 1*, New York: Garland Press.

Millstein, S. and Irwin, C. (1987) 'Concepts of health and illness: Different constructs or variations on a theme', *Health Psychology* 6: 515–524.

Millstein, S. and Litt, I. (1990) 'Adolescent health', in S. Feldman and G. Elliott (Eds) *At the threshold: The developing adolescent*, Cambridge, Massachusetts: Harvard University Press.

Mitchell, J. and Eckert, E. (1987) 'Scope and significance of eating disorders', *Journal of Consulting and Clinical Psychology* 55: 628–634.

Moore, S. and Rosenthal, D. (1991) 'Adolescent invulnerability and perceptions of AIDS risk', *Journal of Adolescent Research* 6: 164–180.

Moore, S. and Rosenthal, D. (1993) *Adolescent sexuality*, London: Routledge.

Mrosovsky, N. (1984) 'Complexities of cause and effect in anorexia nervosa', *Nature* 312: 104.

Mullen, P., Hersey, J. and Iverson, D. (1987) 'Health behavior models compared', *Social Science & Medicine* 24: 973–981.

Mumford, D., Whitehouse, A. and Platts, M. (1991) 'Sociocultural correlates of eating disorders among Asian schoolgirls in Bradford', *British Journal of Psychiatry* 158: 222–228.

Munsch, J. and Wampler, R. (1993) 'Ethnic differences in early adolescents' coping with school stress', *American Journal of Orthopsychiatry* 63: 633–646.

Muuss, R. (1985) 'Adolescent eating disorder: Anorexia nervosa', *Adolescence* 20: 525–536.

Muuss, R. (1986) 'Adolescent eating disorder: Bulimia', *Adolescence* 21: 257–267.

Muuss, R. (1988) *Theories of adolescence* (5th edn.), New York: Random House.

Myers, D. (1989) *Psychology* (2nd edn.), New York: Worth Publishers.

Newcomb, M. and Bentler, P. (1991a) 'Cocaine use among adolescents and young adults, antecedents/predictors of', in R. Lerner, A. Petersen and J. Brooks-Gunn (Eds) *Encyclopedia of adolescence, Vol. 1*, New York: Garland Press.

Newcomb, M. and Bentler, P. (1991b) 'Hallucinogens', in R. Lerner, A. Petersen and J. Brooks-Gunn (Eds) *Encyclopedia of adolescence, Vol. 1*, New York: Garland Press.

Newcomb, M., Huba, G. and Bentler, P. (1986) 'Desirability of various life change events among adolescents: Effects of exposure, sex, age, and ethnicity', *Journal of Research in Personality* 20: 207–227.

Newell, G., Hammig, C., Jurich, A. and Johnson, D. (1990) 'Self-concept as a factor in the quality of diets of adolescent girls', *Adolescence* 25: 117–130.

Newman, B. and Newman, P. (1987) *Development through life: A psychological approach* (4th edn.), Chicago: The Dorsey Press.

Newman, P. and Newman, B. (1988) 'Difference between childhood and adulthood: The identity watershed', *Adolescence* 23: 551–557.

Nix, L., Pasteur, A. and Servance, M. (1988) 'A focus group study of sexually active black male teenagers', *Adolescence* 23: 741–751.

Nolen-Hoeksema, S. (1991) 'Responses to depression and their effects on the duration of depressive episodes', *Journal of Abnormal Psychology* 100: 569–582.

Noller, P. and Callan, V. (1991) *The adolescent in the family*, London: Routledge.

Noller, P. and Patton, W. (1990) 'Maintaining family relationships at adolescence', in P. Heaven and V. Callan (Eds) *Adolescence: An Australian perspective*, Sydney: Harcourt Brace Jovanovich.

Nucci, L., Guerra, N. and Lee, J. (1991) 'Adolescent judgements of the personal, prudential, and normative aspects of drug usage', *Developmental Psychology* 27: 841–848.

Nucifora, J., Gallois, C. and Kashima, Y. (1993) 'Influences on condom use among undergraduates: Testing the theories of reasoned action and planned behaviour', in D. Terry, C. Gallois and M. McCamish (Eds) *The theory of reasoned action: Its applications to AIDS-preventive behaviour*, Oxford: Pergamon Press.

O'Donnell, J. and Clayton, R. (1979) 'Determinants of early marijuana use', in G. Beschner and A. Friedman (Eds) *Youth drug abuse: Problems, issues, and treatment*, Lexington, K.Y.: Lexington Books.

Oswald, H. and Pforr, P. (1992) 'Sexuality and AIDS: Attitudes and behaviors of adolescents in East and West Berlin', *Journal of Adolescence* 15: 373–392.

Papalia, D. and Olds, S. (1989) *Human development*, (4th edn.) New York: McGraw-Hill.

Paxton, S., Wertheim, E., Gibbons, K., Szmukler, G., Hillier, L. and Petrovich, J. (1991) 'Body image satisfaction, dieting beliefs, and weight loss behaviors in adolescent girls and boys', *Journal of Youth and Adolescence* 20: 361–379.

Payne, W. and Hahn, D. (1986) *Understanding your health*, St Louis: Times Mirror/Mosby College Publishing.

Penner, L., Thompson, J. and Coovert, D. (1991) 'Size overestimation among anorexics: Much ado about very little?', *Journal of Abnormal Psychology* 100: 90–93.

Petersen, A. (1988) 'Adolescent development', *Annual Review of Psychology* 39: 583–607.

Petersen, A., Compas, B., Brooks-Gunn, J., Stemmler, M., Ey, S. and Grant, K. (1993) 'Depression in adolescents', *American Psychologist* 48: 155–168.

Petersen, A., Sarigiani, P. and Kennedy, R. (1991) 'Adolescent depression: Why more girls?', *Journal of Youth and Adolescence* 20: 247–271.

Peterson, C., Seligman, M. and Valliant, G. (1988) 'Pessimistic explanatory style is a risk factor for physical illness: A thirty-five-year longitudinal study', *Journal of Personality & Social Psychology* 55: 23–27.

Pleck, J., Sonenstein, F. and Ku, L. (1991) 'Adolescent males' condom use: Relationships between perceived costs-benefits and consistency', *Journal of Marriage and the Family* 53: 733–745.

Puig-Antich, J., Kaufman, J., Ryan, N., Williamson, D., Dahl, R., Lukens, E., Todak, G., Ambrosini, P., Rabinovich, H. and Nelson, B. (1993) 'The psychological functioning and family environment of depressed adolescents', *Journal of the American Academy of Child and Adolescent Psychiatry* 32: 244–253.

Quadrel, M., Fischhoff, B. and Davis, W. (1993) 'Adolescent (in)vulnerability', *American Psychologist* 48: 102–116.

Rauch, J. and Huba, G. (1991) 'Drug use, adolescent', in R. Lerner, A. Petersen and J. Brooks-Gunn (Eds) *Encyclopedia of adolescence, Vol. 1*, New York: Garland Press.

Rauste-von Wright, M. (1989) 'Body image satisfaction in adolescent girls and boys: A longitudinal study', *Journal of Youth and Adolescence* 18: 71–83.

Reifman, A. and Windle, M. (1993) 'Adolescent Type A characteristics and socially problematic behaviors', *Journal of Applied Social Psychology* 23: 21–39.

Reinherz, H., Giaconia, R., Pakiz, B., Silverman, A., Frost, A. and Lefkowitz, E. (1993) 'Psychosocial risks for major depression in late adolescence: A longitudinal community study', *Journal of the American Academy of Child and Adolescent Psychiatry* 32: 1155–1163.

Remafedi, G. (1987) 'Homosexual youth: A challenge to contemporary society', *Journal of the American Medical Association* 258: 222–225.

Resnicow, K. and Reinhardt, J. (1991) 'What do children know about fat, fiber, and cholesterol? A survey of 5,116 primary and secondary school students', *Journal of Nutrition Education* 23: 65–71.

Rice, F. (1992) *The adolescent: Development, relationships, and culture* (7th edn.), Boston: Allyn and Bacon.

Rice, K., Herman, M. and Petersen, A. (1993) 'Coping with challenge in adolescence: A conceptual model and psycho-educational intervention', *Journal of Adolescence* 16: 235–251.

Richard, R. and Van der Pligt, J. (1991) 'Factors affecting condom use among adolescents', *Journal of Community and Applied Social Psychology* 1: 105–116.

Robertson, J. and Simons, R. (1989) 'Family factors, self-esteem, and adolescent depression', *Journal of Marriage and the Family* 51: 125–138.

Roehling, P. and Robin, A. (1986) 'Development and validation of the family beliefs inventory: A measure of unrealistic beliefs among parents and adolescents', *Journal of Consulting and Clinical Psychology* 54: 693–697.

Rogers, R. (1983) 'Cognitive and physiological processes in attitude change: A revised theory of protection motivation', in J. Cacioppo and R. Petty (Eds) *Social psychophysiology*, New York: Guilford Press.

Romeo, F. (1994) 'Adolescent boys and anorexia nervosa', *Adolescence* 29: 643–647.

Ropers, R. and Boyer, R. (1987) 'Perceived health status among the new urban homeless', *Social Science & Medicine* 24: 669–678.

Rosenbaum, E. and Kandel, D. (1990) 'Early onset of adolescent sexual behavior and drug involvement', *Journal of Marriage and the Family* 52: 783–798.

Rosenthal, D. and Moore, S. (1991) 'Risky business: Adolescents and HIV/AIDS', *Youth Studies* 10: 20–25.

Rosenthal, D., Hall, C. and Moore, S. (1992) 'AIDS, adolescents, and sexual risk taking: A test of the health belief model', *Australian Psychologist* 27: 166–171.

Rosenthal, D., Moore, S. and Flynn, I. (1991) 'Adolescent self-efficacy, self-esteem and sexual risk-taking', *Journal of Community and Applied Social Psychology* 1: 77–88.

Rosenstock, I. (1974) 'The health belief model and preventive health behavior', *Health Education Monographs* 2: 354–386.

Rosenstock, I., Strecher, V. and Becker, M. (1988) 'Social learning theory and the health belief model', *Health Education Quarterly* 15: 175–183.

Roth, S. and Cohen, L. (1986) 'Approach, avoidance, and coping with stress', *American Psychologist* 41: 813–819.

Rotter, J. (1966) 'Generalized expectancies for internal versus external control of reinforcement', *Psychological Monographs: General and Applied* 80: whole no. 609.

Rotter, J. (1975) 'Some problems and misconceptions related to the construct of internal versus external control of reinforcement', *Journal of Consulting and Clinical Psychology* 43: 56–67.

Rutter, M. (1986) 'The developmental psychopathology of depression: Issues and perspectives', in M. Rutter, C. Izard and P. Read (Eds) *Depression in young people: Developmental and clinical perspectives*, New York: Guilford Press.

Sadowski, C. and Kelley, M. (1993) 'Social problem solving in suicidal adolescents', *Journal of Consulting and Clinical Psychology* 61: 121–127.

Sallis, J. and Nader, P. (1988) 'Family determinants of health behaviors', in D. Gochman (Ed.) *Health behavior: Emerging research perspectives*, New York: Plenum Press.

Santrock, J. (1990) *Life span development* (4th edn.), Dubuque, Iowa: W.C. Brown.

Sarafino, E. (1990) *Health psychology: biopsychosocial interactions*, New York: John Wiley & Sons.

Sarrel, L. and Sarrel, P. (1981) 'Sexual unfolding', *Journal of Adolescent Health Care* 2: 93–99.

Schafer, R., Schafer, E., Bultena, G. and Hoiberg, E. (1993) 'Food safety: An application of the health belief model', *Journal of Nutrition Education* 25: 17–24.

Schootman, M., Fuortes, L., Zwerling, C., Albanese, M. and Watson, C. (1993) 'Safety behavior among Iowa junior high and high school students', *American Journal of Public Health* 83: 1628–1630.

Schubiner, H., Scott, R. and Tzelepis, A. (1993) 'Exposure to violence among inner-city youth', *Journal of Adolescent Health* 14: 214–219.

Schwartz, G. (1982) 'Testing the biopsychosocial model: The ultimate challenge facing behavioral medicine?', *Journal of Consulting and Clinical Psychology* 50: 1040–1053.

Searight, H., Manley, C., Binder, A., Krohn, E., Rogers, B. and Russo, J. (1991) 'The families of origin of adolescent drug abusers: Perceived autonomy and intimacy', *Contemporary Family Therapy* 13: 71–81.

Shafer, D., Garland, A., Gould, M., Fisher, P. and Trautman, P. (1988) 'Preventing teenage suicide: A critical review', *Journal of the American Academy for Child and Adolescent Psychiatry* 27: 675–687.

Sheridan, C. and Radmacher, S. (1992) *Health psychology: Challenging the biomedical model*, New York: John Wiley & Sons.

Shulman, S. (1993) 'Close relationships and coping behavior in adolescence', *Journal of Adolescence* 16: 267–283.

Siegel, J. (1982) 'Type A behavior and self reports of cardiovascular arousal in adolescents', *Journal of Human Stress* 8: 24–30.

Siegel, J. and Brown, J. (1988) 'A prospective study of stressful circumstances, illness symptoms, and depressed mood among adolescents', *Developmental Psychology* 24: 715–721.

Silber, T. (1984) 'Adolescent health care in Brazil', *Adolescence* 19: 493–499.

Silbereisen, R., Noack, P. and Schonpflug, U. (1994) 'Comparative analyses of beliefs, leisure contexts, and substance use in West Berlin and Warsaw', in R. Silbereisen and E. Todt (Eds) *Adolescence in context: The interplay of family, school, peers, and work in adjustment*, New York: Springer-Verlag.

Simmons, R., Burgeson, R., Carlton-Ford, S. and Blyth, D. (1987) 'The impact of cumulative change in early adolescence', *Child Development* 58: 1220–1234.

Sims, E. (1974) 'Studies in human hyperphagia', in G. Bray and J. Bethune (Eds) *Treatment and management of obesity*, New York: Harper & Row.

Sims, E. (1976) 'Experimental obesity, dietary-induced thermogenesis, and their clinical implications', *Clinics in Endocrinology and Metabolism* 5: 377–395.

Slap, G. (1991) 'Injury during adolescence, risk factors for', in R. Lerner, A. Petersen and J. Brooks-Gunn (Eds) *Encyclopedia of adolescence, Vol. 1*, New York: Garland Press.

Slenker, S., Price, J. and O'Connell, J. (1985) 'Health locus of control of joggers and nonexercisers', *Perceptual & Motor Skills* 61: 323–328.

Small, S., Silverberg, S. and Kerns, D. (1993) 'Adolescents' perceptions of the costs and benefits of engaging in health-compromising behaviors', *Journal of Youth and Adolescence* 22: 73–87.

Smetana, J. (1989) 'Adolescents' and parents' reasoning about actual family conflict', *Child Development* 60: 1052–1067.

Smetana, J., Yau, J., Restrepo, A. and Braeges, J. (1991) 'Conflict and adaptation in adolescence: Adolescent–parent conflict', in M. Colten and S. Gore (Eds) *Adolescent stress: Causes and consequences*, New York: Aldine de Gruyter.

Sobal, J. (1987) 'Health concerns of young adolescents', *Adolescence* 22: 739–750.

Spillman, D. and Everington, C. (1989) 'Somatotypes revisited: Have the media changed our perception of the female body image?', *Psychological Reports* 64: 887–890.

Sprinthall, N. and Collins, W. (1988) *Adolescent psychology: A developmental review*, New York: Random House.

St Lawrence, J. (1993) 'African-American adolescents' knowledge, health-related attitudes, sexual behavior, and contraceptive decisions: Implications for the prevention of adolescent HIV infection', *Journal of Consulting and Clinical Psychology* 61: 104–112.

Steptoe, A., Wardle, J., Vinck, J., Tuomisto, M., Holte, A. and Wichstrom, L. (1994) 'Personality and attitudinal correlates of healthy and unhealthy lifestyles in young adults', *Psychology and Health* 9: 331–343.

Story, M. and Resnick, M. (1986) 'Adolescents' views on food and nutrition', *Journal of Nutrition Education* 18: 188–192.

Stotland, S. and Zuroff, D. (1990) 'A new measure of weight locus of control: The dieting beliefs scale', *Journal of Personality Assessment* 54: 191–203.

Strickland, B. (1989) 'Internal-external control expectancies: From contingency to creativity', *American Psychologist* 44: 1–12.

Strober, M. and Humphrey, L. (1987) 'Familial contributions to the etiology and course of anorexia nervosa and bulimia', *Journal of Consulting and Clinical Psychology* 55: 654–659.

Sullivan, T. and Thompson, K. (1994) *Introduction to social problems* (3rd edn.), New York: Macmillan.

Susman, E. (1991) 'Stress and the adolescent', in R. Lerner, A. Petersen and J. Brooks-Gunn (Eds) *Encyclopedia of adolescence, Vol. 2*, New York: Garland Press.

Susman, E. and Dorn, L. (1991) 'Hormones and behavior in adolescence', in R. Lerner, A. Petersen and J. Brooks-Gunn (Eds) *Encyclopedia of adolescence, Vol. 1*, New York: Garland Press.

Swisher, J. (1991) 'Stimulants', in R. Lerner, A. Petersen and J. Brooks-Gunn (Eds) *Encyclopedia of adolescence, Vol. 2*, New York: Garland Press.

Tanner, J. and Davies, P. (1985) 'Clinical longitudinal standards for height and height velocity for North American children', *Journal of Pediatrics* 107: 317–329.

Taylor, S. (1991) *Health psychology* (2nd edn.), New York: McGraw-Hill.

Terry, D., Galligan, R. and Conway, V. (1993) 'The prediction of safe sex behaviour: The role of intentions, attitudes, norms and control beliefs', *Psychology and Health* 8: 355–368.

Terry, D., Gallois, C. and McCamish, M. (1993a) 'The theory of reasoned action and health care behaviour', in D. Terry, C. Gallois and M. McCamish (Eds) *The theory of reasoned action: Its application to AIDS-preventive behaviour*, Oxford: Pergamon Press.

Terry, D., Gallois, C. and McCamish, M. (1993b) *The theory of reasoned action: Its application to AIDS-preventive behaviour*, Oxford: Pergamon Press.

Thoresen, C. (1991) 'Type A and teenagers', in R. Lerner, A. Petersen and J. Brooks-Gunn (Eds) *Encyclopedia of adolescence, Vol. 2*, New York: Garland Press.

Tiggemann, M. (1994) 'Gender differences in the interrelationships between weight dissatisfaction, restraint, and self-esteem', *Sex Roles* 30: 319–330.

Turtle, A., Ford, B., Habgood, R., Grant, M., Bekiaris, J., Constantinou, C., Macek, M. and Polyzoidis, H. (1989) 'AIDS-related beliefs and behaviours of Australian university students', *Medical Journal of Australia* 150: 371–376.

Urberg, K. and Robbins, R. (1981) 'Adolescents' perceptions of the costs and benefits associated with cigarette smoking: Sex differences and peer influences', *Journal of Youth and Adolescence* 10: 353–361.

Vanderschmidt, H., Lang, J., Knight-Williams, V. and Vanderschmidt, G. (1993) 'Risks among inner-city young teens: The prevalence of sexual activity, violence, drugs, and smoking', *Journal of Adolescent Health* 14: 282–288.

Walker, D., Cross, A., Heyman, P., Ruch-Ross, H., Benson, P. and Tuthill, J. (1982) 'Comparisons between inner-city and private school adolescents' perceptions of health problems', *Journal of Adolescent Health Care* 3: 82–90.

Wallack, L. and Dorfman, L. (1992) 'Health messages on television commercials', *American Journal of Health Promotion* 6: 190–196.

Wallerstein, N. (1992) 'Powerlessness, empowerment, and health: Implications for health promotion programs', *American Journal of Health Promotion* 6: 197–205.

Wallston, B. and Wallston, K. (1984) 'Social psychological models of health behavior: An examination and integration', in A. Baum, S. Taylor and J. Singer (Eds) *Handbook of psychology and health, Vol. IV: Social psychological aspects of health*, Hillsdale, N.J.: Lawrence Erlbaum.

Wallston, K., Maides, S. and Wallston, B. (1976) 'Health-related information seeking as a function of health-related locus of control and health value', *Journal of Research in Personality* 10: 215–222.

Wallston, K., Wallston, B. and DeVellis, R. (1978) 'Development of the health locus of control (MHLC) scales', *Health Education Monographs* 6: 160–170.

Werner, M. and Greene, J. (1992) 'Problem drinking among college freshmen', *Journal of Adolescent Health* 13: 487–492.

Westermeyer, J. (1993) 'Schizophrenia', in P. Tolan and B. Cohler (Eds) *Handbook of clinical research and practice with adolescents*, New York: John Wiley & Sons.

Wichstrom, L., Skogen, K. and Oia, T. (1994) 'Social and cultural factors related to eating problems among adolescents in Norway', *Journal of Adolescence* 17: 471–482.

Wielandt, H. and Boldsen, J. (1989) 'Age of first intercourse', *Journal of Biosocial Science* 21: 169–177.

Wilks, J. and Callan, V. (1990) 'Adolescents and alcohol', in P. Heaven and V. Callan (Eds) *Adolescence: An Australian perspective*, Sydney: Harcourt Brace Jovanovich.

Wilks, J., Callan, V. and Forsyth, S. (1985) 'Cross-cultural perspectives on teenage attitudes to alcohol', *International Journal of the Addictions* 20: 547–561.

Williams, S., Kimble, D., Covell, N., Weiss, L., Newton, K., Fisher, J. and Fisher, W. (1992) 'College students use of implicit personality theory instead of safer sex', *Journal of Applied Social Psychology* 22: 921–933.

Williams, S.R. and Worthington-Roberts, B. (1992) *Nutrition throughout the life cycle*, St Louis: Mosby Year Book.

Wills, T. (1986) 'Stress and coping in early adolescence: Relationships to substance use in urban school samples', *Health Psychology* 5: 503–529.

Wilson, S. and Medora, N. (1990) 'Gender comparisons of college students' attitudes toward sexual behavior', *Adolescence* 25: 615–627.

Winefield, H., Winefield, A., Tiggemann, M. and Goldney, R. (1989) 'Psychological concomitants of tobacco and alcohol use in young Australian adults', *British Journal of Addiction* 84: 1067–1073.

Yamaguchi, K. and Kandel, D. (1984) 'Patterns of drug use from adolescence to young adulthood: III. Predictors of progression', *American Journal of Public Health* 74: 673–681.

Youniss, J. and Smollar, J. (1985) *Adolescent relations with mothers, fathers, and friends*, Chicago: Chicago University Press.

Zani, B. (1991) 'Male and female patterns in the discovery of sexuality during adolescence', *Journal of Adolescence* 14: 163–178.

Zeitlin, H. and Swadi, H. (1991) 'Adolescence: The genesis of addiction', in I. Glass (Ed.) *The international handbook of addiction behaviour*, London: Routledge.

Zelnik, M. and Kantner, J. (1980) 'Sexual activity, contraceptive use and pregnancy among metropolitan-area teenagers: 1971–1979', *Family Planning Perspectives* 12: 230–237.

Zimet, G., Bunch, D., Anglin, T., Lazebnik, R., Williams, P. and Krowchuk, D. (1992) 'Relationship of AIDS-related attitudes to sexual behavior changes in adolescents', *Journal of Adolescent Health* 13: 493–498.

Zubrick, S., Silburn, S., Garton, A., Burton, P., Dalby, R., Carlton, J., Shepherd, C. and Lawrence, D. (1995) *Western Australian child health survey: Developing health and well-being in the nineties*, Perth, Western Australia: Australian Bureau of Statistics and the Institute for Child Health Research.

Name index

Abramson, L. 39
Adams, G. 143
Adityanjee 119–20
Ahmad, S. 82
Ajzen, I. 40, 42–3, 104
Altshuler, J. 57
Anglin, T. 98
Angold, A. 137
Argyle, M. 134
Aro, H. 144
Aseltine, R. 141
Asmussen, L. 50–1
Attie, I. 76
Austin, L. 93
Avison, W. 139

Baer, J. 119
Baghurst, K. 161, 164–5
Baguma, P. 72
Baker, L. 135
Baker, S. 89
Balch, P. 164
Balogun, A. 71
Balogun, J. 71
Bancroft, J. 93
Band, E. 56
Bar-Tal, D. 70
Barber, B. 59
Barling, N. 97
Baron, R. 28
Barr, S. 166
Barth, R. 89, 92–3
Baumeister, R. 75–7
Beck, N. 137

Becker, M. 6, 34–5
Belknap, J. 119
Bennion, L. 143
Benthin, A. 18, 22
Bentler, P. 47–8, 115, 124–5, 121
Benton, P. 91
Beyth-Marom, R. 93
Binder, A. 127
Bingham, C. 143
Blyth, D. 49
Boldero, J. 105–6
Boldsen, J. 89
Borst, S. 147–7
Bowlds, M. 48–9, 58
Boyer, R. 19
Boyle, M. 135, 138
Braeges, J. 51
Brannon, L. 65–6
Brenner, D. 70
Brone, R. 76, 82–3
Brook, D. 121–2, 125
Brook, J. 121–2, 126
Brooks-Gunn, J. 45, 54–5, 62, 76, 97, 135
Brown, B. 24, 151
Brown, J. 44
Brown, L. 83
Brownell, K. 11
Brozek, J. 65
Bruhn, J. 149–50, 167
Brunswik, A. 107–17
Bryant, F. 60
Bultena, G. 165
Bunch, D. 98

Subject index